Police Corruption

Police Corruption
Deviance, accountability and reform in policing

Maurice Punch

Routledge
Taylor & Francis Group

LONDON AND NEW YORK

First published by Willan Publishing 2009
This edition published by Routledge 2011
2 Park Square, Milton Park, Abingdon, Oxon OX14 4RN
711 Third Avenue, New York, NY 10017

Routledge is an imprint of the Taylor & Francis Group

ISBN 978-1-84392-410-4 paperback
        978-1-84392-411-1 hardback

British Library Cataloguing-in-Publication Data

A catalogue record for this book is available from the British Library.

Project managed by Deer Park Productions, Tavistock, Devon
Typeset by GCS, Leighton Buzzard, Bedfordshire

For Geoff and Pat Markham

Contents

List of abbreviations

US
ADA   Assistant District Attorney
CRASH   Community Resources Against Street Hoodlums
DA   District Attorney
DEA   Drug Enforcement Agency
DOI   Department of Investigation
EIS   Early Intervention Systems
FBI   Federal Bureau of Investigation
IAB   Internal Affairs Bureau
IAD   Internal Affairs Division (in New York, in some
               forces 'Bureau')
LAPD   Los Angeles Police Department
LASD   Los Angeles Sheriff Department
NIJ   National Institute of Justice
NYPD   New York City Police Department
OPS   Office of Professional Standards (Chicago)
PBA   Patrolmen's Benevolent Association
PD   Police Department
SIU   Special Investigation Unit (New York)

UK
ACC   Assistant Chief Constable
ACPO   Association of Chief Police Officers
CID   Criminal Investigation Department
CPS   Crown Prosecution Service
DCI   Detective Chief Inspector

DCS	Detective Chief Superintendent
DPP	Director of Public Prosecutions
HMIC	Her Majesty's Inspectorate of Constabulary
IPCC	Independent Police Complaints Commission
IRA	Irish Republican Army
Met	Metropolitan Police Service
OPONI	Office of Police Ombudsman for Northern Ireland
PCA	Police Complaints Authority
PSNI	Police Service of Northern Ireland (since 2001)
PSU	Professional Standards Unit
RUC	Royal Ulster Constabulary (until 2001)
SB	Special Branch
SERCS	South East Regional Crime Squad

Netherlands

CID	Criminal Intelligence Department
IRT	Inter-regional Crime Team
NDA	National Detective Agency
PCS	Plain Clothes Squad
PPS	Public Prosecution Service

Other

ICAC	Independent Commission Against Corruption
NSW	New South Wales
RCMP	Royal Canadian Mounted Police
SAPS	South African Police Service
SOP	Standard Operating Procedure

Preface

Since the late 1960s I've been involved with police officers in various ways and have developed a certain affinity with policing. I believe in the policing enterprise – and in 'good enough' policing (Bowling 2008). But by chance I encountered a corruption scandal in Amsterdam in the 1970s which led to a preoccupation with issues of deviance, control and reform in policing (also with corporate crime and organisational deviance: Punch 1996). The archetypical 'bent cop' of that time, as in the 1970s London novels of G. F. Newman (such as *A Detective's Tale*, 1977), has, however, become increasingly nasty and vicious, going on the contemporary American TV series *The Shield*.

In contrast the officers I know well are committed professionals with an ethic of service and of integrity. I have much respect for Geoffrey Markham, Tom Rogers and Ralph Crawshaw (formerly Essex Police), Stan Gilmour (Thames Valley Police) and for Julian Dixon (British Transport Police). The same was true of Tom Williamson (formerly Nottinghamshire Police and Portsmouth University) and Colin Cramphorn (formerly West Yorkshire Police); sadly both of whom died in recent years. They have all contributed to this book in diverse ways and I thank them for this. Geoff in particular has been a good friend and also a fount of valuable knowledge on policing.

They and other senior officers I have encountered are often impressive people in many ways. How is it, then, that the devious, unsavoury and unlawful practices described in this book take place within the police institution of which they are members? Tom Williamson, for instance, was a man of undoubted integrity, but he worked in the 'Met' (Metropolitan Police Service) when swathes of the organisation were routinely corrupt, and he acknowledged this. How does the 'good' cop survive in such an environment? How are boundaries maintained and what rituals of avoidance take place? One adaptation is exit and among the victims of police deviance are the good officers squeezed out of the police service because they were too straight in a corrupt environment. One officer told me that he blew the whistle, with support from several colleagues, about unacceptable conduct by another officer; but he found himself under threat of legal action because he believes the officer had 'connections'. He resigned, thinking 'why follow the correct path if it is sanctioned?' If he had stayed and faced a similar situation again, he would probably have taken no action. Straight cops with principles are often perturbed not just by the deviance they face but also by the bad faith they encounter within their own organisation.

Generally cops are candid about the moral predicaments faced in policing and the 'dirty hands' dilemma. They are rarely paragons and have usually had a 'wild' period at an early stage of their career with diverse escapades; this is conveyed in a narrative tradition of anecdotes, including 'cock-ups I have known but managed to survive', told with humour and self-deprecation. Nearly all have indulged in the delights of 'grass-eating' (see Chapter 2). So when you meet poised and groomed senior officers fervently espousing 'when you take that first bite of a kebab you lose a portion of your soul and are on the path to damnation,' you can't help visualising them in a Transit van on a cold and dreary night at the back of McDonalds shovelling down hot fries. And later, in the bathos of policing, throwing them up over their shoes, as happened with one unfortunate cop on an otherwise uneventful night that I experienced in Southend in the 1980s. Furthermore, officers who have worked in Complaints and Discipline (cf. Kennison 2001) or in a Professional Standards Unit (PSU) are doubly cynical about fellow cops; they have seen everything.

The only time I interviewed officers who had been arrested and taken to court for 'corruption' was in Amsterdam. Their line was, 'but everyone was at it', and they roundly blamed the organisation. Indeed, virtually every cop will tell you they broke the law in some way at some stage in their career. In classes in London, for example, there are usually officers from abroad. One contingent explained brazenly that they not only routinely take bribes – 'even while we're asleep', one said – but they detailed how they had 'set up' criminals to get a conviction in court. There was, too, a discussion about 'encounters' whereby criminals were shot dead by the Indian police in suspicious circumstances (Belur 2007). These cops from abroad found this perfectly reasonable; it was justified to kill a dangerous criminal especially if he had shot a fellow officer. Indeed, the Deputy Minister for Safety and Security, addressing officers from the South African Police Service (SAPS) about tackling criminals, proclaimed, 'Kill the bastards. You must not worry about the regulations. That is my responsibility' (*Pretoria News* 2008). She received a standing ovation for this 'incitement'.

Even Commissioner Robert Mark, who cleaned up the Met in the 1970s and was a 'sea-green incorruptible' (Whitaker 1979), admits to wrongdoing. As a young constable in Manchester he carried – as did nearly everyone else – an illegal truncheon and during an arrest he broke a man's leg with it (Mark 1978: 28). And at the very time he was fanatically combating corruption in the Met, Mark admits he was prepared to break the law. An Irish Republican Army (IRA) man had died in prison in Britain following a hunger strike and the family intended bringing his body to London for a service that would have amounted to a pro-IRA demonstration. Mark contemplated seizing the coffin to put it directly on a plane to Ireland and comments, 'I had no legal right to take possession of the body but that did not worry me very much' (Mark 1978: 172). Running through policing, including some 'squeaky clean' cops, is a justification that it is sometimes acceptable to break the law. A former Royal Canadian Mounted Police (RCMP) Commissioner, for example, felt that RCMP officers should be able to break the law for a 'noble purpose' (Ericson 1981: 89). What purpose? How noble? And who defines 'noble'?

During the last 30 years I have given presentations, collected material and met police officers, academics and others at seminars and conferences in the US, the UK and elsewhere in Europe. I have also taught courses at Bramshill (Centrex), for the Office of the Police Ombudsman for Northern Ireland (OPONI) and for the *Gárda Síochana* Ombudsman Commission in Dublin (sometimes on University of Portsmouth programmes), and have attended Police Foundation and other seminars in the UK related to accountability, oversight and the functioning of the Independent Police Complaints Commission (IPCC). Over the years I have travelled to the US many times, taught at SUNY Albany, attended conferences, visited police forces, contributed to two National Institute of Justice (NIJ) seminars on police integrity and was involved in the police integrity project of Carl Klockars by helping with the Dutch survey (Klockars *et al.* 2004). These assignments and meetings in Europe and the USA provided the opportunity to speak with academics and practitioners in policing and oversight.

After some 20 years in Dutch universities I became an independent researcher and consultant in 1994; in 1999 I was offered a visiting professorship at the London School of Economics and at King's College London in 2007. I feel privileged to be associated with these two institutions where I can interact with excellent colleagues including Tim Newburn, Robert Reiner, Dick Hobbs, Paddy Rawlinson, Janet Foster, Penny Green, Mercedes Hinton, Elaine Player and Mike Hough. I have learned much from them. Ben Bowling has been stimulating to work with – and dine with – while it is a pleasure to teach with him and his colleagues on the King's MA in Criminology; I'm most grateful for his valuable comments on several chapters. A special word of thanks must go to Paul Rock, who received several chapters on a Sunday morning and returned them later the same day with detailed comments and references. Paul is a scholar of great erudition who is accessible and responsive to all; with others, including David Downes and Stan Cohen, he has set a tone at LSE that high academic productivity is compatible with collegiality, intellectual openness and attention for students.

Finally, through the years in the Netherlands I have gained much from my friends and colleagues Kees van der Vijver, Wim Broer, Geert de Vries, Alexis Aronowitz, Stephen Ellis and Hans Werdmölder. Derek Phillips has been a valuable source of encouragement for my work, and a highly competitive squash partner, since my arrival in the Netherlands. Finally there is my local 'support system' of my dear wife Corry as well as Julio, Maria, George and grandson Jimmy; also George Senior, Netty, Mikey and Zoë and my extended Dutch family, the Vennemans. I thank them all most warmly.

Maurice Punch
Amstelveen

Chapter 1

Introduction

A good police force is one that catches more criminals than it employs.

(Robert Mark, Commissioner of the Metropolitan Police
in the 1970s, *New Statesman* 18 January 1980)

What is really real? Official paradigm and operational code(s)

Policing and corruption go hand in hand. That the two are inextricably linked is a grave matter because the police organisation is the prime agency of the state for law enforcement and social control (Reiner 2000; Loader and Walker 2007). The police are meant to enforce the law and not abuse it. This book explores that worrying but intriguing discrepancy between police as law enforcers and as lawbreakers. Why do officers bend and break rules, procedures and the law and why do some effectively become 'criminals'? It takes a broad perspective on the elastic concept of 'corruption' – which I will define in Chapter 2 – but my position is that we have to abandon atomistic and limited definitions geared to 'individual gain' (Sherman 1974b 5).[1] These are rooted in legal notions of the autonomous individual and of corruption as primarily bribery. In contrast it is necessary to locate corruption within the wider context of misconduct, crime and organisational deviance in policing. It is sociologically unsound to speak of 'individuals' in organisations for there are none. This book is about 'ordinary men' placed in a peculiar institutional context where they are asked to perform dirty work; some remain clean, some become dirty, while others revel in the dirt.[2]

I shall argue that policing presents practitioners with an inherent dilemma in relation to performing their tasks and enforcing the law in a context of rules, resources and laws that restrict them in some way. This 'impossible mandate' (Manning 1977) fosters diverse forms and patterns of deviance and corruption which are related to achieving formally approved goals or covert, illicit ends. Of especial interest is the extent to which the wider environment of policing, the nature of the police organisation, police work and culture conspire to encourage the diverse forms of police deviance. And also to what extent the police organisation is weak, negligent or collusive in the prevention, deterrence and investigation of offences by the police. Given the nearly universal nature of police corruption and its resilience it is patently clear that reform and change in policing are problematic (Walker 2005). That requires, then, a consideration of the issues surrounding investigations of police deviance, prevention, leadership, reform campaigns and especially accountability. In a nutshell I argue that systemic corruption can become 'organisational deviance' so that we can no longer talk of 'bad apples' but rather of 'rotten orchards' (Punch 2003). In some cases, the extent of the deviance and the severity of its consequences, combined with the failure to deal with it, reach the level of 'system failure'.

The book examines a number of cases of police corruption and the diverse forms it takes in several countries; it focuses on the pathways that officers take into corruption; and looks at the issues raised by trying to reform the police organisation and institutionalise accountability (Punch 2000). One strand in this work is the notion that policing *is* accountability and a corrupt police force is essentially unaccountable. This theme has been accentuated in the UK by the rise of new oversight agencies (Markham and Punch 2007a, 2007b). These have played an important role with the Office of Police Ombudsman for Northern Ireland (OPONI), scrutinising the police in Northern Ireland following 30 years of unrest in the Province. In England and Wales the Independent Police Complaints Commission (IPCC), active since 2004, provided an independent agency that critically examined command procedures and also internal communication when the Metropolitan Police shot dead an innocent man during an anti-terrorist operation in 2005 at Stockwell underground station (IPCC 2007a, 2007b; Punch and Markham 2009).

My analysis of deviance in police organisations will draw on the conceptual distinction between the 'official paradigm' and the 'operational code'.[3] In policing, the official paradigm is shaped to bolster institutional values, whereas the operational code espouses how things 'really get done'. This distinction between official paradigm and operational code draws attention to the discrepancy between the public façade that police organisations present to the outside world and the negotiated reality of internal institutional and occupational practices which deviate from that paradigm. Behind the front designed to reassure the outside world there are diverse operational codes. For instance, British cops speak of being 'bent for job' or 'bent for self'; the former is geared to enhancing formal goals – say in ensuring convictions in court through rule-bending – and the latter to rule-breaking for ends that are a perversion of the official paradigm. In all organisations there is an 'informal system', and one strand is the norms and practices that enhance formal goals while another is a subversive 'under-culture' that abuses and profits from the organisational context.

These distinctions alert us to the many-layered reality in police organisations where there are intricate and shifting patterns of meanings and behaviour between formal and informal ends and between deviance 'for' and 'against' the organisation (Punch 2008). Police deviance and corruption shift over time, and are complex, many-faceted and surrounded by ambiguity. The level and nature of deviance is also dependent on the opportunities provided and these vary within police agencies and between diverse environments. This institutional and occupational complexity makes unravelling what is 'really real' in policing a daunting enterprise. The underlying deviant practices have to be camouflaged and concealed to keep the official paradigm intact and to ward off external scrutiny; hence secrecy and deception are usually key features of corruption (Reiss 1971 6).[4] From this perspective the often messy, confusing and frustrating reality of policing becomes a constantly shifting kaleidoscope of personal and institutional performances, of impression management and the construction of accounts for internal or external consumption. The actors at all levels have multiple personalities and identities and slip continually between them, espousing the official paradigm at one moment while acknowledging the operational code at another. Police officers learn to become shrewd and crafty chameleons, opportunistically and instinctively changing colour to fit the arena, audience, and shifting occupational roles. This makes cops no different from actors in other institutional settings (Dalton 1959); what does make them different is that they are law enforcers who have sworn an oath to abide by the law.

The official paradigm of policing is reflected in legal pronouncements about mandate and mission, strategy statements of individual forces and the speeches of police chiefs.[5] The components of the paradigm that contemporary police organisations typically convey contain assertions about the espoused institutional ethos and expected standards of conduct of officers on the following lines.

Officers operate according to the rule of law and are answerable to the courts, aim to enforce the law impartially and apply their assigned monopoly of violence with restraint. They are publicly accountable for policy and operational decisions while cooperating with external oversight. They will provide a service to all citizens, treating them with dignity and respect and will abide by civil and human rights. And they will act with integrity, avoiding conflicts of interest and acceptance of gifts aimed at influencing conduct, eschewing nepotism and favouritism, and will promote standards of professional and ethical conduct. There is a link to the seven 'fundamental values' of democratic policing elucidated by Jones (2003: 606): equity, service delivery, responsiveness, distribution of power, information, redress and participation. There are too the 'Nolan Principles' enunciated by the Committee on Standards in Public Life founded in Britain in 1994 (Nolan 1998); the standards are centred on the principles of selflessness, integrity, objectivity, accountability, openness, honesty and leadership. With the intrusion of 'new public management' into policing (Leishman et al. 1966), moreover, these normative standards are often accompanied by claims of organisational excellence, speed and quality of response to demands from the public, espousing a 'client-friendly' approach and regularly monitoring public opinion on police performance.

In essence, then, the modern police organisation is held to be competent professionally, restrained in the use of its powers and force, legally compliant, responsive to oversight, open to the media, consultative with stakeholders in communities, humane and rights respecting, service and customer oriented but, above all, *trustworthy and accountable*. For instance, the Shared Leadership Vision of the Royal Canadian Mounted Police (RCMP 1998) espouses 'core values' of accountability, respect, professionalism, honesty, compassion and integrity.

If these values are taken as a template but then we hear of officers 'testilying' in court, fabricating statements, tampering with evidence, pressurising a suspect into a false confession or subduing a suspect with excessive force and covering this up, this conveys a stark discrepancy between rhetoric and reality. In Australia in the 1980s, for example, a corrupt cop drove a criminal associate to and from an armed burglary while other corrupt cops attended the scene to cover up for them. In the Sydney 'gang land wars' there were shoot-outs between rival groups of criminals and 'bent' cops; allegedly an officer murdered someone and then investigated his own crime while corrupt cops 'fitted up' innocent people for their own murders.[6] This conduct leads to shock and outrage because expectations of the police are based on trust and when that trust is abused there is a special sense of betrayal. The deviation from espoused norms and the law is a serious violation of a 'fiduciary *relationship*, the corruption of a public *trust*, of public virtue' (Reiss 1977 ix, emphasis in original).

Yet a wealth of material – in academic publications, historical accounts, public inquiries, documentaries and media exposures, court cases, biographies of officers and films – reveals that police officers frequently if not routinely bend and break disciplinary rules and the law. This is a recurring and persistent theme since the commencement of 'modern' public policing early in the nineteenth century. The combined historical and contemporary evidence indicates that police can be venal and violent and can behave irresponsibly while evading accountability.

Indeed, when police research developed in the US in the 1960s – pioneered by several researchers and aided by a number of public inquiries – it portrayed the police as a problem profession characterised by violence, prejudice and corruption.[7] This was reinforced by negative images of baton-wielding police during civil rights and anti-Vietnam demonstrations, leading to the term 'police riot' (Kerner Report 1968). Clearly, then, behind that façade of official presentations conveying a compliant, responsible and controlled institution there are other realities driven by covert codes. For instance, police officers in Albany (New York) would go on patrol with tools to carry out burglaries; they also stole car tyres and batteries (Christianson 1973). There were police burglary rings in several other cities in both the US and the UK (Punch 1985: 10). People in Chicago were blasé about police misconduct but even they were disturbed when their cops became 'Burglars in Blue' (Rokyo 1971: 111). The exposure of police as burglars is glaringly at odds with the official paradigm and with public expectations. This is especially the case with one of the defining images of police deviance in recent decades.

In the infamous Rodney King incident, a citizen with a video-camera filmed officers from the Los Angeles Police Department (LAPD) during an arrest. In the recording officers give a prolonged beating to a black man lying on the ground. What is not visible on the tape shown on TV is that King had strongly resisted arrest. He had earlier tried to evade arrest and this started a car chase that involved some ten patrol cars (Skolnick and Fyfe 2005). There was a helicopter overhead, some 20 LAPD officers were at the scene of the arrest and they watched and shouted encouragement while four of them repeatedly kicked and stomped on King, beat him with metal batons and twice used a 'taser' on him (Collins 2008: 322–4). This was a shocking event and the graphic images attracted worldwide attention. The repercussions of the King case set off widespread rioting in Los Angeles and elsewhere in the US; crucially the violence was viewed as symbolic for the police mistreatment of blacks throughout America. But the official paradigm of a restrained, impartial and law-abiding police force was shattered by those images.

The tape exposed the largely concealed 'backstage' of policing. What was most disturbing to viewers and commentators was that the officers conducted the beating as if it was 'Standard Operating Procedure' (SOP).[8] Indeed, the Christopher Commission (1991), which investigated the King incident, concluded that a significant number of LAPD officers employed excessive violence, that among these were a group of 'repeat offenders' who were not identified as such by the organisation, and that there was a wider institutional failure within the LAPD's management in handling complaints and exercising accountability. The analysis of critical incidents in policing frequently exposes that there is a wider pattern to the deviance, that this has not been dealt with by the organisation and that the institution has displayed negligence, denial and even collusion in the illicit practices.

How can this failure be explained? How can the violent beating of King happen within an accountable and disciplined public agency with ostensibly a semi-military and bureaucratic structure of control? How, indeed, does that institution go about exerting internal control and investigating offences among its personnel? Which paths do officers follow into deviance and in what social arrangements do they become involved? How do they justify the deviance to themselves? How after scandal are police agencies reformed? How indeed is external control of policing exercised? And, finally, how is accountability arranged and exercised?

For one of the most pivotal issues in policing remains *quis custodiet ipsos custodies – who controls the controllers?*[9] There is a general notion in democratic governance that it is undesirable that any public agency investigates itself. This holds particularly for policing because police have the authority to intervene directly in citizens' lives, to deprive them of their freedom and even to take their lives through fatal force. These are uniquely extensive powers and their implementation should surely be subject to independent oversight and transparency. Yet until quite recently the situation in the UK was that there was no external agency to investigate the police; for 175 years police investigated themselves. And it could be argued that that is still largely the case.[10]

The key questions above form the perennial, contentious issues which this book will address; it also explores features of reform and accountability in policing. In the UK, for instance, the architecture of police accountability has altered considerably with the arrival of OPONI in Northern Ireland in 2000 and the IPCC in England and Wales in 2004.[11] In the US, in contrast, the picture remains sombre; for many years there has been considerable hostility among police officers and their representatives to any form of civilian oversight. Some new, promising developments are sketched by Walker (2005).

In this work the official paradigm in policing will, then, be taken to mean the formal structure and the institutional ideology, encapsulating how the organisation wants to appear to the outside world. And the operational code(s) will refer to the diverse practices that deviate from that paradigm and from public expectations.[12] This institutional split personality echoes the lapidary study of managers by Dalton (1959) where, beneath the surface of the corporation, managers were breaking rules all the time. This double life of overt compliance with covert manipulation is evident in Gouldner's (1954) study of a gypsum mine; in Bittner (1965) on the infinite regress of rules in organisations and the muddle in interpreting them; in the 'vicious circles' encountered in institutions (Masuch 1985); and in the 'moral mazes' that executives have to negotiate in corporations (Jackall 1988). It is graphically evident in Geis' (1996) classic study of white-collar crime. The personally law-abiding managers constructed strategic conspiracies to fix prices; they saw it as SOP for conducting business, erased the fact that it was illegal and never thought of themselves as 'criminals' – until their arrest, and even after that. Another way of approaching the discrepancy is to restate the fundamental sociological insight that things are never quite what they seem to be on the surface. Indeed, much research on deviance consists of penetrating to 'backstage' areas of institutions to uncover the reality hidden from the outside world (Goffman 1959). In short, *what is really real?*

This book then, draws on this perspective of ambiguity, muddle, mixed motives and of oscillation between diverse values and layers in organisations to examine police 'corruption'. But to explore all aspects of police corruption, deviance and crime across the globe would involve covering a vast terrain with diverse lenses – political, economic, psychological, anthropological and cross-cultural (cf. Simpson 1977; Duchaine 1979). I shall confine myself to a select number of countries – namely the US, the UK and the Netherlands – and to employing a sociological-criminological perspective. This work does not examine in detail cases of corruption in developing countries, in post-conflict societies, in Africa, Asia, South America or Eastern Europe; nor does it touch on corruption in private policing (see Bayley 1974; Einstein and Amir 2003; Amir and Einstein 2004; Klockars *et al.* 2004; Sarre *et al.* 2005).

First, my research has been on public policing in the countries mentioned. Second, the US and UK have generated the most accessible literature in English. Other area studies would require language skills that I do not possess, except for Dutch. Third, and most important, my research has focused on western democratic societies where police corruption is viewed as a morally reprehensible aberration that reflects negatively on the legitimacy of the state (or local government). It also casts a dark shadow on the trustworthiness of the police agency and the police profession. Typically following exposure through scandal in such societies there are demands from the media, public opinion and politicians that the authorities intervene to restore confidence, trust and legitimacy in the police apparatus.

This plainly does not hold for failed, rogue or totalitarian states where the police agency is the crude instrument of criminal political elites. In such societies police are used by the state for clandestine operations against its enemies and engage in subversion and repression; corruption is deeply ingrained in public life at all levels and bribing the police is routine and accepted;[13] and in some societies, as in Latin America, the state, police and organised crime jointly engage in drug-dealing, torture and murder (Hinton 2005). The police are not seen as legitimate and are not trusted, are engaged in systemic crime and deviance and are, above all, *unaccountable*. They are out of societal control, beyond the law, institutionally corrupt and intertwined with the deviance of the state (Green and Ward 2004). For example, in a volume on policing in developing countries, Hinton and Newburn (2009) convey that police corruption is inextricably linked to political corruption, abuse of human rights, poverty and lack of accountability. Police deviance – such as brutality, discrimination and corruption for political or institutional gain – are tied in many of these countries to repression, negation of the rule of law, no redress for citizens and contempt for democratic values and practices.

In contrast, it is of the essence in western democracies that the state is held responsible for the integrity and legitimacy of public agencies but especially for the police. This holds also for security agencies engaged in 'high' policing dealing with political threats, organised crime and terrorism which are typically less visible than the 'low policing' of ordinary public police; the covert and even clandestine activities of the former are frequently covered by the mantle of national security (Brodeur 1983; Bowling and Newburn 2006). The understanding in a democracy is that police officers who break the law can be called to account in open court. In the societies I examine the police agencies are not held to be irredeemable when found to have committed offences but are assumed to be capable of reform and of having public confidence in them restored. In this process the crucial test for policing in a democratic system is *accountability*. A police force that covers up corruption is unaccountable. For without genuine accountability there can be no legitimacy; and without legitimacy the police cannot function effectively in democratic society.

Furthermore, if the focus is moved from the societal to the institutional and operational level, then a central theme here is that police corruption is not typically individual but collective, is largely fostered by the nature of police work, police culture and the police organisation, and is a constantly recurring feature of policing. But if corruption is an inherent and near universal facet of policing then it cannot simply be the product of some '*bad apples*'. This much used image, often employed defensively following scandal, conveys that the problem is one of human failure confined to a handful of reprehensible and unrepresentative deviants who if removed will no longer contaminate the otherwise healthy majority. But in cases of serious, widespread and prolonged corruption the more appropriate metaphor should be '*bad barrels*', if not '*bad orchards*' (Punch 2003).

That in turn should raise some questions. Why do the good apples not protest and kick out the bad apples that are causing them to rot? Why do the bad apples attack a good apple complaining of contamination? Whose duty was it to inspect the fruit and who neglected to apply the insecticide? Why do some particular orchards continually produce rotten fruit; what contaminated the soil and can healthy fruit ever grow there? And, finally, the key questions: who was in charge of the orchard; why did they confine themselves to polishing the apples and ignoring or concealing the rotten ones; and how can they be held to account?

9

Indeed, this theme of near universal, recurring and somehow ingrained deviance in policing is reinforced in Newburn's authoritative review of the literature (1999: 14):

> It [corruption] is pervasive – corrupt practices are found in some form in a great many police agencies in all societies; it is a continuing problem – there is evidence of corrupt practices from all stages of police history; it is not simply a problem of lower ranks – corruption has been found at all levels of the organisation; there are certain forms of policing, or areas of the police organisation, which are more at 'risk' of corruption; it is not simply financial: activities (including 'process' activities) extending beyond bribery and corruption have been examined.

Sherman (1978: xxii) also maintains that corruption is a feature of 'every police system in the world' and that almost every urban police department in the US has experienced a 'major scandal'. The views of Sherman and Newburn establish the important conclusion that *corruption is found in virtually all countries, in all forces and at every level of the organisation at some time.*

But having said that we have to face the fact that there is no reliable and valid instrument for ascertaining how much police corruption there is in a society or individual police force. This is not a subject that elicits reliable information in surveys – cops are understandably devious about their deviousness (as we all are) – and research data are typically based on attitudes to corruption or perceptions of its extent. There are studies based on perceptions such as the cross-national study of police attitudes to corruption (Klockars *et al.* 2004). In this work officers in several countries were presented with a number of scenarios of police deviance, and asked to rank them on a number of dimensions including seriousness. There are methodological problems related to the distribution of the survey and representative nature of the sampling – in the US certain proposed research locations were barred by the police unions, which also had to approve the questions – but also cultural issues with regard to the meaning and significance of certain offences in diverse societies (such as the relative monetary value of 'kickbacks'). Usually the police forces themselves were responsible for distributing the surveys and for administering their completion. Despite these limitations there are discernible differences in response on the lines one would expect; e.g. Dutch officers show a higher level of 'integrity' in their ranking of seriousness of offences in response to the survey than American officers (Huberts *et al.* 2003).[14]

Kutnjak Ivkovic (2005) reinforces some of these expected differences with an exhaustive scrutiny of surveys and other indicators of cross-national differences in relation to corruption. There is too the Transparency International Index of *perceptions* of political corruption which can be taken as a likely indicator of corresponding police corruption (TI 2007). The least corrupt countries in the Index were New Zealand, Denmark, Finland, Singapore, Sweden, Iceland, the Netherlands, Switzerland, Norway and Canada; the UK ranked 12th and the US 20th. The most corrupt were Myanmar, Iraq, Haiti, Tonga, Uzbekistan, Chad, Sudan, Afghanistan and Somalia.

This book is looking primarily at highly negative practices in police forces and it may convey the message that everyone is 'bent'. As mentioned above, this cannot be known with any reliability, while there are agencies that are not only relatively 'clean' but also professional and ethical or simply not into serious deviance. But delegates at the National Symposium on Police Integrity in Washington DC in 1996 lamented that there were no reliable data on police departments that were relatively free from corruption (Gaffigan and McDonald 1997: 50).

I shall return to the definition of corruption and the diverse forms it takes in Chapter 2. But here I want to convey that my focus reaches far wider than the ostensibly financially based transactions of bribery. The material presented reflects the broader spectrum of police deviance and crime where officers engage in serious offences against citizens, suspects and criminals including undue violence, abusing rights, committing perjury, planting evidence, recycling confiscated or stolen drugs, burglary, sexual harassment,[15] cooperating with organised criminals and even murder. There is plainly a disturbing discrepancy between these practices and the ideal in a democratic society that police will adhere to the rule of law and will be accountable.

Corruption in this wider sense of serious police deviance, if not police 'crime', is then inextricably linked to *abuse of official power, to abuse of trust* and in some cases to the notion of *system failure*. The incidents reveal not just individual or group failure but also wider institutional deficiencies. A graphic illustration of such abuse and failure is portrayed by the case of Officer Michael Dowd. He testified before the Mollen Commission (1994) which investigated corruption within the New York City Police Department (NYPD).[16] The US has a rich history of police corruption (Fogelson 1977) and the NYPD invariably catches much attention. This is because New York has displayed a cycle of corruption scandals roughly every 20 years; those scandals usually elicited public inquiries which illuminate the shifting patterns of police corruption. And Michael Dowd is an officer whose personal deviant career powerfully reveals the wider deficiencies in the police system in New York.

Officer Dowd (New York)

Dowd was a uniformed officer who would drive into work, sign on for duty and then just *disappear*. He never seemed to do any police work. His routine was to meet some of his criminal contacts to drink and/or take drugs. In addition, Dowd and up to fifteen officers would meet at a desolate location to drink, fire their weapons, meet their girlfriends and plan criminal activities. His criminal career inside the police started early and he became adept at stealing at the scene of burglaries. He and his police cronies indulged in violence, known as 'tuning up' a suspect. Dowd also graduated to becoming a close associate of criminals, cooperated with them and performed services for them such as 'green-lighting' drug deliveries, 'riding shotgun' on them and using violence and intimidation against their competitors. Effectively he had become a criminal in a police uniform. The Mollen Commission (1994) detailed Dowd's activities and those of several groups of corrupt officers in a number of precincts in New York.

Patrolman Dowd – who took bribes from drug traffickers, became a drug dealer and actually assisted and protected major drug operations – came into the limelight during the Commission's hearings. Although he was not offered immunity and faced a prison sentence,[17] Dowd was prepared to talk about deviant practices. Dowd was apparently liked and even admired by his colleagues; indeed, some of the bent cops looked like ideal recruits and even had seemingly exemplary records. But their working style was dominated by deeply deviant behaviour. Dowd was clearly aware of the 'slippery slope' process involved in deviance and carefully introduced his partners to a form of criminal apprenticeship; all fourteen partners took the bait and then agreed with Dowd to share any proceedings from crime. The path into 'cop crime' which emerged from the Commission's report began with simple break-ins covered by making fake emergency calls of a burglary, or there was theft during legal searches. But the corrupt cops graduated to breaking in to promising locations looking for drugs, money and weapons; they also become dealers themselves or cooperated with dealers. Dowd, for instance, was asked if he was a cop or a drug dealer; he answered 'both'. Asked if his allegiance was to the city he was policing or the drug traffickers, he replied, 'I guess I'd have to say the drug traffickers' (Mollen Commission 1994: 32).

Dowd explained to the Commission that force was employed partly to exhibit police control over their territory but also partly as a *rite of passage* for newcomers. Some officers explained in hearings that the brutality was how they initially learned to 'cross the line'. After that first step it was easier to progress to other deviance, including corruption. Brutality was used to see if a new officer was a tough and 'good' cop, meaning one who could be trusted not to report any wrongdoing. Dowd, like others, clearly perceived brutality as strengthening the bonds of loyalty and the code of silence among officers and this in turn fostered tolerance of corruption; he stated that brutality 'is a form of acceptance. It's not just simply a beating. It's the other officers begin to accept you more' (Mollen Commission 1994: 47).

Dowd and the officers portrayed by the Mollen Commission were uniformed cops and low in the formal rank hierarchy whereas serious forms of corruption have usually been associated with detectives, special units and 'political' policing. Some of their activities were visible or known to colleagues and supervisors; their conduct was predatory and voracious; they had to all intents and purposes *become criminals*. The working style, with its accent on action, excitement and revelling in the 'dirt', was near addictive and echoed Katz (1988) on the 'seductions of crime' for criminals. For Dowd being a cop had become a convenient cover for being a full-time, professional, organised criminal in uniform.

The significance of this unedifying portrait is twofold. First, this was not individual deviance, for Dowd functioned within a small group of highly deviant officers and there were a number of such groups. And second he avoided police work and almost never made any arrests. These two factors indicate institutional failure if not implicit or explicit collusion in his deviance. For Dowd seemed not to have been supervised; his lifestyle (he owned several houses and lived lavishly), intimate contacts with criminals, drug use and violence seemingly went unnoticed. And surely, one might think, there should be a red warning light flashing if an officer is not making any arrests and is going absent while on duty. Instead there was a glowing appraisal of him from the personnel department of the NYPD, which viewed him as an officer with 'excellent street knowledge ... relates well with his peers ... empathetic to the community ... could excel within the NYPD ... become a role model for others to emulate if he maximized his inner drive to fulfill job responsibilities to the fullest ... must improve attendance and arrest activity ... good career potential' (Mollen Commission 1994: 81). This appears to indicate that the personnel department was not closely appraising the person being evaluated and was using formulaic phrases in a ritual assessment. But this could also be said of the Internal Affairs Division (IAD), because Dowd had attracted fifteen investigations following complaints; but all were unsubstantiated and he was continually held to have 'met standards'.

Perhaps Dowd as an individual may have had a personal predilection for rule-bending; we don't know this. But irrespective of any personality characteristics, he was placed in an environment of wide open opportunities for unbridled deviance with seemingly no supervision, unlimited autonomy, a chronic inability to pick up any negative signals about his conduct and that of his cronies, an evaluation system that saw him as the near ideal officer and an internal control system that parried every complaint against him. In other words, Officer Dowd failed as an individual by turning to a career in crime within the NYPD, but that career was fostered by manifest organisational failure. At the basic level of front-line supervision, for instance, *where were the sergeants?* And at the level of internal control, what was the IAD doing?[18] And what did the other officers in the precinct think of Dowd and his gang?

In short, corrupt officers were venal, violent and out of control and were the antithesis of the professional, impartial, law-bound model of the responsible public servant that police forces project in the official paradigm. And these 'bent cops' could thrive on the opportunities provided for deviant activity because the system failed to prevent, locate or investigate them; indeed, the system can be held to be *collusive* in their crimes. Despite the 'red flags' vigorously waving about his conduct, from informants and from the pattern of complaints, Dowd was able to follow his corrupt career for at least six years after someone should have stopped him. And that was largely because other cops did not dare to 'rat' on him and no supervisor wanted to intervene. Above all, the conduct of Dowd and others was patently far more than some cosy form of being on the take for so-called 'individual gain' with the local gambling syndicate. They were super-predators engaged in a range of serious criminal offences.

This material leads me to the defining of 'corruption' in the next chapter. Later, in Chapter 2, I go on to detail the features of the police organisation and occupational culture that are potentially conducive to deviance and corruption.

Notes

1 Many authors use this definition but then give umpteen examples of corruption by collectives of officers where there is no discernible 'individual gain' and/or there is far more involved than some form of instrumental 'gain'.

2 This refers to *Ordinary Men* (Browning 1992), on atrocities committed in Poland by a German battalion of 'ordinary' reserve police officers in World War Two. Also in nearly all accounts of corruption female officers play no part; Maas (1974: 251) does mention a female officer involved in a scandal in the NYPD.

3 This draws on Reisman`s study of bribery within American multinationals in the 1970s and his distinction between the 'myth system' and the 'operational code'; e.g. a corporation may state explicitly it is strongly opposed to bribery while covertly and routinely engaging in bribery.

4 Reiss (1971) does note that certain forms of police deviance including crimes were observed by the researchers during the project for his book. Whyte in *Street Corner Society* (1955: 124) mentions that cops in Boston rarely paid for groceries and one cop would openly fill up his car with free groceries before the weekend: 'I mean he really loads up – one family couldn't eat all that stuff. He must take care of all his relatives on that.'

5 The British Police Services Statement of Common Purpose and Values is: 'The purpose of the police service is to uphold the law fairly and firmly; to prevent crime; to pursue and bring to justice those who break the law; to keep the Queen's Peace; to protect, help and reassure the community; and to be seen to do all this with integrity, common sense and sound judgement. We must be compassionate, courteous and patient, acting without fear or favour or prejudice to the rights of others. We need to be professional, calm and restrained in the face of violence and apply only that force which is necessary to accomplish our lawful duty. We must strive to reduce the fears of the public and so far as we can, to reflect their priorities in the action we take. We must respond to well founded criticism with a willingness to change.' National and International Police Associations have codes of conduct for police officers and many individual forces have 'mission statements'.

6 Personal communication from Martin Voyez (Western Australia Police); with thanks to Martin for material he has sent on police corruption, commissions and reform in Australia and on the anti-corruption efforts in Western Australia.

7 Westley's research on police violence was conducted earlier but was only published as a book in 1970. Important in establishing the field were Skolnick (1966), Bittner (1967), Reiss (1971), Van Maanen (1973), Manning (1977) and Rubinstein (1973) in the US and Banton (1964) and Cain (1973) in the UK. Of the four commissions the *President's Commission*

on Law Enforcement and Administration of Justice: Task Force Report on the Police proved especially influential in setting out norms for professional policing (Goldstein 1977: 5).

8   In some countries and some forces it is 'SOP' to beat someone who gives police a hard time during a chase, perhaps even baiting the cops, and especially if the driver does not submit readily; see Collins (2008: 89) for his concept of 'forward panic' in such incidents. 'SOP' also relates to the documentary film based on the book '*Standard Operating Procedure*' on the ill-treatment of prisoners in the US-controlled prison Abu Ghraib in Iraq (Gourevitch and Morris 2008).

9   The Roman satirist Juvenal was referring to a man who employs guards to protect his wives; but who would guard the guards – against the *wives*!

10 The United Kingdom of Great Britain and Northern Ireland consists of three separate jurisdictions – England and Wales, Scotland and Northern Ireland.

11 A Commissioner for Complaints in Scotland and since 2007 a *Garda Síochána* Ombudsman Commission for the National Police Service, Irish Republic.

12 The distinction also echoes the concepts of 'formal' and 'informal system' in the organisational literature (Salaman 1979).

13 Discussions with, and theses from, officers from the Indian subcontinent convey the routine of 'baksheesh' or 'speed money', taking tips for services to prisoners in custody and claiming 'expenses' for performing routine duties; bribes are elicited on threat of planting evidence while suspects with money can bribe to have almost any criminal charge dropped. Officers are also pressurised from above to change their political loyalties and show favouritism to particular politicians and officials.

14 But then in the US free meals, tipping, discounts and 'moonlighting' (the latter often allowed by the police department) are more pervasive and more likely to be seen as natural perks of the job than in the Netherlands. In the UK and the Netherlands, moreover, a range of formally negotiated discounts with service and other firms are available for police.

15 In New Zealand several officers were accused of 'pack-rape' and of covering up the offences; Operation Austin, launched in 2004, investigated accusations by women of sexual assaults by officers or former officers, a number from the 1980s when some victims were minors (one was 13). Following 'Austin' several former officers were jailed and some serving officers have resigned (*New Zealand Press Association*, 12 December 2007).

16 I return to the Mollen Commission in Chapter 3.

17 Dowd spent ten years in prison; on leaving he was repentant of his misdeeds, was no longer married, no longer saw his children and was in a halfway house looking for a job (*New York Daily News* 2004).

18   The IAD comprised some 1,200 personnel which made it a sizeable internal control unit for the roughly 40,000 employees of the NYPD (sworn officers and civilians). In comparison the Department of Investigation (DOI) for everyone employed by New York City had about 1,000 operatives for 350,000 people (personal communication Kevin Ford who worked for DOI).

Chapter 2

What is corruption?

Corruption was their profession: police work was an incidental activity.

(Alex 1976: 93)

Definition and forms of corruption

Throughout this work a central thread will be that the corrupt activity of police officers will be viewed both as 'individual' failure but also, to varying extents, as institutional failure. I say 'individual' as in western society the autonomous individual is held morally and legally responsible for his or her decisions; and if anyone can be held to know what is not legal then it surely has to be a police officer. Yet there are no 'individuals' in organisations, meaning that people in a collective entity adjust and adapt to social pressures and institutional expectations (Punch 2009). Indeed, these pressures and expectations are particularly strong in the police occupational environment, with its emphasis on solidarity and inclusion, as will become evident. Let us now turn to the definitional issue of what 'corruption' is and the forms it takes.

Bribery and 'conventional corruption'

Police corruption in its narrow, legalistic sense generally refers to: *an officer knowingly doing or not doing something that is against his or her duty for some form of financial or material gain or promise of such gain.* This limited focus is geared principally at bribery and ostensibly financial arrangements for not enforcing the law. I say 'ostensibly' because many arrangements with organised crime in relation to prostitution, gambling and other illegal activities are typically lubricated by 'bungs' and favours, but the 'gain' is also amplified by the ways in which cops endeavour to regulate, make more predictable and manage their working environment in a range of relationships with criminals and others.

The offence of bribery is posited on an external briber, one who is bribed and *some form of reciprocation* from the one who is bribed. It implies that the initiative for the transaction comes from someone outside the police organisation. Generally the nature of the reciprocation is vital for proving that a criminal offence has taken place; simply accepting gifts or small amounts of money without evidence of reciprocation might then fall under internal disciplinary regulations. For instance, showing that an officer altered a statement so that the briber will not be prosecuted for an offence would be an indication of reciprocation. That proof of reciprocation would require the briber to testify against the one who is bribed unless there is other evidence or a confession; but criminals are unlikely to incriminate themselves, while police officers generally follow the occupational wisdom of 'you never cough' (never admit anything).

The slant of legislation and regulations is clearly to deter officers from accepting external inducements. But the briber may be positioned within the police force itself. In Providence, Rhode Island, for instance, officers seeking promotion would pay another officer for the answers to the sergeant's exam (Stanton 2003); and in some forces supervisors take money for tailoring duties to individual requests.[1] The offence is then internally based rather than externally driven. Furthermore, it may be the police officer who requests the bribe so that the direction of the corrupt initiative is reversed. This can lead to an amicable and mutually agreeable arrangement; but given that the officer has a degree of power over enforcement it can also foster extortion by the police official of a bribe from a citizen.

Another element in many definitions of corruption is that it is geared to 'individual gain'. Yet the material on the subject conveys that deviant and criminal practices in policing can at times be individual but are overwhelmingly collective. These practices can occur in a small group, a specialist squad, a substantial segment of the force or even throughout almost the entire organisation. And the definition of 'gain' may vary considerably and not be financial. Indeed in some of the more serious forms of police deviance there is no briber and no tangible financial or material gain; the 'gain' may be getting an arrest or a conviction, achieving status and receiving praise, public acclaim and perhaps a recommendation. Already it is clear that 'corruption' is more complex and intricate than is formulated in many of the legal and existing academic definitions.

Three typologies

As well as this traditional definition geared largely to bribery and gain in return for favours, there is a more elastic if not all-encompassing definition of corruption as *'deviant, dishonest, improper, unethical or criminal behavior by a police officer'* (Barker and Roebuck 1973: 3). Corruption then overlaps with police misconduct that may not be illegal and with police 'crime' in the widespread and even systematic deviation from the law by officers. Deviant behaviour is conduct that violates normative expectations in a group or organisation; its definition is then relative to the audience judging the digression (Downes and Rock 2007). What is deviant within the official paradigm may not be deviant within the operational code; and some forms of police deviance may fall under internal police regulations rather than the criminal law. Crime is, of course, formulated in the criminal law; but the formal definitions are 'law in the books' as opposed to the 'law in action' which is a matter of investigation and prosecution in a process of negotiation and definition within a specific context. Furthermore 'crime' in the legal sense means offences that potentially infringe the criminal law if they were approached and defined by the authorities as crimes and were taken to trial in a criminal court. And conventional corruption in its limited sense is also normally defined as criminal in law. But for a range of reasons police misconduct that is potentially definable as crime is often redefined as a disciplinary offence and handled in the 'private' justice of an internal tribunal, or is never even formally registered but is handled through informal means. This implies that there is a considerable 'dark number' of police crimes.

To touch on the range of practices contained in the wider notion of police corruption that I wish to use I consider three typologies. The first is a typology of types of officers; the second is a well-known classification by Barker and Roebuck (1973); and the third looks broadly at three levels of deviance.

Grass-eaters, meat-eaters and birds

The first part of this section derives from the testimony of a senior officer before the Knapp Commission (1972), which investigated corruption within the NYPD. He typified three sorts of officers (quotes from him are in italics; Barker and Roebuck 1973: 35).

Grass-eaters. The 'grass-eaters' did not look for graft or kickbacks but passively accepted them as the natural perks that were spontaneously on offer. *'Well, they'll accept a cup of coffee or a free meal or a television wholesale from a merchant, but they draw a line.'* These benign grazers had no moral qualms about accepting free food and reductions on purchases; this was widespread and any officer who refused such offers became the deviant for foolishly rejecting 'easy money' and 'easy pickings'. Serpico was such a 'foolish' cop and his story illustrates graphically the dilemma of a straight officer who becomes the 'deviant' in a corrupt environment (Maas 1974; and see Chapter 3).

Meat-eaters. The 'meat-eaters' were proactive carnivores; they went after the graft in order to organise and regulate arrangements. *'The meat-eaters are different. They're out looking. They're on a pad with gamblers, they deal in junk, or they'd compromise a homicide investigation for money.'*[2] They set out to make deals either of mutual benefit to the parties involved or in aggressive forms of extortion such as enforcing the 'licensing' of illegal enterprises in return for payments and/or offering protection from enforcement or from harm from competitors.

Birds. The 'birds' tend to be forgotten whereas the previous two categories are frequently cited; yet this is an interesting category because it conveys a class of officers who avoid deviant practices. The officer testifying spoke of the 'birds' who glided above without looking down and without taking part. *'The birds just fly up high. They don't eat anything either because they are honest or because they don't have any good opportunities.'* These officers doubtless had reasons for consciously or instinctively keeping their hands clean and their consciences unsullied; perhaps it was from serious moral or religious convictions or else sensitivity to long-term career prospects.[3] Or, as the officer said, they did not work in an environment with opportunities to tempt them.

But it could also have meant indifference or fear of getting involved. With the birds gliding up above it presumably led to the carnivores intimidating or even exploiting the herbivores. The latter could hardly point to the former because the meat-eaters possessed knowledge of the grass-eaters' deviance and could effectively blackmail them into silence or else lean on them heavily.

There are three factors of interest in relation to this categorisation. First, did the givers of 'freebies' to officers do this from natural kindness or did they expect some form of reciprocation? An almost universal response from police officers is that there is invariably a latent expectation by the owner of an enterprise frequented by cops that there will a quick police response to any trouble, a sympathetic hearing if the owner gets into a dispute with clients and a blind eye turned to minor infringements.[4] In effect, police officers have power and discretion in enforcement so that *all relationships* lubricated by gifts and goods, work-related but also personal, may be seen as carrying an implicit benefit at some stage for someone wanting something from the officer. There is always the chance that a favour from someone to a police officer will lead to a demand for some form of reciprocation. This makes the police officer both powerful and eternally vulnerable.

Second, did this backdrop of grass-eaters in some way provide an encouraging environment for the meat-eaters? Did the grass-eaters turn a blind eye or was there ever disapproval of the rapacity of the carnivores? This is related to questions such as, when do people start on a deviant path? And why do some people remain at a certain level of deviance without going on to the next phase? The purists, for instance, warn against taking that first cup of coffee as it might mean the start of a criminal career. When and how does deviance in policing start and what turns an officer into a meat-eater?

And third, if a 'bird' was promoted to a higher rank, did he or she continue to soar above the reality of the street and remain (wilfully) ignorant of deviant practices in the lower ranks? This could form an obstacle to perceiving the existence of corruption and dealing with it effectively. And if a meat-eater was promoted or moved to where it was difficult to carry on with the former illegal deals, how did he or she cope with the guilty knowledge of malpractice imbibed in their deviant days? Did it mean that they were forewarned to look for the signals of deviance in their subordinates so that they could become transformed and crack down on corruption? Or did they experience a form of near miraculous amnesia – Australian cops say, 'he's had the injection' – which allowed them to slot into their new identity in a supervisory function as if they had never cut corners, taken backhanders or roughed up a suspect in their previous role? Or did those officers who engaged in deviance lower down remain deviant on promotion but in new ways and at a higher level, exploiting the fresh opportunities that come with high office?

This born-again transformation is more likely in those systems, notably in the UK and US, where all officers begin at the base of the organisation before proceeding up the ranks on promotion.

In the more paramilitary or *gendarmerie* type of forces in much of Continental Europe and elsewhere, in contrast, there is a two-tier system of recruitment and training for the lower and upper ranks. Senior officers do not start at the street level and are to a certain extent insulated from certain corruptive influences.

Dirty Harry and other types

> Just what I needed, a college boy... What's your degree? ... Sociology? You'll go far. That's if you live ... Just don't let your college degree get you killed.
>
> ('Dirty Harry' in the 1971 film of the same name; quoted in Moskos 2008: 1)

Here I look at diverse profiles of police officers to glean the motivation that draws them into rule-breaking. For example, an iconic figure in the genre of cops using 'dirty' means for 'good' ends is the legendary 'Dirty Harry' (the fictional detective played by Clint Eastwood in several films; Kleinig 1996). In addition, drawing on my fieldwork in Amsterdam and on classifications of police officers in the literature, I have constructed a typology of police officers and their relationship to deviance and corruption.

Uniform carrier. This cop is between a ritualist and a retreatist in the sense that he (or she) has joined policing primarily for instrumental reasons and tries hard not to work too hard. In the British force they are called 'uniform carriers'; and in Baltimore a 'hump' (Moskos 2008). They put in minimum effort, avoid difficult assignments and evade informal socialisation; but they are unlikely to be involved in serious forms of deviance as they choose marginality and are not sought after as partners. They do play a role in fostering disillusionment among the young, keen officers. In some accounts, including Chan (2003) and Moskos (2008), it is plain that 'old hands' take it easy and do not exert themselves.[5] They may, then, form the first step in disillusionment among those cops who wish to be active and assertive officers but begin to see other colleagues are indifferent, complacent and poorly motivated.

Mister (sic) Average. When I was conducting research in Amsterdam, probably most of the patrol officers seemed straightforward, conformist workers who did the job in a satisfactory fashion. But typically they were fairly laid back about policing; they were pleasant and reliable colleagues but were not overly motivated. They might take part in some mild grass-eating but stayed out of relations that would lead to more serious forms of deviance. The majority of officers were like this and there was something of an attitude of not overexerting oneself and of sarcasm against 'rate-busters'.

The other types listed below were more likely to be involved in rule-bending and rule-breaking; they were also more likely to be in plain-clothes or detective work than in uniformed patrol so this pattern is plainly related to the nature of the work and the opportunity structure. But first there is a group that tends to get neglected among the uniform carriers and devious 'duckers and divers'.

Professionals. The professionals (also referred to at times as 'legalistic' officers) are involved in policing as a profession that they find challenging and fulfilling; they believe in achieving results by 'good' – meaning skilful and honest – policing and are reflective if they fail. If they do not get a confession or are not making progress in a case they tend to be self-critical and are resolute about doing it better next time. Niederhoffer (1967) also uses the category 'professionals' in his typology while Shearing speaks of the 'good officer' (1981: 33). In particular they do not get too frustrated by setbacks and refuse to be drawn into rule-bending and corrupt practices. They see the use of violence against a suspect as 'bad policing' which will only gain poor, if not useless, information. Perhaps it seems strange that they exist alongside patently 'bent' colleagues – this is one of the mystifying features of policing – but either they turn a blind eye for career reasons or they develop techniques of avoidance with judgements on who can be trusted and who not.

The deviants came from the following groups. It is possible that people passed from one group to another and changed their spots during their time in the police for a variety of reasons.

Dirty Harrys. In the 'Dirty Harry' syndrome police work is viewed as a conflict between good and evil where tough or devious methods are deemed appropriate to achieving a result such as an arrest and confession (Kleinig 1996: 52–64; Klockars 2005). Dirty Harry Callahan was the archetypal cynical but dedicated cop who believes the 'system' is too lax and that you have to use unorthodox methods to get 'good' convictions against real 'villains'. Callahan views policing as a form of crusade where cops' prime task is to fight crime by taking criminals off the streets, with extreme violence if necessary. But Dirty Harry has a 'moral' code in that he would never take a bribe to drop a case; and would never ever set someone up – unless, of course, the suspect fully 'deserved it'.[6]

Noble causers. 'Noble cause' is a term used in the UK and elsewhere to express the 'dirty hands' justification of officers like Dirty Harry on using devious means to achieve supposedly just ends. In an article entitled 'The Necessity for Dishonesty', Goldschmidt (2008) analyses interviews with ten British cops who with one exception are rule-benders and who maintain that only in this way can they enforce the law; and, they argue, it serves the 'public good'.

Innovators and number-crunchers. Some officers who get into trouble are dedicated and respected cops who are innovators seeking the boundaries of the law and practice to achieve results. And some cops and units are so keen to 'score' that they falsify data. The pressure to bend rules is largely self-generated; there is no external briber, no bribes and no one is seeking direct material gain. What they want is institutional success and the corresponding kudos.

Crusaders. These officers are not necessarily deviant but they are obsessed with crime-fighting – they despise criminals whom they hunt remorselessly – and with a one-sided 'war' against crime; this can lead them into deviance and law-breaking.

Ideological combatants. A variant on the crusade metaphor is when the police become engaged in a conflict with an 'ideological' component. Here the politically driven cause replaces the fight against crime and the participants feel they are justified in using devious means in a 'war' for righteous ends against a dangerous enemy that threatens their way of life and values. In Northern Ireland during the 'Troubles' (1968–98) it was held that the predominantly Protestant Royal Ulster Constabulary (RUC) was institutionally biased against the largely Catholic population and engaged in serious deviance in response to the violence of the Irish Republican Army (IRA) (Ryder 2000). Ellis (1988) details politically motivated police deviance in South Africa during the apartheid regime; police engaged in a range of grave offences including murder, torture and subversion in covert operations that were instigated by racially motivated politicians against their opponents in the African National Congress (ANC) campaigning for the rights of the black majority.

Lone wolf. Some deviance can be conducted by an individual driven by a sort of personal crusade. In Rotterdam one of the 'best detectives' was involved in a major investigation that was halted by the authorities. But he continued to pursue it on his own and was eventually arrested passing information to a criminal for money. He had posed as a corrupt cop in order to infiltrate the drugs gangs: 'I was really mad that the crooks would get away with it because the investigation had run aground; my anger led me to infiltrate the group on my own. I lived in a sort of state of intoxication, in a tunnel, and I had only one aim – catching crooks. I sold the

25

police files to crooks to build up my credibility. If you give them something and ask for nothing in exchange then you`ve blown it with them.' Claiming this was part of the original investigation, and was solely designed to secure convictions, he presented himself in court as 'a lonesome avenger for whom no mountain was too high in his battle against the drug trade'. The court heard he had a rather rigid personality, had become lost in his own reality, could not easily accept disappointments and had developed a form of 'tunnel vision' regarding work. The judges were not convinced and sentenced him to two years in prison (*de Volkskrant* 1999). This form of near obsessive behaviour was 'individual' and forms an extreme perversion of the police culture's emphasis on crime-fighting.[7]

'*Cowboys*'. In my research station in Amsterdam the officers referred negatively to some other cops as 'cowboys' (using the English term). Shearing (1981: 34) speaks of 'real cops' who are the opposite of the 'good cops', and who can become folk heroes. In the literature, 'cowboys' is also sometimes used for highly aggressive officers (Collins 2008: 370). The cowboys could be picked out in the station; they were into the macho police identity with their nonchalant stance, used underworld slang profusely and were only interested in 'thief-catching'. They were typically undisciplined, drove too fast, played practical jokes on others, treated supervisors with near contempt, intimidated the weaker brethren and were recalcitrant about following instructions. They displayed a hunting instinct and constantly sought out opportunities for the chase, scuffle and the bravado of entry into the station triumphantly brandishing their prisoner. They were rebellious, keen to get out of uniform and become detectives, enjoyed delving into the watering holes of the underworld in the inner city of Amsterdam, became friendly with the bouncers in the clubs and socialised in cliques outside of work in clubs and bars that were formally off limits. There was ambivalence about them as they were seen both as undisciplined 'troublemakers', especially by supervisors, but also as colleagues who could be relied on to respond rapidly if any cop was in trouble.

These types are distilled from my own experience and from other classifications of types of officer in the literature (Wilson 1968; Muir 1977; Reiner 2000). The style adopted can be related to personality, or to behaviour in a specific group or station, and it can change over time. A Dirty Harry, for example, might become a 'meat-eater' from frustration and disdain about inept superiors and lax enforcement. And being a 'cowboy' could be a phase that dissipates with maturation; some of them in the research station in Amsterdam cleaned up their act and kept out of trouble to get accepted for detective training; several eventually became first-class detectives; but other 'cowboys' ended up in deep trouble (as we shall see in Chapter 4).

Barker and Roebuck

The second classification, which contains eight categories, refers to one of the most widely used typologies of police corrupt practices (Barker and Roebuck 1973).

1 *Corruption of authority.* Officers receive gain by virtue of their function without violating the law (free drinks, meals, services, etc.).

2 *Kickbacks.* Gain for referring business to particular firms.[8]

3 *Opportunistic theft.* Stealing from arrestees (also known as 'rolling' in the past), from victims of crime or of accidents, from dead bodies, from the scenes of crime and from colleagues.

4 *Shakedowns.* Gain for not following through on a criminal violation such as an arrest, impounding property or filing a charge.

5 *Protection of illegal activities.* Protection of those involved in illegal activities (typically prostitution, drug-dealing, gambling, illicit bars), enabling the enterprise to continue (this could also apply to legitimate firms, bars, restaurants, groceries, etc. which occasionally break the law).

6 *The fix.* Undermining criminal investigations or proceedings, loss of evidence, fixing parking tickets, and so on.

7 *Direct criminal activities.* Committing a crime in clear violation of criminal norms.

8 *Internal pay-off.* Officers pay supervisors for favourable adjustments to holiday arrangements, working duties including shifts and hours of works, for promotion and for easy assignments.

I added a ninth category to reflect deviant police practices particularly in drug cases.

9 *Flaking and padding.* Planting or adding to evidence to 'set someone up', to ensure a conviction or a longer sentence for a criminal (Punch 1985: 11).

This second typology is useful and touches on the main standard practices of conventional police corruption; but the classification is by no means exhaustive – there is overlap between the categories and confusion from the terminology. In 'corruption of authority' Barker and Roebuck are referring primarily to 'grass-eating', which they see as non-criminal. But 'corruption of authority' is not the most judicious term for a category that could also be applied to serious criminal offences. And why is the theft in the third category dubbed 'opportunistic' when cops have sometimes set out deliberately and repeatedly to burgle and steal? Then 'direct criminal activities' raises the question, what are *indirect* criminal activities? Also, Barker and Roebuck categorise this as for 'gain' but there are a range of other motives for a cop to commit a crime. In brief, much of what is termed 'corruption' by Barker and Roebuck and others is both abuse of authority and criminal and not always for 'gain' (in the sense of some direct financial or material gain or promise of such gain).

The third typology I have developed sets out to cover a wider range of deviant and criminal practices and to pitch them at diverse levels. Much of the literature and many of the categories, as above in Barker and Roebuck, refer to offences committed primarily by front-line patrol officers or detectives in operational functions. There is not a great deal of attention paid to external pressure for police deviance, the diverse motives for rule-breaking, the essentially criminal nature of serious police corruption, or to the broader societal consequences of police deviance.

Three-level typology of police deviance/corruption

Externally driven
State domination. Police are linked to state or local politicians and their illicit aims, with sometimes clandestine units, death squads and violence against political opponents and rivals in criminal enterprises and against out-groups such as terrorists, left-wing movements, street children and journalists (e.g. the RUC in Northern Ireland, GAL in Spain, 'Third Force' in South Africa).[9]

Capture by deviant elite. This is where deviant politicians and organised criminals have 'captured' the police agency; in his classic study of 'Rainfall West' Chambliss (1971) portrays the police as part of a 'cabal' of politicians, organised criminals and city officials who ran the town (Seattle) for illicit gain and to maintain and exercise their power.

Within the police domain
Grass-eating. The low-level deviance of accepting 'freebies' on offer to officers, usually viewed as a disciplinary and not a criminal offence; there can be considerable cross-cultural variations on how widespread the practices are and how seriously they are viewed by the agency.

Volume or conventional corruption. The wider range of more serious practices such as bribery, kickbacks, shakedowns, mostly covered by Barker and Roebuck (1973) and generally understood to form the bulk of conventional 'corruption'.

Process corruption. Newburn (1999) refers to 'process corruption' – such as lying in court, altering evidence, making false statements – which can lead to charges of perjury, conspiracy and 'perverting the course of justice'. These practices can vary greatly in the extent of their organisation and may shade over into the next two categories.

Meat-eating: predatory (strategic) corruption. Understood as proactive, aggressive efforts to regulate criminal markets and extort money from illegal but also legal enterprises; can also mean close cooperation with some segments of organised crime with direct involvement in criminal activities and conducting crime and preying on competitors (say stealing their drugs and recycling them).

Noble cause: combative (strategic) corruption. Typically assertive efforts to gain convictions and achieve results against organised gangs, major criminals or terrorist suspects by illicit means.

System failure: labelling, and wider impact, of corruption
Police institutional failure. On exposure, the deviance is seen as symptomatic of an institutional failure but largely confined within the police system. For instance, Stephen Lawrence was a black teenager who was murdered by a gang of white youths in London in 1993; for a number of reasons these youths were never convicted. An inquiry set up to look into the killing came to the conclusion that the Metropolitan Police was 'institutionally racist' (Macpherson 1999). Although the case was not primarily about corruption, the inquiry into this critical incident had a major impact on policing in London with regard to hate crimes and offences against blacks (Foster *et al.* 2005). It was viewed as a substantial and damaging institutional failure.

Police and criminal justice failure. The scandal expands beyond the police to touch on wider failures in the criminal justice system (investigations, forensics, prosecution, judiciary, appeal system), as in the 'miscarriage of justice' cases in the UK. These miscarriages were related to people who were suspected of IRA bombings in Britain, some of whom spent sixteen years in prison before being released; the cases also generated dissatisfaction about police investigating the police (see Chapter 5). The Inter-regional Crime Team ('IRT') affair in the Netherlands raised criticisms of police methods in tackling organised crime and critical attention spread to the wider criminal justice system and led to new legislation (Punch 2003; and see Chapter 4).

System failure with societal impact. The scandal goes beyond the criminal justice system, sponsoring demands for fundamental reform of the system but also raising demands to change the manner in which the state itself is governed. For instance, in Belgium the Dutroux case concerned a convicted rapist who was released early from prison; he abducted, abused and murdered four young girls (and an accomplice of his). For Belgians he was the ultimate folk devil. And if the police and judicial investigation had been competent and coordinated then it should have been possible to rescue the girls while they were still alive; despite tips about concealed compartments in his houses and searches of them the girls died in horrific circumstances (two were rescued). It also took some time for him to be linked to the abductions and for him to be arrested. There was such seething outrage throughout Belgium about incompetence, miscommunication and failings in the police and justice systems that there were nation-wide protests and huge demonstrations demanding reform not only of the institutions involved but of the wider manner in which Belgian society was governed. The father of one victim stated, 'I hold the Belgian state responsible for the murder of my daughter' (Punch 2005: 367). As with the Lawrence affair this case was not about conventional corruption, although there were rumours of corrupt relationships between Dutroux and some police officers, but more about a profound societal protest that viewed the system failure as a symptom of a deeper national malaise in Belgium, and led to significant institutional reform.

Forms and components of corruption

Drawing on this material and categories I shall view corruption as having the following components. It is the abuse of authority, of the oath of office, of trust (of fellow officers, the police organisation and the public) and of the rights of colleagues, suspects and citizens. It involves the misuse of police power and authority, utilising organisational position and resources largely to avoid preventing crime, to encourage crime by others, to engage in crime, to combat crime by illegal means or simply to exercise power for illicit ends. It can be individual but is typically collective with conspiracies to achieve diverse ends for the individual, group, unit or organisation to achieve formally approved goals and/or covert but informally approved institutional goals, to reach ends that subvert the official paradigm and to obtain some form of advantage or satisfaction through illegal means.

In this sense police corruption is not one thing as it takes diverse forms and can alter over time. It relates centrally to *abuse of office, of power and of trust* and manifests itself in many ways but most frequently in consensual and exploitive relations with criminals, in discrimination against certain groups, in excessive violence and in infringements of the rule of law and due process. Controversial use of police force leading to injuries and deaths can also occur in aggressive use of police dogs, high-speed chases, firing at an assailant during a foot chase, shooting from a moving car or firing at a fleeing vehicle (Walker 2005). Although misuse of force may appear remote from conventional notions of corruption it is often that 'beating leads to cheating' by cover-up or by charging the victim with assaulting the police. In a notorious past case of police violence in Sheffield in 1963, it was not just that a 'rhino-whip' was used but there was 'wholesale covering-up' including fabricating statements and destroying evidence (Whitaker 1979: 254). And at the National Symposium on Police Integrity in 1997 (Gaffigan and McDonald 1997), excessive force and brutality were included under 'corruption'.[10]

In terms of equitable and accountable law enforcement in democratic society these are grave matters. We have to abandon simplistic and atomistic notions of 'individual gain' and of primarily 'financial' arrangements. In essence I will use four concepts:

Deviance. An umbrella term for all forms of police activity that transgress internal regulations, the law and public expectations of legal and ethical conduct by the police.

Misconduct. It is clear from the literature that many of the low-level practices discussed as forms of corruption are types of 'occupational deviance' found in many other organisations. They are usually not infringements of the criminal law but are covered by internal disciplinary codes and regulations; and in practice some offences that might have led to a criminal investigation are negotiated down to the disciplinary arena. The 'misconduct' offences typically relate to drinking on duty,[11] poor punctuality, disrespect to a superior, neglect of duty, damage to property and so on as defined in codes of conduct.[12] Such offences are also sometimes dealt with informally by front-line supervisors; but it is difficult to find evidence on this largely concealed behaviour. It is the case that such disciplinary codes are frequently catch-all regulations demanding, for instance, that an officer accepts nothing in pursuance of his or her office. The sanctions that can be applied by an internal tribunal can range from no action or a caution to reduction in rank or even dismissal.

Corruption. This term will be used for a range of offences involving abuse of power and authority; this makes it much broader than bribery and the offences fall under the criminal law. For example, the IPCC defines 'serious corruption' for purposes of classifying the incidents to be referred to it for investigation under the Police Reform Act 2002, as attempts to pervert the course of justice, receiving payments or favours, corrupt handler–informant relationships, leaking confidential information, 'extraction and supply of seized controlled drugs, firearms or other material' and conspiracies in relation to all these (see www.ipcc.gov.uk). However, whether or not the label 'criminal' is attached, or how the alleged offence is processed internally, investigated and prosecuted, is a matter of internal definition and negotiation. As suggested above potential crimes by police officers have often almost certainly not been defined as such and have been dealt with informally or redefined as disciplinary matters. Furthermore, if one adopts a strict definition of 'criminal' as meaning a conviction in a criminal court then police officers tend to have an advantage in trials and are given the benefit of the doubt in relation to witnesses who are often perceived as untrustworthy (Kutnjak Ivkovic 2005). If these suppositions are accurate then it implies that only a small proportion of those officers who could potentially be convicted of a crime are perceived of, and investigated as, criminal suspects, ever appear in a criminal court as a defendant and hear a guilty verdict pronounced (Brodeur 1981).

It is clear that for me corruption relates to a range of serious offences. There is a vast difference between the banality of cops stealing rings from the dead and the hard-core corruption of falsely imprisoning a 54-year-old grandmother in order to force her sons to confess to a crime (Lamboo 2000: 153; Leuci 2004: 37).[13] If the accent is placed not so much on the offence but on the abuse of authority by enforcers of the law to break the law and then on police officers' ability to use their special status to avoid detection and investigation, we are speaking of abusing the office to commit crime and entering a criminal conspiracy to avoid detection. The key is employing the special status and authority, the knowledge and the resources for criminal intent. This takes us primarily into group offences such as 'process corruption' to fix cases and achieve convictions by illegal means which may be done for a variety of motives such as so-called 'noble-cause' corruption to put suspected serious criminals or terrorists in prison. Excessive violence can also serve a number of ends such as retaliation for some perceived offence against the police or simply exerting control over an area. For in all this it is the special status of the police officer that converts crimes by him or her into corruption. For example, the police officer is in a unique position to stimulate crime through an *agent provocateur*, to alter evidence, to intimidate witnesses and to engage in illicit activities that are a clear contravention of the rule of law and of due process. And this abuse of office and law-breaking is committed by someone whose principal function and oath of office holds him or her to abiding by both. It is a perversion both of the ends and means of policing (Newburn 1999: 6); or, as Goldstein states, the corrupt police officer 'is like a fireman setting fires or a physician spreading disease' (1977: 190).'[14]

Police crime. This term is used for serious offences that have little to do with almost any police-related ends (such as 'noble cause') but are a gross abuse of power. I am thinking of gratuitous violence, armed robbery, rape and murder (including murdering another officer);[15] also where offences relate to innocent victims chosen at random, and where they would be roundly condemned by nearly all police officers. People refer to the 'fog of war' and officers speak of an 'orgy' or a 'frenzy' of corruption where it has become near irrational, out of control, addictive and with the 'badass' element of the criminals described by Katz (1988). But there is no watertight definition. For instance, if these offences are conducted while on duty or off duty but using police knowledge, resources and authority then they would fall under 'corruption' if its main component is abuse of office. But the various codes and regulations governing police behaviour are so broad and all-encompassing that virtually any deviant act, however minor, can be viewed as abuse of authority and of office. Then police crime would also be synonymous with corruption.

That is why I wish to make a distinction between relatively minor incidents that are not 'criminal' (misconduct), more serious offences deemed 'corrupt' and are formally criminal, and those very serious 'crimes' that are deeply criminal in the sense that they are seen as unjustifiable even for most 'bent' cops. For example, if an off-duty officer uses his police badge and firearm to commit murder during

33

an armed robbery then this is 'crime by cop'; if it led to covering up the crime with the collusion of other officers and the altering of evidence then those other officers would also be corrupt.

Police organisation, police culture and dirty work

This broader notion of corruption is informed by notions of 'organisational' and 'occupational' deviance (Ermann and Lundman 1996). There is deviance and rule-bending in all organisations; when this is for employees' advantage at the expense of the organisation it is generally referred to as 'occupational deviance' (Green 1997; Ditton 1977; Mars 1982). Some of the informal practices found in police agencies – such as sleeping on the job, pilfering, work avoidance – fall under occupational deviance. And there is a police vocabulary of expressions such as 'mumping', 'cooping' and 'easing' to describe these practices (Manning 1977: 151–5; Holdaway 1980). Formal organisations in western societies are predominantly efforts to achieve stated aims by establishing control through 'rational-legal' bureaucratic structures. But research repeatedly reveals that control is often problematic and there are vestiges of both traditional and charismatic authority in organisational life (Salaman 1979). Moreover some organisations, particularly large public bureaucracies, simply function poorly and hence unwittingly foster deviance, or they may encourage or pressurise personnel to bend and break rules in the interests of the organisation. This is referred to as 'organisational' deviance in the sense of systemic rule-breaking either by negligence or lack of control or else as part of a conscious formal or informal strategy (Shover 1980). In other words, some of the forms of police deviance and their causes are related to the nature of the work, the occupational culture and the organisational ethos and structure and are, moreover, consistent with patterns in other organisations and institutions. This takes me into a consideration of the police organisation, police culture, 'dirty work', 'moral career' and 'inclusion' (Newburn 2003, 2005).

Police organisation

The literature indisputably indicates that police forces and the officers in them frequently if not routinely deviate from the official paradigm and the law (Newburn 1999; Sherman 1974a). Ostensibly the power of the police is regulated by law and by checks and balances but there is continual concern particularly with regard to abuse of that power, excessive violence, invasions of privacy and undermining of civil and human rights. What features in the organisation of policing distort the implementation of the official paradigm and lead to the sorts of deviations outlined above?

Impossible mandate. Many stakeholders define the primary mission of policing as combating and reducing crime but there is a wealth of evidence that the police alone can have only a limited impact on crime reduction (Manning 1977; Bayley 1994).

Goals and means. The emphasis on one dominant goal can pressurise the police organisation to adopt illicit means; defining goals as a 'war' or a 'mission' that must be won can lead to an overemphasis on goal achievement (Gross 1980; Sheptycki 2000b).

Control. Control is problematic in all organisations and this is often true in policing due to institutional fragmentation and sub-unit autonomy.

Fragmentation and autonomy. Descriptions of police agencies convey fragmentation, 'silos' that inhibit coordination, rivalry between units, turf wars, a strong sense of status with factional interests, powerful personalities pursuing their own agendas and building fiefdoms based on personal loyalty. There is a myriad of sub-goals, strong sub-unit identities and short-term immediacy focusing on means and not ultimate ends.[16] Fragmentation and lack of coordination can lead to considerable autonomy for specific units with low visibility and high operational freedom.

Leadership and layers. As an emergency organisation with considerable powers one might expect that leadership would be forcefully present in policing. In practice the top layers of police organisations are, like other organisations, arenas for egos and power-plays, and inter-personal factionalism fosters divisiveness, infighting and paralysis at the top echelon.[17] Police chiefs often demand a quick result from subordinates, sometimes turning a blind eye to rule-bending, but if anything should go wrong they retreat behind the formal paradigm as a 'cover your ass' (CYA) shield.

Management cops and street cops. Reuss-Ianni (1983) argued that traditionally there was a measure of solidarity across police ranks with a common 'cop culture.'[18] In the late 1970s in New York, however, there was the beginning of public management in policing that was strongly geared to external stakeholders. This increased the gap

35

between high and low in terms of culture, attitudes to work, internal control and dealing with the outside world. It could be argued that developments have led to accentuating this rift with 'strategic' cops at the top and management cops in the middle with both having considerable social distance from where the 'real' work takes place.

Decision-making. Many of the most important decisions are taken at the base of the police organisation, not at the apex as in many other organisations. The lower ranks are often indifferent if not disdainful of supervisors seen as inadequate at taking key decisions in operations.

Mock bureaucracy/front-line organisation. Much of the material on the police organisation shows it as a 'mock-bureaucracy' with the edifice of a semi-military, centrally led bureaucracy when in reality it is a 'front-line' organisation run by 'street-level bureaucrats' (Lipsky 1980). The police organisation does not always seem that impressive on the inside and displays a number of weaknesses in enforcement and delivering services; one explanatory factor is that in a front-line organisation the lower personnel have considerable power to shape what work is carried out – and how – and also to undermine control and hinder change.

The pivotal point here is to emphasise that police organisations are not always rational, tightly controlled and well led; life within them can exhibit irrationality, contradiction, paradox and even absurdity (Lyman and Scott 1970). Such features can enhance both the opportunities for deviance and the likelihood that it will not be detected and investigated. Those corruption-conducive features are reinforced by some of the tenets of the occupational culture.

Police culture

When you put on that uniform, you're not white or black. You're blue. We're one big happy family, right? Dysfunctional as hell. But what family isn't?
> (Academy instructor to police recruits in Baltimore,
> cited in Moskos 2008: 2)

Certain facets of officers' views about their work, crime, criminals, justice, punishment and the publics they serve are reflected in the tenets of police culture (Young 1991; Crank 1998; Chan 2003). If we take culture to refer to the norms, values and practices tied to the 'way we do things around here' (Schein 1985), then there may be many variations in police culture related to national cultures, specific force cultures, diverse branch cultures within a force (such as Uniform,

Traffic, Detective Branches), district and specialist unit cultures and to small group cultures (Waddington 1999b). This leads to a complicated matrix of diversity and variety. In its broadest sense there are positive features to police culture – loyalty and solidarity can be positive and can provide comforting mutual support – but here I concentrate on features that serve as a backcloth for accepting, promoting and justifying deviant behaviour. In that particular sense the fundaments of police culture are generally held to rest on the following:

A sense of mission. Policing is seen as a vocation if not a noble mission; this enhances a view of being separate and different and of doing valuable work that is not fully appreciated by outsiders.

Danger and sacrifice. Although policing is not a particularly dangerous occupation compared to some others, the awareness of potential danger is embedded in the culture; there are areas and assignments associated with danger but there is also a sense that danger is unpredictable and can arise at unexpected moments (Crank 1998).

Solidarity. A powerful feature in policing is that the nature of the work, operating in uncertain situations of potential conflict, generates strong solidarity. In the 'cop code' officers must always back up partners and respond rapidly when an officer is in trouble (Reuss-Ianni 1983).

Rule of silence. A major domain assumption is that an officer will follow 'the code' or 'blue wall', meaning the rule of silence; indeed loyalty can mean lying for another officer (Kleinig 1996: 67). Breaking the code elicits strong informal sanctions such as threats, ostracism, damage to personal property, malicious rumour and discrediting black propaganda and even violence (Reiner 1992: 93).[19] Serious deviant behaviour in a police agency is a perversion of the official paradigm and there has to be camouflage to conceal it. Part of the cement that holds police agencies together is the code of silence; of course, this is also prevalent in other contexts including school playgrounds, prisons, the military and organised crime.

Cynicism. The work brings officers in touch with the seedy and disreputable side of society with exposure to human frailty and suffering related to drink, drugs, violence, sexual abuse and poverty; the work may appear pointless – 'it's shovelling the same shit up against the pipe' – and lead to cynicism. As with Dirty Harry, the cynicism may mask an underlying motivation to gain results, be an occupational thick skin developed in response to the sights and sounds of human pain, or even indicate an underlying concern and commitment (Manning 1977: 119). But some officers become jaded, bitter, hardened or indifferent by all this (Moskos 2008).

Hedonism. There can be an emphasis on, and tolerance for, drinking, drugs and sex (both on and off duty). In the closed society of policing there may be fast driving in patrol cars with races and dares, wild parties, pranks, sexual escapades and other forms of 'backstage' behaviour.[20]

Machoism. Policing was predominantly a male occupation until comparatively recently and there are many accounts of the strong masculine ethos with bullying, sexism, harassment and intolerance. Certain roles enhance a strongly masculine ethos as in assertive squads against street crimes, special detective units and SWAT squads.[21] Macho norms and behaviour can lead to wild and aggressive incidents when off-duty cops get drunk, trash hotels, get into fights and beat up civilians (Hopkins-Burke 2004: 2).

Female exclusion. A noticeable feature of corruption is the rarity of female officers becoming closely involved. The conspiratorial male bonding with out-of-work socialising tends to exclude females from corrupt circles; the occupational culture deems them to be 'untrustworthy' and stereotypes them as 'too emotional' or unable to 'keep quiet.'[22]

Pragmatism. The culture can support an anti-theoretical view that practical knowledge gained on the streets is the key to police craftsmanship; 'theoretical' knowledge is suspect; and innovation and change are resented (Skolnick 1966; Lee and Punch 2006). This may begin when recruits hear experienced officers telling them that formal learning is 'bullshit' and they should forget all they have learned at the training academy when they go out on the streets (Van Maanen 1973). This makes 'rookies' vulnerable to learning deviant values and practices from the 'old hands'.

Taking it easy/work avoidance. In accounts of policing there are norms and behaviour that replicate the rather truculent views of blue-collar, industrial workers about not working too hard and resenting 'rate-busters'. What first disturbed Serpico as an eager rookie in New York was that many cops were avoiding work and 'cooping' at night (sleeping in comfortable spots out of the cold; Maas 1974: 54–5).[23]

Social isolation. The nature of the work, together with hostility from the community and patterns of shift work can lead to social isolation with officers preferring to socialise together outside of work, becoming negative about outsiders, feeling that only a fellow officer can truly understand 'what it is really like'. In some remote or rural units, and where officers are stationed in barracks or police housing, this can mean functioning in an occupational community with little separation between personal life and work and even amounting to a form of 'total institution' (Goffman 1961). In some communities cops face hostility and are seen as pariahs (Manning 1977: 134).

Suspicion. The possibility of danger and interaction with untrustworthy people impregnates the working personality with an inherent suspiciousness. Officers look out for 'symbolic assailants' (Skolnick 1966), discount the accounts and motives of suspects and others and substitute the assumption of innocence with the supposition that suspects are guilty until proven innocent.

Dichotomous thinking. Dividing the world into simplistic, rigid categories based on a dichotomy between good and evil, rough and respectable, trustworthy and untrustworthy, 'them and us' is common – with a battery of negative epithets (assholes, scum, animals, toe-rags; Van Maanen 1978b). To Leuci average New York citizens were an 'ungrateful bunch of hypocritical assholes' (2004: 71).

Excitement/action. Routine work is disparaged, with a predilection for action and for the chase, scuffle, arrest, delivering the prisoner at the station with accolades for a good arrest, proudly showing off the injuries from a valiant struggle.

'Real' police work. This is held to be crime-fighting and 'catching crooks'. Other tasks are denigrated as 'shit work' and officers in non-operational roles are disparaged as 'empty-holster guys'.

Rough justice/just deserts. There are norms about distributing 'rough justice'; for instance against suspects fleeing arrest and giving the pursuers a hard time, those resisting arrest, abusing officers and their families, attacking a female officer, refusing to be subdued in custody, spitting at an officer,[24] threatening officers with retaliation, and so on. People behaving in this way are likely to receive more than usual force. In the interaction with serious criminals there may be norms about ripping them off as informal punishment or on releasing an informant's name because he has crossed the police in some way even when the police know he will be severely punished, if not eliminated, by criminals. These views rationalise gratuitous violence and 'dirty tricks', including using false statements, planting of evidence and perjury in order to get a conviction against a suspect with the rationalisation that 'he deserved it'.

Moral/political conservatism. Police officers usually come from relatively conventional backgrounds (Reiner 1978) but the occupational identity can shape a 'conservative' view of the world favouring stability, order and a tough approach to crime with antagonistic stereotypes of certain groups based on an ideological standpoint (including in the US right-wing or racist groups; Beigel and Beigel 1977: 150).

'Ducking and diving'. The culture is often posited on the view that the work requires cutting corners and bending rules (utilising the so-called 'Ways and Means Act'). Officers face a web of rules in a blame culture; an officer in London said 'you can't go eight hours on the job without breaking the disciplinary code' (Manning 1977: 165). Cops learn to bend rules for a variety of reasons without necessarily perceiving this to be illicit (Young 1991). Those skilful at rule-bending may be revered within the operational code with a degree of tolerance for certain forms of deviance. Officers learn to 'gild the lily' in statements in court or arrest someone on a 'resource charge' bearing little relation to the actual incident (Chatterton 1976). This is viewed as the craft of 'making the case' and shaping report writing, interrogation and presentation of evidence to garner a desired outcome (Barker and Carter 1990). This manipulation and fabrication becomes the routine style of lubricating work and is seen as legitimate, while there is respect for cunning, artful 'duckers and divers'. In Hobbs' (1988) description of detective work in east London in the 1980s the cops were wheeler-dealers, doing 'business' in negotiation with crooks and informants and adopting the linguistic conventions and appearance of entrepreneurial villains in East End culture.

Routinisation and commodification. Features of police work associated with pain, suffering, death and victimisation become routine (as with other emergency workers). This routinisation and instrumentality can apply to exchanging prisoners or information as commodities or gearing arrests to making money through overtime – in the US referred to as 'collars for dollars'. A Baltimore cop referred to court overtime as 'our heroin' (Moskos 2008: 122). Three factors are of importance. First, where there is a permanent reservoir of available 'suspects' there is also a constant source of arrests and these form a supply of 'collars' to suit personal or institutional needs. Second, this generates a mercenary attitude to arrests and information that can be traded for cash or bartered for favours. This pattern appears strongly in accounts of policing in the US.[25] But third, and importantly, this manipulation with regard to arrests means falsifying statements and lying in court. Does this send officers down a 'slippery slope' and how 'slippery' is the slope (Kleinig 1996: 174–81)?

In elucidating these factors, which crop up widely in the literature but which may not be universal, it might seem that the average police officer is a distorted male chauvinist who drives too fast and is into heavy drinking, wild sex, scatological language, snorting coke in the patrol car, highly creative report writing, lying in court, arresting the innocent for gain and abusing prisoners. This negative stereotype emerges from a compilation of the darker underpinnings of police culture and practice. Yet it is the case that in a survey of police and public commissioned by the Met of London in the early 1980s there was considerable reporting of sexism, racism, drinking on duty, bribery and persistent rule-bending (Smith and Gray 1985).[26] Furthermore, the archetypical cop in movies is invariably idiosyncratic,[27] displays contempt for the formal rules and superiors and goes outside routine to solve the case. The universal cultural message conveyed by fiction is that cops habitually bend or break the law.

Elements of the standard tenets of police culture are repeated in accounts of policing in several societies, although there will be some national variations. It is possible to see these norms as arising 'naturally' from the nature of the work. Indeed, many ethnographies of policing are empathetic portraits of wily cops trying to make sense of an impossible job under difficult circumstances and doing so with guile, comradeship, wit and even compassion (Bittner 1967; Rubinstein 1973; Punch 1979). Also an officer may espouse police culture *in extremis* while in the company of other officers yet perform in a relatively restrained and correct manner in interaction with citizens. Culture possibly shapes attitudes more than actual behaviour and operational codes can contain a portion of occupational myth rather than the working reality.

Of particular interest here, however, are those elements espoused by elements of the standard police culture – especially solidarity, rule of silence, cynicism and rough justice – which promote or tolerate rule-bending and rule-breaking; and also make cops refrain from intervening in deviant situations involving colleagues of which they disapprove. Allied to this is the concept of 'dirty work' and how it steers police into deviance and corruption.

Good people and dirty work

When considering why certain people choose to engage in deviant behaviour it is possible to look at individual personality variables. For instance, perhaps some of the highly deviant police officers in the cases mentioned in this book – such as Dowd in New York and Putnam in London (see Chapter 5) – had a predilection for rule-bending and might well have become deviant in any setting. The sociological and criminal perspective commences from an alternative premise that the social environment is crucial in making people become deviant. It poses certain questions. What is the nature of the work and organisation? What is the opportunity structure for deviant activities. What are the social groupings that construct deviance and recruit others for their deviant enterprise? How widespread is the deviance and how strongly supported is it? And what are the social and material rewards for participating?

This perspective assumes that the social context is crucial and that 'good' people can be induced to do almost anything if they become convinced that it is appropriate in a setting with others pressurising, encouraging and rewarding them (Browning 1992). Each context will have its own opportunities, inducements and rationalisations; and it is held that people enter the context as 'moral' and rule-abiding individuals but allow themselves to be persuaded by social pressures to do things they would possibly not do outside of the group. As Jackall (1988) remarks of managers, they leave their conscience behind when they enter the corporation where they are prepared to do whatever the company asks of them. In short, good people are induced to do bad things in certain settings in response to group and/or institutional pressures (Hughes 1963; Punch 2008, 2009).

In policing, for instance, the nature of the work seems to subvert the officers' oath of office and training and divert them from the official paradigm – geared to professional impartiality and dispassionate legality – to stereotype people, to discriminate, to use undue force and to engage in rule-bending and rule-breaking. This would seem to arise primarily from the social and occupational pressures of the context, because in the accounts of corrupt officers about their deviant careers they frequently say that they only began to slide into deviancy because of the strength of the occupational culture, peer-group pressure, their disillusionment with the police organisation and because of the nature of the work.[28]

A wealth of research reveals that much police work is routine if not mundane (Bayley 1994; Waddington 1999a) but that the work does at times involve facing violence, sudden death and serious injury, body parts and dead bodies (some badly decomposed), acts of cruelty, major accidents with appalling injuries, people in trouble and people causing trouble. Cops enter and deal with the 'dirty' and even menial jobs largely in marginal segments of society. Moreover officers find that some groups cause them more trouble than others and it is difficult to remain impartial and restrained and treat them with respect and courtesy (Chan 2003). This is especially true because they learn that those they encounter can be devious, unreliable, untruthful, aggressive and abusive. They tend to divide people into 'moral' categories, which generates powerful negative feelings about those involved in certain gruesome crimes and leads to feelings of contempt if not hatred for criminals who exploit the weak and the vulnerable and who cause serious harm. They are also asked at times to engage in unsavoury and seedy tasks such as intervening in industrial disputes, repressing dissent and using subterfuge and dissimulation to spy on citizens (Marx 1988; Fijnaut and Marx 1995).

Their work also brings cops into close contact with criminals and they enter the 'underworld' to gain information and to recruit informants – the old saying is, 'you don't meet crooks in church'. They spend time in bars, interact with criminals, are surrounded by the temptations of the flesh and are tasked to build relationships with 'villains'. Those relationships may be conducted in an instrumental and professional manner but can also lead to deals, compromises and even friendships.[29] In some cases criminals and detectives come from similar backgrounds and share a common world view (Hobbs 1988; Leuci 2004). Organised crime is essentially about exploiting the weaknesses of others by controlling access to illegal markets and exercising power over those markets. In the 'underworld' the natural order deems that the strong exploit the weak; this echoes the Sicilian concepts of *fesso* for the naive whereas the opposite, *fuerto* or *scaltro*, means that people are 'sly, nimble, quick-witted' and possess 'the sly knowingness which is able to fox authority, to get things done, to bend rules' (Steinberg 1989: 13). Some cops imbibe that world-view and wish to be *fuerto*, even seeing it as essential to surviving in tough environments, to gaining respect and to achieving results. Rather like Sicilians, they react to the vagaries of the criminal law, the weaknesses in the police hierarchy and coping with the cast of loathsome or amenable criminals with wily ruses in the culture of ducking and diving.

Corruption has, moreover, always been closely associated with the so-called 'victimless crimes', where society forbids certain pursuits but the inelastic demand encourages criminals to set up illicit enterprises, typically with regard to prostitution, gambling and intoxicants. If the police are faced by the popular use of such enterprises, weak enforcement and resilient criminals who skilfully manage to remain in business, then it makes sense in the eyes of some officers to come to some form of arrangement with the gangland operators and bosses (either by amicable consensual deals or by extortion).

This leads to close relations with 'villains' and some officers start to revel in the 'dirt'; they frequent bars where they rub shoulders with criminals. In east London detective work was conducted in a pub where the saloon bar was the territory of cops and crooks and other customers stayed out of it (Hobbs 1988). In the UK heavy drinking if not alcoholism has been a serious occupational hazard, especially among detectives. And going undercover means that the officer has to look, think and act like a criminal and perhaps even engage in criminal acts. Major 'villains', moreover, are sometimes charming and manipulative people who can exert an influence on cops who may start to look up to the 'godfathers'; it is not unknown that an officer passes to the 'other side' and joins the 'Mob' (organised crime).[30]

It is noticeable that much corruption is associated with recurring and hence in some respects predictable areas that involve face-to-face relations with criminals, contacts with criminal enterprises and with 'legitimate' enterprises that do not always conform to the law (typically clubs, discos, bars, restaurants, places of entertainment, shops and casinos in inner-city areas) and that are willing to come to arrangements in order to remain in operation and avoid prosecution. The predictably risky areas are undercover work (and 'going native'), informant handling (where the informant ends up running the handler) and corruption-conducive areas, particularly licensing and regulation of premises, 'vice' (gambling, prostitution and pornography) and, above all, drugs. As we shall see, the immense profits in drugs and the power of certain drug-dealers has made tackling drugs the prime hazard where police are likely to succumb to doing deals, to combative corruption, to meat-eating and to being 'turned' (Manning 1980).

This material implies that the context helps to determine corruption and that originally good officers can become contaminated by – or attracted to – the dirty work and 'invitational edges' of opportunities and inducements on offer and/or the conviction that dirty means are necessary to achieve good ends (Manning and Redlinger 1978).

Inclusion, moral career and slippery slope

In this final section I wish to accentuate two important points that are interrelated and recur throughout the literature and in the cases to be presented. First, a key element of solidarity is 'inclusion'. And, second, in unravelling the pathways officers take into deviance, there is the notion of a 'moral career' with the accompanying image of the 'slippery slope'.

Inclusion

I was told there would be $200 a month extra; I knew it was from gambling. It was seen as 'easy money' and you were stupid if you didn't do it. I refused. But then there was temptation and peer pressure – 'do you want to be in or do you want to be out?'

(Former corrupt cop in *Bad Cops*, 1993)

Running through the cases and literature is the powerful pull of officers wanting to belong to a group or clique and how that solidarity can be related to the code of silence and to engaging in deviance as a condition of that acceptance. This example graphically illustrates the process of inclusion/exclusion: in 1988 a young officer on patrol on his own at night in South Yorkshire faced a serious assault:

> Two armed men in military fatigues, faces hidden by balaclavas, dragged him to waste ground. They forced him face down in the mud, hands cuffed behind his back, a gun to his head. His trousers were pulled down. He feared the worst. Shaking uncontrollably, expecting to die, he heard the click, saw the flash: not a gun, but a camera. Prostrate and terrified on the ground the young officer turned his head to see the armed men removing their balaclavas. They were laughing. Laughing policemen. (Scraton 1999: 15)

This was an initiation ceremony by fellow officers of the sort also found in some military units. The behaviour was intimidating to the point of bullying but the 'target' was faced with a stark choice. What if he complained? For the not so subtle message was, 'if you keep quiet you are one of us'; hence keeping silent was also an instantaneous test of membership.[31] So the choice for the young cop was, did he want to be in or be out? The incident also raises some questions. Where were the supervisors? Did they know, did they approve, did they find it amusing to see the photos (perhaps having taken part in similar ordeals themselves), or did they turn a blind eye? But, most important, did this nocturnal 'prank' bear any relation to a broader pattern of tolerating deviance and keeping quiet in other areas of work? Was the group behind the feigned attack involved in other dubious activities?

The crucial point is, to what extent does acceptance into a police group involved in deviance imply that the 'rookie' engages in the deviance and keeps silent simply to attain and retain membership? How far does that take him or her down the path into corruption; does it start the slide down that 'slippery slope'?

45

Moral career/slippery slope

The concept 'moral career' is employed to allude to the process by which someone is introduced to deviant group behaviour. There are stages of recruitment, initiation, learning techniques, relating to other members in terms of roles and hierarchy, becoming proficient in deviant activities and finally becoming fully accepted. It implies a path of steps to be overcome, a graded learning process, assimilation to a group, subordination to group discipline and group leaders, distancing from the 'straight' world and acceptance of the group's justification for its deviance. The deviant behaviour is then rationalised in 'vocabularies of motive' (Sykes and Matza 1957).

A key concept related to 'career' and entering deviance is the 'slippery slope' metaphor. This conveys the social-psychological process by which the deviant begins with relatively small deviant acts that may initially be found disturbing. But the deviant finds that rule-breaking becomes easier with each successive act so that he or she 'slides' ineluctably down the slope until far more serious forms of deviance become habitual and accepted. A New York cop eloquently expressed this slide: 'Then before you know it, you're up to your ears. I can't even remember where the money was coming from. You know, taking money is like getting laid. You remember the first time with a broad; after that it's a blur' (Shecter and Phillips 1974: 87–88).

An alternative metaphor is that of a 'ladder' (Sherman 1974c: 199). The slope image is rather deterministic, as once on the slope the deviant will continue to slide if not accelerate, and one clearly cannot slide back up a slope. The ladder has attractions as an alternative image to sliding. First, some cops go part of the way but then stop, for instance those grass-eaters who do not graduate to meat-eating. And, second, some accounts of entering deviance accentuate that the first step was especially difficult to take, caused considerable doubt and required some moral anguish to overcome (Matza 1969).

This ladder suggests a series of steps, where the first step is difficult to surmount but where the steps become progressively easier to take; some cops take just one or a few steps and then remain on a plateau, but others go the whole hog and reach the top (say, the meat-eaters). Perhaps there is also a slide at the top of the ladder back down to even deeper depths of deviance, depositing the slider onto a carousel in perpetual motion and where the only exit is to jump off. So cops climb, slide, plunge or drift into corruption with varying degrees of awareness and of doubt.

Conclusion

In the section above I have examined the key process of inclusion and the crucial concept of moral career. In the following chapters I explore the contours of a number of scandals from several societies – in the US (Chapter 3), the Netherlands (Chapter 4) and the UK (Chapter 5) – and also examine pathways into police deviance (Chapter 6) as well as reform and accountability in policing (Chapter 7) before concluding with Chapter 8. It will become evident that each individual case contains a large number of contextual variables while the deviance covers a wide range of practices and offences related to opportunities, relationships among those concerned, nature of the transactions, level of organisation, susceptibility to control, types of harm, as well as the diverse accomplices and victims involved.

First, it will become patently clear that there is on occasion substantial if not systemic deviance from the official paradigm. Second, this implies that officers had to be recruited, to be initiated, to come to accept and to rationalise the deviant behaviour which was often greatly at variance with the edicts of the paradigm and their oath of office. And, third, the extent of the deviance can be so extensive that it fosters 'system failure' in the sense of a wider institutional failure to see the deviance, and prevent or deal with it. In short, the checks and balances meant to deal with deviance malfunctioned. Of central significance in these processes is the role of police culture and especially norms on solidarity, loyalty and silence; these norms and practices are in turn reinforced by the conspiratorial nature of police deviance. But, as we shall see, corruption also leads to certain officers abandoning the solidarity of the deviant group and betraying it; the poacher goes to work for the gamekeeper and stalks his fellow poachers in a double role. The hunter turns to hunt his own; deviance begets deviance.

Finally, I use 'corruption' not in its narrow sense of individual advantage based on financial gain but in the broader sense as defined above. Corruption is not one thing, it takes diverse forms and can alter over time. Essentially my focus is on serious deviations from the official paradigm, from the oath of office, from official rules and/ or the criminal law and from the public trust in the police. They manifest themselves in many ways but most frequently in consensual and exploitive relations with criminals, in discrimination against certain groups, in excessive violence and in infringements of the rule of law and due process. I abandon simplistic and atomistic notions of 'individual' and of primarily 'financial' arrangements and reject the

47

'bad apple' analogy. Rather I shall be examining bad barrels and bad orchards – and those responsible for those orchards – and showing that corruption is serious collective deviance with diverse motives, several forms that shift over time, and with diverse consequences including severe consequences for its multiple victims.

In essence, my view is that 'bent cops' are not born but are predominantly made by the culture, the work and the institutional context. Indeed 'a bad cop has to be a good cop first' (Wood 2003). Part of that context can be external to the police organisation, and part of it is that police organisations are at times dysfunctional and are into denial on the existence of corruption, they fail to put adequate resources into internal control, have an adversarial or non-cooperative attitude to oversight and in some respects can be held to passively or actively condone deviance while even colluding in it (Cohen 2001).

The police *organisation* is to 'blame' for much corruption; it has failed to see it, to prevent it, to control it and to stop segments of the institution entering recidivism. This may appear to reify the organisation but actors in institutions tend to perceive the organisation as real and give it an existence outside of themselves (Gross 1980). Of course, corrupt practices have to be articulated by groups of police officers who break the criminal law and sometimes behave like criminals (yet often evading the criminal label of a court conviction). And in common with nearly all deviants they have to rationalise and find justifications for breaking the law in order to make it acceptable to themselves. As one British cop put it, 'If I act dishonestly, with the intent of the good of society, I am not wrong. I am at the top of my game. I am confident, I am right, and I will win more of my cases than I lose. Honesty does make the job easier, and it makes you feel better about what you do. *But I am willing to do what I have to do to make the case*' (Goldschmidt 2008: 127, my emphasis).

Notes

1 In the US when patrolmen had to phone the sergeant regularly a cop who wanted to 'coop' (sleep) at night without being disturbed would tip the sergeant not to have to call him.
2 The 'pad' refers to the organised system of 'graft' – the payments from organised criminals for protection from enforcement – and 'junk' means drugs.
3 The NYPD's reforming police chief following Serpico's press revelations and the Knapp investigation, Patrick Murphy, apparently kept out of

plain-clothes work to evade the deviant practices (Maas 1974: 21). See Chapter 3 on Murphy.

4 A retired British copper told me that when he joined the police his first task each morning, as the new boy, was to collect bread and bacon from the shops without paying and make breakfast for his shift. With a laugh he said that if the baker or butcher got into a dispute with someone then there was a tendency to settle the matter 'impartially' in their favour.

5 When Leuci (2004: 30) joined the NYPD he wanted to see action; but he was put with an old-timer in a remote precinct who never made arrests because he had a painting business on the side and would lose money by attending court on his days off.

6 When Ralph Crawshaw was lecturing on human rights to police in a developing country they stated, 'But we only use torture when we are absolutely sure of the suspect's guilt' (personal communication).

7 Other 'lone wolf' cases include an officer planting evidence in order to 'discover' it himself, placing a bomb under his own car and shooting at fellow officers in order to create an incident. One can only speculate on the motivation but perhaps it relates to making oneself important by becoming the centre of an incident (Ryder 2000: 92); or else gaining kudos for locating weapons or explosives as was the case with several officers of the Irish National Police in Donegal who had planted them themselves (Morris Tribunal 2004). McLaglan (2004: 318) speaks of individual 'Lone Rangers' who resort to leaking classified information as intensified control and surveillance have made collective deviance more visible and risky.

8 In Britain the 'golden hook' refers to the tow-truck when officers recommend a particular garage to someone whose vehicle has been damaged; the cops receive a kickback. This also happens with undertakers, when an officer recommends a funeral service to people confronted with a sudden death.

9 For the so-called 'shoot to kill' cases involving the RUC and people suspected of involvement in IRA terrorism in Northern Ireland see Stalker (1988). GAL was a covert police unit in Spain set up to assassinate suspected ETA activists; ETA uses violence to gain independence for the Basque region of Spain (de Volkskrant 1998c). GAL was held responsible for abductions, torture, bombings and 27 assassinations with much of its activity taking place in South France where many ETA members hid out and planned operations (de Volkskrant 1998b). The 'Third Force' in apartheid South Africa was involved in violent clandestine activities against ANC members who were fighting to overthrow the regime (Ellis 1998). In all three cases high-level government politicians and officials were involved in some way. In Spain officers facing long sentences changed their evidence and implicated senior officials and even government ministers (de Volkskrant 1998a).

10 Sometimes the violence is prolonged and racist. In Leeds in 1971 two officers persistently hounded and abused a homeless man of Nigerian origin with a history of mental illness; they beat Oluwale, urinated on him and chased him towards a river where he was later found drowned. Many see this as an early example of racist police violence in the UK and as leading directly to his death. But the officers were cleared of manslaughter and convicted only of assault (Whitaker 1979: 279–80). In the Selmouni case in France a suspect of North African origin (with Dutch nationality) was abused for several days in a Paris police station; he was beaten, publicly humiliated in front of several officers including a woman, urinated upon and had a rubber truncheon thrust in his anus. The French government was subsequently held responsible for this 'cruel and degrading treatment' by the European Court of Human Rights (Crawshaw and Holmström 2006: 186–97).

11 This was a severe problem in the early decades of policing in Britain (Bailey 1981: 14).

12 For England and Wales see *The Police (Complaints and Misconduct) (Amendment) Regulations 2008* published by the Home Office.

13 She served three years before she was released following the cop's confession.

14 Beigel and Beigel (1977: 69) write of a 'black neighbourhood' in Chicago which had been improved with facilities and resources leading to crime reduction; 'the police openly and actively transported prostitutes and drug addicts from another part of the district to this block'. The police profited from this as the deterioration led to requests for police protection which 'gave more power and discretion to the police, facilitating bribery, extortion, and other corrupt activities'.

15 An off-duty female officer of the New Orleans PD shot dead a male colleague, moonlighting as a security guard in a restaurant, during a robbery; she also shot dead two of the owner's children; she later went on duty and returned to the scene but was recognised by a family member who had hidden from her (*New Yorker* 1997: 99).

16 In a British force it was common until fairly recently that if an officer from Traffic tried to enter the territory of the Detective Branch he was made to feel unwelcome, if not chased out.

17 Certainly fictional and film presentations tend to depict police chiefs unfavourably as either slippery careerists or as bumbling bureaucrats.

18 I'm not sure how accurate this is and it may be something of a myth; surely in old-style police organisations based on formal, bureaucratic and even militaristic discipline there was a chasm between officers and men?

19 A promising female recruit at the NYPD Academy faced sexual harassment from an instructor (as had other female cadets). She discussed this 'in confidence' with a leading member of staff but her

complaint was leaked; as a result of persistent hostility she resigned from the police (Mollen Commission 1994: 51).

20 One hears of orgy-like CID parties in the UK with an amount paid beforehand for damages and cleaning given their history of wildness causing damage to carpets and property. A review of a novel by a former copper states that it 'presents its policemen as indistinguishable from the people they police; its best joke is... the unexpected metamorphosis of a cell full of unwashed and foul-mouthed louts, sleeping off the previous night's drinking and brawling, into a squad of policemen' (Hayward 2000).

21 SWAT means 'Special Weapons and Tactics'.

22 It could also be that female officers exclude themselves for a variety of reasons but it will be of interest to see if that pattern of female exclusion and distancing from deviant behaviour will alter as more female officers enter the areas of police work most associated with corruption.

23 On cold nights Serpico found a school's warm boiler-room was full of cops, some with fold-down cots – and alarm clocks because they had to phone the sergeant at arranged times.

24 Spitting has changed its significance with the rise of HIV and it has been considered a 'dangerous weapon' in recent US courts' decisions where suspects during arrest have spat in cops' faces or mouths.

25 Leuci (2004: 242) says that in New York you never told cops in another unit about a case you were working on because they would poach it and sell it; once a case he was working on was sold three times.

26 Apart from this overview there were four publications detailing the Policy Studies Institute's survey, by Smith (1983), Small (1983), and Smith and Gray (1983a, 1983b).

27 The fictional Swedish detective Wallander is divorced, listens to Callas and cannot cope with computers; the highly popular British TV detective Morse drives a vintage Jaguar, is single and never seems to develop a lasting relationship with women. They are both lonely outsiders in society and within the police force; both are dogged by superiors who disdain their individualistic, 'intuitive' approach and unorthodox methods.

28 In her study of recruits during their first two years in an Australian police force that had been through a reform process and had renewed its training accordingly, Chan and her colleagues show that although there was diversity in adaptations to and views on policing, just about everyone in the sample – whatever their gender or background – moved closer to the tenets of the practical police culture with negative stereotyping of out-groups (Chan 2003).

29 In Northern Ireland an RUC officer treated his informant almost like a 'brother', inviting him to his home at Christmas and giving him clothes; allegedly he would suggest crimes to the informant and even take part

with him in some of them; the officer was convicted but freed on appeal (Ryder 2000: 265).

30 In the Netherlands a former cop from my research station in Amsterdam became the bodyguard of Klaas Bruinsma, a drugs baron and so-called 'godfather' of the Amsterdam underworld; the ex-cop then became involved with a rival gang and was convicted of murdering Bruinsma (Middelburg 1993).

31 In fact this officer suffered a nervous breakdown which meant the story came out and several officers were sanctioned. This behaviour and rituals are not unusual among young men being admitted to insider groups, as in the military, schools, colleges and sports teams.

Chapter 3

The US: from pad to crew

Certain precincts in Harlem ... comprised what police officers called the 'Gold Coast' because they provided so many payoff-prone activities ... In contrast, the Twenty-Second Precinct, which is Central Park, has clearly limited payoff opportunities. As Patrolman Phillips remarked, 'what can you do, shakedown the squirrels?'

(Knapp Commission 1972: 67)

Police corruption in America

Corruption, like violence, is a recurring feature of American society. It surfaces continually in city, state and national government and even at the presidential level. President Nixon was forced to resign the presidency in 1974 or he would have faced impeachment and prosecution.[1] There is as well a long and rich history of police corruption in the US (Richardson 1974). Corruption also arises periodically in other segments of the criminal justice system – in corrections, among prosecutors and the judiciary as well as federal agencies such as the Federal Bureau of Investigation (FBI) (Ermann and Lundman 1996). Several authors have traced this umbilical link between policing and corruption. Uchida (1993), for example, views 'the large-scale corruption that occurred in most police departments' as a common theme characterising US policing in the nineteenth century. And Kappeler *et al.* (1994) echo this: 'To study the history of police is to study police deviance, corruption and misconduct'.

Historically much civic and police corruption can be linked to the weakness of the central state and to the manner in which urban politics developed (Gardiner and Olson 1974). The US developed as a highly decentralised society compared to most Western European states, with the federal government in Washington DC having low significance. The early independence of the US from Britain also meant that it did not experience the reform of policing ushered in by Peel in the mother country. Rather than one institutional style for public policing there developed a patchwork of diverse policing agencies at the federal, state, county, city and local community levels (Klockars 1985).

Typically the burgeoning American cities of the nineteenth century were run on the lines of 'machine politics' where the party in office and officials associated with it were determined to remain in power (Banfield and Wilson 1963). For instance, the infamous Tammany Hall in New York, representing the Irish-American hold on the Democratic Party, became a byword for machine politics lubricated by 'graft'. The incumbents of office in the cities and their ward bosses induced people to vote for them and to contribute to their coffers by the distribution of favours and jobs to faithful supporters. The police chief, commanders in the wards and often ordinary officers owed their positions to patronage and even paid for the appointment as in pre-modern times.[2]

In the early days of policing, moreover, the qualifications for becoming a cop were minimal and it was easy to reward supporters with a job in policing.[3] This context meant, however, that there was often a mercenary, venal culture where jobs, licences and decisions in court were up for sale and public life was thoroughly corrupt (Gardiner 1970). 'Corruption' was how the system functioned and for many it was legitimate, 'honest' graft; indeed, for many cops being corrupt was effectively a condition of employment (Goldstein 1977: 189). And it was said that in many cities the main functions of the police were to hand over the graft to whichever party was in office and to 'keep the blacks in their place'.

It also meant that police chiefs were dependent on the mayor while the ward bosses could control the appointment of the local commander.[4] Pat Murphy, NYPD Commissioner in the early 1970s (at the time of the Knapp Commission, see below), saw this legacy as generating insecurity, conservatism and a failure of leadership in American police chiefs. He wrote scathingly:

What we have here is a pathetic spectacle, and those of us in the police world know that the insecurity and weakness of the nation's police chiefs is one major reason why police departments are so readily (a) compromised and (b) corrupted, and, therefore (c) controlled by the politicians. The police chiefs do not, cannot, and seemingly will not stand up to the political establishments ... A tiger in the street, bullying the troops and the other unfortunates, the chief is a lamb in the major leagues, cowering and simpering like a court jester in the halls of the mighty. (Murphy and Plate 1977: 23)

In a country that is so diverse we should be wary of overgeneralising. The patterns of civic governance, graft and cronyism varied from city to city and state to state (Goldstein 1977). What can be concluded, however, is that city politics in the USA typically reflected localism, political pluralism, ethnic diversity and corruption (Manning 1977). Race, for example, is clearly a crucial theme in US urban life and policing. In a city with a large population of blacks which was run by a white civic elite and a police force that were corrupt, the black community might feel not only doubly discriminated against – being both repressed and exploited by the police – but also neglected by them.

Viewed historically there have, then, been examples of rampant corruption in many of the large cities.[5] In addition scandals have occurred in recent years in several major police departments including Miami, New Orleans, Cincinnati, Detroit, Oakland (California) and among sheriffs in Los Angeles and Pennsylvania state troopers (Walker 2005). This pervasive police corruption in America has to be placed within the broader environment of civic, judicial and business corruption (Reisman 1979).

Furthermore, whether or not this pattern of police misconduct leads to media exposure, political debate and efforts at reform depends on the shifting alliances between city politics, police leadership, the media and public tolerance for police deviance (Sherman 1977). In Chicago, for instance, it was said the public *preferred* a corrupt police; 'Most Chicagoans considered the dishonesty of the police as part of the natural environment. The Chicago River is polluted, the factories belch smoke ... and the cops are crooked, so what else is new?' (Rokyo 1971: 107). In Philadelphia the public believed that officers slept on the job, were rude, took bribes and sexually harassed defendants, yet 'still rated the police department very high'! (Gaffigan and McDonald 1997: 62).

There has also been a pattern in the US of passing moralistic legislation in the area of 'vice' (gambling, prostitution, pornography and alcohol) which was difficult to enforce while prosecutions typically led to mild sanctioning. This often had the unanticipated consequence of encouraging organised crime and stimulating corruption, with Prohibition in the 1920s as the prime example (Moskos 2008). Also, low-level 'graft' emerged from complex local ordinances related to health, Sunday trading, traffic and building regulations which impacted on ordinary citizens and legitimate firms and which the police could exploit through discretionary enforcement. People who broke some petty regulation could pay a small 'fee' to the local cop or face a fine as a reprisal for not playing the game (Ward 1975). Above all, 'vice' shaped large illicit markets based on inelastic demand from a wide public while ensuring considerable profits. The police and organised crime would, then, frequently decide that it made sense to come to an agreement; rather than combating crime the police regulated it, 'licensed it' and profited from it.[6] Enforcement became a negotiable commodity to be traded and also selectively employed as an inducement or sanction to such agreements (Brodeur 1981).

To illustrate these processes I shall focus especially on New York. Of course, New York is not America – just as Amsterdam is not the Netherlands and London not the UK – but the NYPD has provided both a rich vein of corruption and a prime example of the cyclical nature of scandal and reform. This can be illustrated by two commissions of inquiry in particular, namely the Knapp (1972) and Mollen (1994) Commissions. These provide valuable and contrasting analyses of changing patterns of corruption and of proposals to tackle it.

I also briefly consider two more recent scandals within the Chicago PD and the LAPD. And, to illustrate that police corruption does not only occur in large cities, I look at corruption in the tiny police department of Sea Girt (New Jersey). In fact most of the 1,800 police departments in the USA are very small, many with under ten officers. Finally, the examination of the developments between Knapp and Mollen reveals both how corruption adapts to the control regime and how the organisational reforms following scandal can be short-lived.

New York and the NYPD

In New York there have been periodic corruption scandals

involving the NYPD since its formation in 1854 and roughly every 20 years since the first major exposure of systemic corruption by the Lexow Commission in 1894.[7] That Commission called many witnesses:

> Coaxed, prodded, and sometimes bullied by Goff [counsel to the Commission], the witnesses told a shocking story. According to them: the police secured appointments and won promotions through political influence and cash payments. In return for regular payoffs they protected gambling, prostitution, and other illicit enterprises. Officers extorted money from peddlers, storekeepers, and other legitimate businessmen who were hard pressed to abide by municipal ordinances. Detectives allowed conmen, pickpockets, and thieves to go about their business in return for a share of the proceeds. Officers also assaulted ordinary citizens with impunity. As Captain Max Schmittberger, a twenty-two-year veteran whose testimony was the high point of the investigation, charged, the department was 'rotten to the core.' (Fogelson 1977: 3)

The police were also flagrantly partisan and intimidated Republican voters, ignored Democratic repeat voters, interfered with ballot boxes and openly displayed their Democratic allegiance. But apart from a ritual cleansing little was done to alter policing and the refrain of abuses was to become familiar. In 1950, for instance, there was the 'Gross scandal', which virtually echoed the situation recorded by Lexow over 50 years earlier. Gross was a bookmaker who had paid the police a million dollars yearly to protect his gambling empire valued at $20 million. 'Before the affair was over, the Police Commissioner had resigned, most of the department's high command was implicated, more than a hundred policemen, including inspectors and captains were dismissed or quit under fire, and three of them committed suicide' (Maas 1974: 113).

There is, then, a constantly recurring and cyclical nature to scandal and reform in New York (as elsewhere in the US; Sherman 1978). For the revelations typically lead to a clean-up but, within time, the deviant practices re-emerge until a fresh scandal unleashes the repetitive dynamic of exposure, special commission and new broom at the top with tighter control. And each time faith and confidence in the formal paradigm are reconfirmed; and usually with the ritual casting out of the 'bad apples' and high praise for the majority of 'honest and law-abiding officers'.

For the US is also the land of periodic reform movements determined to clean out the stables. The major police scandals in New York, for instance, have nearly all elicited a commission to investigate the deviance – in 1894, 1912, 1932, 1949, 1970 and 1994 – and initiated changes (Kutnjak Ivkovic 2005). The inquiries repeatedly itemise police skulduggery. There has been the sale of police jobs, case fixing, blackmail and extortion, brutality, stealing confiscated property, use of false witnesses, judicial corruption related to bail and bondsmen and continually corrupt relations with the 'Mob' and with politicians. Another feature of American political and social life is an appetite for scandal going back to the 'muck-raking' journalists of the early twentieth century (Steffens 1957). This in turn has fostered crusades of 'sound and fury' by politicians and moral entrepreneurs which condemn the practices and argue for new measures to tackle the problem (Reisman 1979).

This book emphasises of necessity the murky side of American urban life but there have also been periodic efforts to reform civic affairs (Fogelson 1977). Generally these follow scandals but scandals are social constructs geared to a selective process. They are usually sparked off by diverse sources such as media exposure, a campaign against certain 'deviant' practices by moral entrepreneurs, a public inquiry, a political move by parties out of office to embarrass the rival party in power or by a whistle-blower (Sherman 1978).

Whistle-blowing is rare in policing given the strength of the code of silence. By whistle-blowing I am not referring to those officers who are prepared to talk as a result of immunity against prosecution or have been 'turned' and cooperate or even work undercover for the authorities. These have usually chosen to cooperate having been caught in law-breaking; this could be related to plea-bargaining, which provides immunity or a reduced sentence for cooperating. In contrast the Knapp Commission was founded following revelations to the press by two NYPD officers who were prepared to expose unacceptable police practices in which they had personally not been involved. One of those officers was Frank Serpico and he was, according to Maas (1974: 11), the first police officer in the history of the NYPD, if not of any police department in the US, 'to step forward to report and subsequently openly testify about widespread, systematic cop corruption – payoffs amounting to millions of dollars'.[8]

Serpico

Serpico, whose parents were Italian, joined the NYPD in 1959.[9] He was proud to be a cop and was eager, diligent and ambitious. From early on he avoided grass-eating as demeaning; he felt the police officer should be respected rather than be viewed with contempt or fear. He developed cosmopolitan tastes and was unconventional compared to most of his colleagues. His dilemma was that he was committed to policing and keen to become a detective but access to that area exposed him to corrupt practices.

Initially he solved this when he joined the plain-clothes squad by agreeing to 'park' the graft on offer with one of its organisers. But at heart he held a strong belief in the integrity of policing. However, the cops around him were cynical and disillusioned; they had adopted a purely mercenary attitude, following the old saying in policing that 'the job is only good for time or money'. One officer, Stanard, tried to get Serpico to accept money and was astounded by his refusal. He patiently explained how the system worked almost 'as if he were an executive explaining corporate benefits to a newly hired employee'; the monthly amount for each officer was about $800. This openness revealed that 'graft and corruption had become so entrenched in the department, so completely a way of life for a cop like Stanard that he could not conceive of another policeman's questioning of what he did, much less doing anything about it' (Maas 1974: 128). Serpico's distancing from the code of practice did not go unnoticed; he was threatened and subject to rumours about his sexual preference.

Serpico discovered that corruption throughout the Plainclothes Division (with some 450 members) was near universal. It was highly organised, well regulated and almost bureaucratic. Officers received nothing at first, to see if they could be trusted, and a sum was given later if they moved on; those transferred to less lucrative areas received something like 'severance pay' in compensation (Barker and Roebuck 1973: 33). The system of graft was known as the 'pad'; an individual officer's payment was his 'nut'; and a 'bagman', often a former cop, regularly picked up the graft from the establishments contributing to the pad. This was classic, 'straightforward' corruption viewed as easy and 'clean' money. 'Clean' had meant that it was not from drugs, but that was changing. In drug enforcement there was the 'score' which was the amount taken in a single transaction and, unlike the more egalitarian pad, it was usually retained by the individual officer or several officers. Generally there was widespread grass-eating and also the trading of arrests for favours; but principally the system was based on the regularised and lucrative graft of the pad with amicable relations with the 'cousins' under police protection from enforcement. There was too a working style that was nonchalant, with officers signing in and then perhaps going to a film or going home for a swim; in the office they sat around drinking coffee and playing cards. Serpico concluded that the main function of the Plainclothes Division was to manage the pad while looking after their criminal clients:

> What Serpico found so ironic was that the other plainclothesmen he met were really professional in the sense that they were first-class investigators, and they brought to their craft all the requisites this entailed – instinct, patience, technique, determination, and accurate intelligence provided by a carefully nurtured network of informers. If they had wanted to, they could have wiped out a major portion of the number one target – illegal gambling – practically overnight. But their motivation instead was that there was money in it for them. Serpico was constantly impressed by the way they could ferret out operations no matter how cleverly concealed, but their purpose was always to extort money from the people they caught. (Maas 1974: 137)

To a degree this was goal displacement or role reversal, with working the informal system taking over from law enforcement as the 'core business'. The operational code had effectively become elevated to the 'SOP' for the entire plain-clothes unit. Almost everyone was bent; the choice was participate, look away or move out. This was a very rotten orchard indeed; and it was the one healthy apple that proved 'deviant'.

At one stage Serpico tried to communicate this unwholesome situation to his superiors, aided by a colleague, David Durk. Durk was more articulate than Serpico and 'was able to verbalise easily and impressively much of what had been churning inside Serpico' (Maas 1974: 108).[10] Invariably there were promises from these senior officers about taking it further up the hierarchy but nothing materialised. There was also contact with someone from the Mayor's Office. Durk was seconded to the City's Department of Investigations (DOI) which investigates corruption among those working for the City of New York; and the DOI reported directly to Mayor Lindsay.[11] There was no response from anyone consulted and Serpico finally decided to testify against fellow officers in court.

Serpico was probably too straight and motivated to function in this city of sharks and within the messy, manipulative and mercenary world of the NYPD. In a sense he was a 'misfit' and this stigmatising epithet is often applied to whistle-blowers.[12] Serpico's message had fallen on deaf ears, while tension was rising between him and his colleagues when he was suspected of 'ratting' to superiors. In 1970 he and Durk decided to approach the *New York Times*, where editors pondered whether or not to run the story. Mayor Lindsay was forewarned about the likelihood of damaging articles appearing and swiftly announced an independent, blue-ribbon committee to investigate the accusations, the Knapp Commission. The impact of the articles in the *New York Times* (1970) by David Burnham, with the first headline, 'Graft Paid to Police Here: Said to Run in Millions', was so dramatic that the affair became national news.[13]

Both Serpico and Durk were prepared to appear before the Knapp Commission. Serpico also testified in court against several officers. They were low in the police hierarchy and no link was made to corruption among senior officers or their failure to act against it; effectively they were scapegoats. By now Serpico was ostracised at work and received threats. Then in May 1971 he took part in a raid on an apartment of suspected drug-dealers; he went in first but got caught in the doorway facing armed dealers. He called for assistance but received no backup; he was shot in the face and was fortunate to survive. In hospital he experienced harassment from fellow officers and received hate mail. There was information that the 'Mob' had a contract from fellow cops to eliminate Serpico. There remains a strong suspicion that he was deliberately set up in the raid, although Serpico himself has rejected this.

Some months later he was the prime witness before the Knapp Commission. In 1972 he received the NYPD's highest award, the Medal of Honor, but shortly afterwards retired and moved abroad, partly to recuperate from his injuries.[14] In 1980 he returned to the US and occasionally speaks in public on police abuse of power.

Serpico's story is significant for two main reasons. First, it indelibly conveys the unenviable position of the straight police officer who works in a thoroughly corrupt environment. The usual options are retreat or exit but Serpico did not want to abandon his chosen profession and opted to speak out. Second, it reveals that breaking the code of silence can elicit severe sanctions. The warm solidarity and comforting inclusiveness of the police 'family' for those who remain faithful to the operational code can instantly alter to exclusion, to pariah status and to facing sanctions for those who break ranks. Some corrupt cops will consider killing a colleague for washing their dirty linen in public.

Knapp Commission

The Knapp Commission, formally the Commission to Investigate Alleged Police Corruption and the City's Anti-Corruption Procedures, was set up by Mayor Lindsay. Knapp was a federal judge and the Commission started work in 1970 although the public hearings did not commence until autumn 1971. The inquiry began with limited resources and only a six-month deadline; but the Department of Justice moved in with federal funding to extend its deadline. The Commission heard testimony from 183 witnesses. It faced legal challenges from the Policemen's Benevolent Society and was unable to subpoena officers to testify until April 1971.[15] The public hearings attracted considerable interest because they were televised and people could view testimony from an array of police officers, city officials, victims of police shakedowns, Serpico and Durk as well as several corrupt cops who had agreed to work for the Commission. Its final report was published in December 1972.

This report was unequivocal. As Serpico and Durk had stated and others confirmed, deviance was widespread with systemic corruption related to both organised crime and legitimate businesses. Payments to the police were picked up weekly, everyone in certain units was on the 'pad' and the individual 'nut' was graded according to rank. Although some officers saw this as 'easy' money and its recipients as grass-eaters, there was also a culture of doing deals on serious cases with criminals paying for investigations to be dropped. Some officers still saw drugs money as 'dirty' but the report ominously stated that there was increasing involvement with drugs gangs.

In essence, the report concluded that corruption was widespread within the NYPD. Particularly plain-clothes officers in gambling enforcement displayed the pattern of organised payments; their individual 'nut' could reach $800 per month or more and supervisory officers were included. The individual 'scores' in narcotics 'could be staggering in amount' with one pay-off amounting to $80,000 (Knapp Commission 1972: 2). Generally uniformed officers were not involved in a pad but they could often enjoy many small, regular payments from legal and illegal establishments and occasional payments from 'after-hour bars, bottle clubs, tow trucks, motorists, cab drivers, parking lots, prostitutes and defendants wanting to fix their cases in court' (1972: 3).

The Commission used the grass-eaters/meat-eaters distinction but argued that the former are at 'the heart of the problem'. This was because the code of silence and threat of sanctions amounted to a situation where for the newcomer 'it is easier for him to become corrupt than to remain honest' (1972: 4). Grass-eaters formed a backcloth of widespread, petty deviance for the meat-eaters; the herbivores never interfered and hence silently condoned the practices of the carnivores.[16]

The Commission used a number of corrupt officers to work undercover for it; they had been caught but could not be offered immunity from prosecution. One of these was Patrolman Phillips and he acknowledged that his 'entire career had been one of virtually unrelieved corruption'; he called himself a 'super-thief' (1972: 51). Phillips gave testimony backed by film and tape recordings of corrupt transactions he had made with other officers. He had taken part in relatively 'petty' graft that involved 'construction sites, bars, restaurants, bowling alleys, and other establishments making regular payments to officers on patrol'. He was involved in the 'organised shakedowns' of gamblers and had negotiated deals with the criminal leaders of gambling operations who were willing to pay for immunity against enforcement: He had 'engineered innumerable "scores" of gamblers, pimps, loan sharks, illegal liquor dealers, and other violators who had paid him as much as several thousand dollars for their freedom following arrest', and had 'arranged for the alteration of testimony in criminal trials'. Phillips also enjoyed free hotel rooms and free meals at decent restaurants. He knew all the establishments in his area and was fully aware of the regulations that could be used to extract money from them by threatening enforcement for an infringement. He also had an extensive network of acquaintances throughout the department to supply information on the 'reliability' of other cops if he approached them about a corrupt deal (1972: 51).

Phillips had been caught taking bribes and agreed to work undercover. With a transmitter and under surveillance he worked undercover for around five months, taking corrupt payments and attending meetings at which crime bosses negotiated deals with the police. This material led to several trials and convictions, including that of officers who had accepted bribes from two 'mobsters' for getting them off a murder charge: 'Those indicted included three police officers, two retired detectives, and the two men who paid the bribe – one of whom was also charged with murder' (1972: 51). It became clear from the invaluable testimony of Phillips that the officers he dealt with while undercover discussed, or participated in, illicit arrangements as the taken-for-granted routine. Another officer who was asked to talk to the Commission, Bob Leuci, became diverted to another investigation where he was persuaded to cooperate with the authorities (a Joint Task Force with city and federal personnel). Leuci was a member of the SIU (Special Investigation Unit of the NYPD) which investigated major drug cases.[17] His undercover work ran parallel to the investigations of the Commission; I deal with Leuci and SIU later (in Chapter 6). Leuci's activities for the Task Force indicate that next to the Commission there were several agencies investigating corruption although Knapp was not always informed about them.

As well as the testimony of Serpico and Durk there were, then, several officers who set out in detail how extensive the corrupt practices had become within the NYPD. This decisively demolished the 'bad apples' defence. The main conclusion of Knapp amounted to saying that in New York there were rotten barrels if not a rotten orchard: 'Police corruption was found to be an extensive, Department-wide phenomenon, indulged in to some degree by a *sizeable majority* of those on the force and protected by a code of silence on the part of those who remained honest' (1972: 61, my emphasis).

The Commission's findings further elaborate the patterns of corruption with regard to gambling, narcotics, prostitution, sabbath laws, construction, bars, tow trucks, parking and traffic, gratuities, internal pay-offs and a miscellaneous category that included theft from burglarised premises. Some officers even stole rings from dead bodies or items from premises where someone living alone had died, or they searched the pockets of a 'DOA' (dead on arrival) at a hospital, took the keys and went to burglar the home.

There are three elements of the work of the Commission that are of particular interest: how attitudes to taking drugs money was changing; what reasons accounted for corruption flourishing; and what recommendations did Knapp make on reform?

Narcotics enforcement

Initially, taking money from drug-dealers was seen as 'dirty money', which reflected a similar attitude to that initially taken by the 'Mob' (Mafia).[18] But the Mob found the profits to be made with drugs irresistible. Traditional police corruption had been mostly focused around 'vice' – especially gambling, prostitution and liquor – but was shifting towards drugs. Senior officials within the NYPD perceived it to be 'the most serious problem facing the Department' (Knapp Commission 1972 91). Indeed, confirmation about the level of deviance in the narcotics area emerged with the news that over two hundred pounds of drugs had disappeared from the Police

Property Office during a number of years.[19] A senior officer from the Inspections Division of the NYPD was quoted by Knapp:

> Police officers have been involved in activities such as extortion of money and/or narcotics from narcotics violators in order to avoid arrest; they have accepted bribes; they have sold narcotics. They have known of narcotics violations and have failed to take proper enforcement actions. They have entered into personal associations with narcotic criminals and in some cases have used narcotics. They have given false testimony in court in order to obtain dismissal of the charges against a defendant. (1972: 91)

The corrupt practices included keeping confiscated money and/or drugs; selling drugs to informants in return for stolen goods or for resale to addicts; 'flaking' or planting evidence on a suspect or 'padding' the quantity of drugs seized in order to upgrade an arrest; illegal telephone taps to help incriminate suspects or to blackmail them; offering freedom from taps for a monthly rate; taking money for registering informants whose 'cooperation' with the police was faked to help them gain amnesty for previous misdeeds; determining the strength and purity of drugs by getting addict-informants to test it on themselves; kidnapping witnesses before a trial to stop them testifying; providing armed protection for dealers; obtaining 'hit-men' to kill potential witnesses; and disclosing the identity of a government informant to criminals resulting in his murder (1972: 91–2).

The evidence presented indicates that corruption in narcotics was widespread and organised and affected whole units of the NYPD; the patterns also reappeared after measures had been taken against corruption. Initially the Narcotics Division was seen as relatively corruption-free, but in 1968 it came under an internal IAD investigation and almost all the officers in the SIU were transferred; yet within three years the deviant patterns had re-emerged (Glazer 1995: 1054). This strongly suggests that narcotics enforcement is highly conducive to corruption if not almost predictably corrosive of integrity. In the drugs area the pattern is based on cooperation with certain drug-dealers, the exploitation of other dealers and the reliance on informants who are themselves dealers or are an addict and hence vulnerable to manipulation (for instance through becoming dependent on supplies from a police handler and/or being threatened with prosecution for non-cooperation). The resilience and extent of the corrupt practices are fuelled by the large amounts of money involved. An individual 'score', taking money off a dealer at the time of arrest, could amount to $20,000 although much larger sums were also mentioned (Knapp Commission 1972: 65). The Commission's Report signalled indisputably that drugs were fast becoming the pivotal factor in police corruption in New York.

The Knapp Commission's explanations

Knapp and his colleagues endeavoured to explain how such rampant deviation from the official paradigm, the formal rules of the NYPD and the criminal law could occur. Their focus was on several key elements.

First, there was the manifest failure of senior officers to take adequate measures against corruption. This was closely allied to a combination of hostility to outside interference and 'an intense desire to be proud of the Department'. This mixture created 'the most serious roadblock to a rational attack upon police corruption: a stubborn refusal at all levels to acknowledge that a serious problem exists'. As one officer put it, corruption was spoken of 'with all the enthusiasm of a group of little old ladies talking about venereal disease'. The department's reaction to exposure of deviance was based on the mantra of 'bad apples', as if swift action would remove the malignant ones so that the majority would remain unaffected, with the organisation returning rapidly to business as usual (Punch 2003). Knapp decisively rejected the bad apple analogy (Knapp Commission 1972: 6–11).

Second, a spin-off to this defensive yet self-confirming position was the clear failure of unit leaders and of front-line supervision. Often senior officers were remote and bureaucratic while distancing themselves from the front-line reality. And they were not held to account for trouble on their 'patch'. Indeed, it was the failure of senior officers to respond to the warning signals from Serpico that had led indirectly to the Commission. One consequence of this blind-eye remoteness was to isolate the front-line supervisory ranks who became drawn into corrupt practices. First-line supervision was all too frequently just not functioning.

Third, the self-cleansing ability of the Department through its prime internal control unit, the Internal Affairs Division (IAD), was low, given that the IAD of the time was centralised, reactive, slow and highly bureaucratic. Indeed, there were several units for internal investigations but these were 'widely dispersed, poorly coordinated, undermanned and, in many instances, were so misdirected that they were almost totally ineffective at rooting out corrupt policemen' (1972: 205). The Commission also examined the records for four and a half years to see how many cases had led on to a prosecution; in that time there had been 136 proceedings against 218 officers resulting in 91 convictions and 31 jail sentences (only one in five sentences were longer than one year; 1972: 252). In short, these diverse units displayed little cutting edge; there was a patent failure in internal investigations related to discipline offences and possible crimes; and subsequent prosecutions were meagre and usually led to dismissals, acquittals, suspended sentences or short custodial sentences.

Fourth, Knapp paid considerable attention to the strong loyalty and solidarity among officers; accepting a pay-off, for example, was a means of proving an officer could be trusted and was 'one of the boys'. This was cemented by the strength of the 'code' or blue wall of silence which prevented straight and honest cops from speaking out. In turn this was backed up by the seriousness of the threats and intimidation against those who broke the code.

Finally, Knapp spoke of the pervasive if not total cynicism among New York cops about policing, the NYPD and the criminal justice system.

In response to the revelations and to the impact of the Knapp Commission, Mayor Lindsay appointed a reforming chief, Patrick Murphy, who launched a thorough clean-up of the NYPD with a range of tough measures.

Murphy's Law

Patrick Murphy was a respected police leader who started as a patrol officer with the NYPD but was police chief in Detroit when he was recruited to take over the scandal-racked NYPD. He returned to New York as a reformer to clean out the stables. His reforms drew on his ideas about leadership, the manifest failures within the NYPD and on Knapp's recommendations. Indeed, he admitted that he *needed* the Commission and the accompanying publicity to implement change (Daley 1979: 37–46). For the mayor it was also vital to his political standing to be seen to be firmly supporting the reform process.

Murphy set out to make corruption the focal point for fundamentally altering the structure and culture of the Department. First, he introduced a new policy of decentralisation allied to command accountability. He sternly informed 180 commanders: 'I hold you personally responsible for any misconduct within the ranks at any level of your command' (Murphy and Plate 1977: 167).

Second, there were massive transfers of senior officers, the rotation of officers working in sensitive areas, and the autonomy of the detective and plain-clothes branches was significantly reduced.

Third, he reinvigorated the internal investigatory system, which had seemed 'deliberately designed not to work', and sponsored a proactive stance with integrity testing and 'field associates' (Sherman 1978: 157). Integrity tests included handing wallets containing money to officers as lost property to see if the officers would subsequently turn them in.[20] Field associates were covertly recruited from newcomers training at the Academy and were asked to 'spy' on their fellow cops. Commanders were not informed of their identity and perhaps one in ten of recruits became a field associate (Murphy and Plate 1977: 237).

Finally, he set out to alter the opportunity structure by employing wide discretion in simply not enforcing gambling laws and sabbath day ordinances. He also provided sufficient funds for paying informants and commenced a campaign to arrest those offering bribes (Kennedy School 1977a, 1977b).

What Murphy tried to accomplish sounds familiar in the light of other reform campaigns. There is little doubt of Murphy's resolve and integrity; but did it work? In essence, like all reformers after a scandal he was trying to get people doing the work they were supposed to be doing and getting the institution to reach the goals and standards it was supposed to be pursuing. It was like trying to physically steer the ponderous NYPD, like some sluggish freighter with a recalcitrant crew that had drifted dangerously off course, back into safe waters and with new élan; yet sensing that to relax the hold on the tiller would have the freighter drifting off course again. Initially, however, Murphy attracted political, media and public support. Indeed, Sherman (1978: xxxix) contended that 'from all indicators, the most recent episode of scandal and reform in the NYPD has reduced police corruption to a very minimal level'.

Certainly in conversations with NYPD officers in the early 1980s I was told with conviction that the Department had been cleansed. Some spoke of a 'revolution' and in the *New York Times* (1982) an officer said of corruption: 'But as a widespread and organised thing, as something that was once accepted, that's gone. The whole climate of the department has been reversed since Knapp'. Yet in a 'corruption profile' compiled by the IAD's Intelligence Section just *one year* after Knapp, mention is made of other forms of deviance replacing gambling graft; there was an increase in thefts from suspects and from impounded cars. In one precinct a 'major growing problem' was the procurement of prostitutes' services 'under threat of arrest' (Command Corruption Profile, NYPD: 1973). Nevertheless, Commissioner Maguire could claim in 1984 that 'there is in the whole country no other police force of this size that is so free of corruption as this one, and that spends so much effort on integrity' (in *Vrij Nederland* 1984).[21]

Indeed, the most significant line in the Commission's report was: 'Will history repeat itself? Or does society finally realise that police corruption is a problem that must be dealt with and not just talked about once every 20 years?' The answer came, almost punctually, just over 20 years later, with a new scandal and a new investigation by the Mollen Commission.

Mollen Commission

The Mollen Commission, 'The City of New York Commission to Investigate Allegations of Police Corruption and the Anti-Corruption Procedures of the Police Department', was formed by Mayor Dinkins in 1992, held hearings in 1993 and reported in 1994. By that time Rudolph Giuliani, who had been a District Attorney in New York and involved in the prosecutions arising from the undercover work of Leuci, had been elected mayor. The scandal unfolded not from internal control activity but when several NYPD officers were arrested during an investigation into a drug ring on Long Island outside the NYPD's jurisdiction. These arrests led to focusing on deviance in precincts in Manhattan, Brooklyn and the Bronx (including the 30th, the 'Dirty Thirty') and the 9th, 46th, 75th and 94th precincts (the latter two were the terrain of Officer Dowd). The Commission read thousands of documents, interviewed many witnesses within and without the Department, held public hearings, interacted with a number of investigatory and prosecuting agencies and used surveillance, undercover officers, informants and 'turned' cops in its investigations. Its analysis and recommendations form a strong echo of the Knapp findings. This could only mean that many of the changes implemented by Murphy had been blunted, deflected, reversed or never fully implemented. The report stated baldly:

> What we found was that the problem of police corruption extends far beyond the corrupt cop. It is a multi-faceted problem that has flourished in parts of our City not only because of opportunity and greed, but because of a police culture that exalts loyalty over integrity; because of the silence of honest cops who fear the consequences of 'ratting' on another cop no matter how grave the crime; because of wilfully blind supervisors who fear

the consequences of a corruption scandal more than corruption itself; because of the demise of the principle of accountability that makes all commanders responsible for fighting corruption in their commands; because of a hostility and alienation between the police and community which breeds an 'Us versus Them mentality;' and because for years the New York City Police Department abandoned its responsibility to insure the integrity of its members. (Mollen Commission 1994: 2)

I shall briefly look at three features of the Commission's finding: on the changing nature of police corruption since Knapp, the analysis of causes and the proposals for reform.

Mollen: the changing nature of police corruption

A fundamental point of difference with the Knapp era is that the Mollen Commission contended that corruption had altered in structure and style. In some respects the corruption had become *more criminal*. The extensive and regulated 'pad' for large groups had effectively vanished; now corruption was less widespread and revolved around a 'crew', or small, cohesive group. Drugs had become central to corruption; this was illustrated earlier with regard to Officer Dowd (see Chapter 1).

The Commission detailed such activities in several precincts in New York and concluded that corruption within the NYPD had become structured around small, cohesive groups or 'crews'. These crews engaged in violence and various forms of serious crime. South American drug-dealers dominated the scene and the crews either cooperated or competed with them. Of interest is Mollen's delineation of these 'crews':

> Virtually all of the corruption that we uncovered, however, involved groups of officers – called crews – that protect and assist each other's criminal activities. This was accomplished in a variety of ways, including: identifying drug sites; planning raids; forcibly entering and looting drug trafficking locations; and sharing proceeds according to regular and agreed-upon principles. The crews varied in closeness, purpose and size. In the 30th Precinct, a large group of cops worked in quasi-independent groups of three to five officers, each protecting and assisting the other's criminal activities. In the 73rd Precinct, a tightly knit group of eight to ten officers who worked on

steady tours of duty, routinely conducted unlawful raids on drug locations while they were on duty from 1998 to 1992. Sometimes most of the squad, ten to twelve officers, would attend clandestine meetings in desolate locations in the precincts ... to drink, avoid patrol duties and plan future raids.

The 75th Precinct gathered in a similar location ... This 'crew' corruption displayed a new and disturbing form of organisation. Whereas pads were standardised and hierarchical – almost bureaucratic – crews were *more akin to street gangs: small, loyal, flexible, fast moving, and often hard hitting.* (Mollen Commission 1994: 17–18, my emphasis)

They planned operations; they structured their police work to locate promising targets; they used the police radio and developed code names to coordinate operations. They were capable of manipulating fellow officers and their supervisors: 'And they fuel each other's corruption through their eagerness to prove their loyalty and toughness to one another (1994: 18).

Patrolman Dowd came into the limelight during the Commission's hearings but he was not alone in his appetite for corruption:

Former police officer Kevin Hembury did not only steal drugs, guns and money in the course of a series of unlawful searches; he was part of a gang of cops that raided drug locations almost daily for the sole purpose of lining their pockets with cash. Former police officer Bernard Crawley – nicknamed 'the Mechanic' by his sergeant because he so openly and frequently 'tuned people up', or beat them – not only used informants to identify drug locations for robberies, but beat people indiscriminately in crime-infested housing projects in his precinct. And it is alleged that former police officer Alfonso Compres, one of the fourteen officers arrested thus far in the Commission's year long 30th Precinct investigation, did not just steal from drug dealers on the streets; he demanded regular payments to allow them to operate freely in his precinct and robbed those who did not pay – he even used his service revolver to shoot a dealer while stealing a package of cocaine while in uniform. To cover up their corruption, officers created even more: they falsified reports and perjured themselves to conceal their misdeeds. (Mollen Commission 1994: 2)

In essence, the Commission argued that corruption had become 'more serious and threatening than ever before'. The path into 'cop crime' that emerged from the report began with simple break-ins or theft during legal searches. But these officers graduated to breaking-in to promising locations more often and in a more organised fashion; this was known as 'booming' or 'doing' doors. They were looking for what they called 'the gold mine', which was the main secret location of drugs, money and weapons. The 'score' from a successful search could bring in between $30,000 and $100,000.[22] Some of these crooked cops engaged in off-duty robbing during which they would use their police badge and service weapon. In one case this ended in a murder.[23] At one level there was a strong sense of solidarity related to small, cohesive units with a division of labour, patterns of initiation, loyalty and a code of silence; at another level the conspirators did not fully trust one another. A prime motive was doubtless greed. Dowd was taking thousands of dollars a month. But their rationale was that this was 'vigilante justice'; it was punishing crooks and others, intimidating them, showing them who was 'in charge' and exerting police power.

Mollen: explanations

Mollen echoed many other reports on police deviance by pointing to the central factors – namely *group loyalty, the code of silence* and *cynicism about the criminal justice system.* The loyalty to the working group, precinct or fraternity of cops was dominant. The police union bolstered this defensiveness by predictable legal action against the Commission; the lawsuit came from the Captain's Benevolent Association, indicating that hostility also came from senior officers. The 'code' meant that the worst offence an officer could commit was to 'rat' on a fellow officer; this is an endemic feature of many groups but is especially strong among police. The consequence was that 'good' cops, and supervisors, who disapproved of the criminal activities of Dowd and his like dared not speak out; banishment from the police family, years of lonely ostracism, threats and intimidation would have been the result. Officer Crawley, widely referred to as 'the Mechanic' for his habit of 'tuning up' people, testified that he was never concerned that another cop might divulge his illicit activities; he felt unassailable behind the 'blue wall'. Indeed, his nickname illustrates moreover that alongside the 'code' there was a tolerance for 'street justice'. The Commission reported that an 'excessive use of fists to face, nightsticks to ribs, and knees to groin' were accepted almost universally, including among officers who would refuse a free cup of coffee, as the reality of policing the streets in the tough areas (1994: 49).

But the report added several other factors, namely *greed, power, excitement* and *vigilante justice*. The police gangs seemed to exult in their control over their territory while they justified their abuse of people as a form of 'rough justice'. They were the street 'enforcers' doling out fines and punishments to those who richly and rightly deserved it. But at times the violence and burglaries had no obvious reason and appeared gratuitous, conducted merely for the thrill or 'buzz'. Clearly greed also played a role. Dowd, whose police pay was around $400 a week, was particularly rapacious and was enjoying an illegal income of $4,000 per week with his partner; this was just from pay-offs for protecting drug-dealing in his area, and with 'scores' his untaxed income was probably $8,000 per week.

The Commission Report also elaborates on the multiple institutional failures that allowed practices to continue undetected. Senior officers were 'wilfully blind' to signals of deviance and were not held accountable for deviance on their patch. First-line supervision was often abysmal while many sergeants were young, inexperienced and lacking in authority (due to recruitment policies). And the IAD (Internal Affairs Division) had once more become slow, reactive and ineffective, with the report referring to the 'collapse' of internal control with no cutting edge in investigations. Members of the IAD explained that they received strong signals from above not to embarrass the Department by pursuing cases that would attract negative media attention. In response they tended not to look closely at deviance by senior ranks; and where a group was involved its members were investigated individually to avoid the picture of systemic corruption. About forty of the most serious and sensitive cases were never formally recorded or forwarded to prosecutors; it was an IAD officer who alerted the Commission to the existence of a 'Tickler file', which concealed these cases to help preserve the NYPD's public image. It is clear that Dowd and others would have been exposed earlier if complaints against them had been examined professionally. The Commission even speaks of the 'abandonment of responsibility' (1994: 70).

Corruption had changed its shape but the organisation had also reverted to being collusive in ways familiar from Knapp. Allied to this were the cynicism, disillusion and hostility of officers, not just about criminal justice but also about the NYPD. They did not feel supported by the Department; there was a glaring discrepancy between promises and delivery; there had been a significant drop in standards of recruiting; and getting on in the Department was related to favouritism. This sounds much like the universal cop lament (Alex 1976), but the cynicism, disillusion and hostility doubtless amplified a general attitude of protecting one's own and not making waves.

Mollen: proposals

In its proposals for preventing and tackling corruption the report produced a familiar list of measures. These included a strong plea for independent investigation of police deviance; this has always been a strongly contested issue in US policing with the powerful police unions persistently opposing civilian review, especially in New York. The Commission also favoured a strongly proactive stance in internal investigations. Mollen called for the reinstatement of command accountability as Murphy had done earlier. And there followed a list of recommendations including the improved selection of recruits, strengthening front-line supervision, preventing and detecting drug abuse among officers, enhancing sanctions for corruption and brutality and legislative reform.

Above all the Commission demanded 'organisational commitment' to implement the changes. Given that the analysis and recommendations virtually repeat the words of Knapp and Murphy, uttered at a time of palpable commitment to reform, one can only conclude that that commitment had a limited 'shelf-life'. For within 20 years of Knapp corruption within the NYPD had proved resilient, altering its structure and style, while the organisation had slipped back to multiple failures which effectively condoned, and colluded with, serious criminal behaviour in its ranks.

Chicago, LAPD and Sea Girt

Many portraits could be sketched of police corruption in a range of American cities but I confine myself to scandals in two cities, Chicago and Los Angeles. These reinforce the shift from pad to crew and to the dominance of drug-related corruption detailed by Mollen. And I also touch on corruption in a minuscule police department.

Chicago

Chicago and Illinois have been associated with repetitive

exposures of 'boodling' (taking bribes) reaching back to the 1800s.[24] Machine politics and patronage dominated city life with organised crime playing a social and political role in the wards and in appointments to office. Indeed, Chicago School sociologists reported on intimate links between upper- and under-world in the 1930s, with politicians and cops carrying the coffin at a leading gangster's funeral (Landesco 1929). A generation later Rokyo wrote that it wasn't 'uncommon for Chicago politicians to join in the mourning at the funerals of gangsters – with aldermen weeping and judges praying', because they were now dependent on his successor (1971: 43).

In Chicago in the 1960s, moreover, this pattern was once more evident when an investigation led to over sixty convictions after it had revealed a thriving relationship between the police, organised crime and city politics involving a swathe of offences including bribery, extortion, perjury and conspiracy (Beigel and Beigel 1977). Invariably these episodic exposures led to a commission, to a significant turnover of personnel and to efforts at reform. For in 1997 Mayor Richard M. Daley[25] had to form yet another commission in the light of police corruption scandals related to extorting money and drugs from dealers. The report focused on the strong link between narcotics enforcement and corruption not only in Chicago but also elsewhere in large US cities; old-style 'passive' corruption had shifted 'dramatically' towards more aggressive forms: 'Today's police corruption is most likely to involve drugs, organised crime and relatively sophisticated but small groups of officers engaged in felonious criminal activities' (Commission on Police Integrity 1997: 11).

Indeed, within a decade there was a new scandal in Chicago when in 2005 charges were filed against four officers on federal drug and conspiracy charges. Around that time attention also focused on the inappropriately named 'SOS', the Special Operations Section of the Department. SOS was an aggressive, proactive unit for street enforcement but some of its members began harassing people, using trumped-up charges and burgling their property. There was a pattern of illegal entry, verbal abuse, humiliations, threats, planting evidence and forcing victims to name another victim to be targeted. Officers would stop someone, give no reason for this, find his address, enter his house without a warrant and steal money. Six officers of this 'elite' squad faced charges and it emerged that SOS had spawned a predatory group with a *modus operandi* of sudden and unjustified intervention, illegal detention and search, armed robbery and false charges aimed at silencing the target while those they beat up were charged with battery (the unit was later disbanded; *Chicago Tribune* 2007).

Yet the then Chicago Police Superintendent stated that the SOS had done a wonderful job and should not be disbanded. This was despite the fact that on one occasion some thirty SOS officers entered a bar where they searched everyone, selected two men whom they arrested on false charges; while the men were locked up, their houses were burgled by cops from the unit. Indeed, there was a pattern of Chicago cops getting into bar fights and then threatening the victims with arrest if they lodged complaints. One drunk off-duty officer was caught on the security camera viciously beating a female bar attendant for refusing him a drink. Rather like the description of criminal 'crews' in the Mollen Report, the situation in Chicago was one of aggressive and predatory groups of officers who seemed to be poorly supervised and who operated almost like a violent criminal gang.

Much attention was paid by the authorities to the fact that the Office of Professional Standards (OPS) of the Chicago Police, working closely with federal investigators, had taken the initiative in tackling several cases. Superintendent Cline, then chief of police, spoke of the head of the Department's 'unwavering commitment to rid itself of officers engaged in wrongdoing ... The fact that the Chicago Police Department initiated this investigation and worked closely with federal authorities, underscores that commitment. The arrests announced today should send a clear message to the public and to the Department's 13,500 honorable men and women that officers who violate their oath of office will be held strictly accountable' (FBI 2005).[26] Yet a national expert on internal affairs asserted that Chicago officials had 'deliberately ignored corruption within the ranks, giving cops a sense of security to commit crimes on the job without being caught'. He was hired by plaintiffs suing the city and alleged there was a 'practice of indifference' making cops engaged in misconduct 'feel protected' (*Chicago Tribune* 2006). This was reinforced by a Chicago academic, Craig Futterman, who had examined how the Chicago PD dealt with complaints. He held that a small number of officers were responsible for a large number of complaints but they seemed to operate with near impunity; he based his findings on OPS files. This material had made Futterman sceptical about pronouncements on improvements promising a sharper cutting edge in internal affairs: 'There's a big police scandal, and you'll get these big pronouncements, "internal investigation," "no stone unturned," and "we're going to do all these great things" ... And then the dust settles, and it ends up as being business as usual' (*Chicago Tribune* 2006).

In Chicago, then, the focus moved from the incidents themselves to the weaknesses in internal investigations of complaints. Faced by continued criticism on this, the mayor brought in a new chief from the FBI and the first chief from outside the department in 40 years. This new 'broom' rapidly moved 21 of the 25 district commanders, while three top deputy chiefs have resigned. The mayor has also revamped the OPS and appointed a lawyer from LA to lead it who is specialised in investigating police misconduct. A mayor of Daley's standing does not want the Police Department to tarnish his record. Persistent accusations of a lack of police integrity reflect ill on mayors, particularly if police violence and arrest patterns appear to be disproportionately focused on minorities. There is usually a swift reaction to political danger with a ritual house-cleaning, new police leadership and a massive turnover of the 'old guard'.

Los Angeles

Until the Rodney King affair, the LAPD had the reputation of being a well-disciplined and well-equipped agency. Under Chief Parker in the 1950s it had become a model as a centralised agency with an almost paramilitary style; this was partly to avoid corruption. Unlike many US cities the police chief had civil service tenure and could not be removed by the mayor; as a result the LAPD had an air of political independence compared to many other police departments.

But then in 2000 a report – the 'Rampart Inquiry' – concluded that LAPD officers had been involved in a range of serious offences in the Rampart area of the city. They had stolen drugs, severely beaten suspects in custody, fabricated evidence, planted guns on unarmed suspects and intimidated witnesses (LAPD 2000). The report details a list of criminal offences committed by a network of officers associated with a special unit; these were committed on duty, off duty and sometimes with civilian accomplices. The cases came to light as a result of three serious incidents. An officer named Mack was involved in an armed bank robbery (with an inside accomplice). Another officer, Hewitt, badly beat a handcuffed prisoner in custody. And when six pounds of cocaine disappeared from the Property Office the trail eventually led to Officer Perez.

Perez agreed to cooperate in return for a reduced sentence on the cocaine theft and gave extensive testimony that implicated some 70 officers. The core group were in a personal network and were members or former members of 'CRASH' ('Community Resources Against Street Hoodlums'), a special anti-gang unit for an area of LA with a large immigrant population and a thriving gang culture (Skolnick 2002). Indeed some officers had come strongly under the influence of the gang and rap culture and mirrored their style and conduct on it. Several were on the payroll of the 'hip-hop mogul' Marion 'Suge' Knight of Death Row Records who had links with the Bloods gang.[27] The testimony of Perez revealed a disturbing list of offences including unprovoked shootings and beatings (the latter with an element of sadism), planting evidence, framing innocent people, stealing drugs, armed robbery, covering up incidents and perjury (*Economist* 1999). In several cases of shootings by police officers the persons involved were unarmed and not taking part in a crime but they attracted the attention of officers or were mistaken for drug-dealers. In one case Perez and his partner shot a handcuffed young man, causing partial paralysis; they then planted a gun on him and the victim subsequently received a long prison sentence on their testimony. Several officers including Perez were implicated in the drive-by shooting of the rapper Notorious BIG. This is both predatory corruption and police 'crime'.

On several occasions supervisors colluded in the cover-ups of these police crimes. Indeed, the active involvement of supervisors in providing cover stories is one of the more disturbing elements in the Rampart affair. But it went even further when at off-duty celebrations of shootings, supervisors would reward officers concerned with plaques for wounding and killing people. The culture and style of CRASH officers that emerged from subsequent investigations was of an extremely aggressive stance, gratuitous violence with sadism, planting evidence, framing innocent suspects with perjury in court, affiliations with the gangs and the active collusion, if not encouragement, of supervisors. Perez claimed that 90 per cent of the officers in CRASH, many of whom were tattooed with the CRASH logo, took part in such practices. Two other features of the Rampart case are of significance.

First, police deviance elicits various forms of harm and creates diverse victims. Here victims of police violence were robbed, beaten, seriously injured, shot at, wounded and even killed. There were innocent victims who were set up for crimes they did not commit and for which they received long prison sentences. The CRASH members seemed to operate on the principle that anyone they encountered was a suspect – unless from a gang they were associating with – and that they were *a priori* guilty. This guilt by location meant that it was justifiable to attack them, rob them and send them to prison on trumped-up charges. But as a result of these illegal practices there were subsequently around 140 lawsuits mounted against the city, over \$125 million in compensation was paid and some 106 convictions were quashed in cases brought originally by CRASH officers.

Second, corruption causes damage to the reputation of a police force (Weitzer 2002). This can be limited by an adequate, transparent and forceful response in investigations and institutional reform. But if these measures are not convincing then the scandal escalates by the failure to cope with the original scandal. Within the LAPD there was apparently a swift, initial response with investigations and an internal inquiry. But this was marred when allegations surfaced that Chief Parks and others had obstructed the inquiry. Parks headed the IAB (Internal Affairs Bureau) when reports came in of CRASH misdeeds but it was claimed he was slow to react and suppressed a report linking Officer Mack to the murder of the rapper Notorious BIG. A detective on the Rampart Corruption Task Force resigned in protest from the LAPD about this omission. Furthermore Erwin Chemerinsky, a distinguished law professor who had walked off an advisory panel on the Rampart affair, published an independent report claiming that the LAPD tried to minimise the scope of the corruption and had effectively abetted the corruption by its weak internal anti-corruption strategy.[28] Chief Parks, who could not be removed from office, was subsequently not reappointed when he came up for an extension of his contract.

In Los Angeles a special squad in the Rampart area had begun to operate almost literally as 'outlaws', a criminal gang outside the law (Skolnick 2002). There was collusion from supervisors regarding serious crimes, a tardy and inadequate response from those responsible for internal control and an ambivalent reaction from the leadership. On the surface there was an internal investigation and cooperation with external investigators but underneath were rumblings about weak internal control and obstruction of an investigation. The extent and depth of the police deviance in the Rampart area was such that it raises the question how it was possible that this swathe of misconduct from one particular unit did not set off glaring warning lights? One answer in the Rampart Report was 'mediocrity', which in the LAPD had led to 'lack of commitment, laziness, excessive tolerance and kid gloves'. Supervisors had failed to hold officers responsible and accountable for standards and conduct and other cops began to take an easy path when they saw colleagues getting away with poor conduct that went unchecked (LAPD 2000). This conclusion laid the blame indisputably at the door of the organisation and its management.

Sea Girt

> I'm a cop. I can't get caught. Who's going to catch me? Me?
> (Former corrupt officer in *Bad Cops*, 1993)

The documentary film *Bad Cops* (1993) tells of a scandal far removed from large cities, in the tiny force of ten officers in the seaside town of Sea Girt, New Jersey. And in the report of the National Symposium on Police Integrity (Gaffigan and McDonald 1997: 7) mention is made of problems in small departments and sheriff's offices in Citron County (Florida), West Hampton (New York), Southgate (California) and Anchorage (Alaska).

The Sea Girt case can be viewed through the eyes of an officer who had become a drug addict. It conveys the weakness of control in a department of such small size. In the documentary the officer says the following (the question is in italics):

> *Did you realise you were breaking the law?* No. I knew it was against the law, but it didn't really occur to me. The police were involved in drugs; we knew the main players and the users. There's so much temptation in a small town. At night there were only two cars out and we would arrange to meet on the premises of the New Jersey Police Academy and we spent most of the night sniffing coke in the patrol car and playing cards ... we would line up the two cars on the state police dock down by the water so we could see if anyone was coming, and then line up the coke on the dashboard. (Former corrupt officer in *Bad Cops*' 1993)

He became addicted to drugs, stole from his family and then from the safe in the station. The deviant officers became involved with the local drug 'circle' and used the station for weighing, cutting and distributing the drugs. They became less and less cautious and their theft of drugs from the safe was filmed on surveillance cameras. The officer cooperated with investigators and was given a suspended sentence and ordered to perform community service.

The point of the Sea Girt case is that in a tiny department – ten officers policing only one square mile with 2,000 inhabitants (although this doubled during holidays) – one might expect high informal control. But there was in fact unlimited autonomy based on trust. At night there were perhaps only two officers on duty with no one else to control them; and the three officers caught in a drugs sting not related to cops were all supervisors (a sergeant, lieutenant and captain). Unknown to the investigators these cops had become part of a drug ring, protected it and sold drugs.

Who was to stop them? And as the former officer says, 'there is so much temptation in a small town'. In such a small department there is a high level of trust; certainly the police chief and mayor emphasised this and said they were devastated. Everyone knew everyone else in the community and the officers were well known and trusted by all; indeed, the officer in the documentary gave advice in schools on the dangers of drug use. Sea Girt is, then, a reminder not to make the assumption that corruption is mostly related to policing in large cities. That may well be the case. But as we do not know and can never know how much corruption there is anywhere, then the fixation on well-documented cases in major cities may only serve to deflect attention from the opportunities for, and patterns of, corruption in tiny police departments functioning in small communities or in rural areas (Walker 2005).

Violence, drugs, police crime and corruption: New York, Miami and Los Angeles

In New York and elsewhere, such as Miami and Cincinnati, the form of police deviance that has attracted most attention in recent years has been excessive violence. In particular, three cases in New York have attracted critical comment and wide protest and have also been linked to the aggressive, 'zero tolerance' approach. First, Abner Louima, an immigrant from Haiti, was severely abused in a police station;[29] he required hospital treatment for extensive internal injuries (Skolnick 2002). Second a young immigrant from Guinea, Amadou Diallo, was apprehended by members of a plain-clothes unit for tackling street crime. The officers felt he fitted the description of a suspected rapist; when asked to raise his hands Diallo reached inside his jacket, probably for his identity card. Thinking he was going for a gun, the officers started shooting and fired 41 bullets of which 19 hit Diallo.[30] And third, three unarmed young black men were shot with some 50 bullets; one was wounded, one seriously injured but the third man died (it was to have been his wedding day). There was confusion when a scuffle broke out late at night between the three-man stag-group and two white men at a spot under surveillance by an undercover police unit. The police thought a weapon was involved and then the car of the stag-group was said to have driven at an officer while it collided with a police vehicle. The police opened fire with one officer firing 31 shots (*Guardian Unlimited* 2006).

It does appear, then, that the emphasis on special units with a mandate to tackle and reduce street and drug crime – and that consequently adopt an aggressive style, as with CRASH – fosters the likelihood of such incidents occurring. But of crucial significance is that all three victims were black and in America the police mistreatment or shooting of sometimes unarmed black people and migrants from minority communities is highly emotive.[31] With the increased self-consciousness of Afro-Americans, with media exposures of police violence against minorities and with clear patterns that youths from minorities are disproportionately likely to become the victims of police shootings, attention has shifted away from conventional corruption and more towards abuse of authority and excessive violence. This was evident at the National Symposium on Police Integrity in Washington DC in 1996 where the main emphasis was on the abuse of power and excessive violence and particularly on the impact these have on minorities with regard to confidence in the police. As one contributor stated, 'Regarding the public's perception of policing, this is the worst period for policing I have seen since the late '60s and early '70s' (Gaffigan and McDonald 1997: 50).

Another feature has been the escalating amounts of money and drugs available at the scene of a 'bust' which began to encourage single-officer or small-group 'scores' (ripping off the dealers' money and/or drugs). In turn the 'war' on drugs can also elicit police violence. This can be illustrated by two major scandals with contrasting styles, one with high violence and the other with a mercenary orientation. In the Miami River affair of 1985 the officers specialised in ripping off wholesale dealers with the help of an informer and graduated to raiding drugs boats coming up the Miami River transporting large amounts of drugs from South America. The stolen drugs were recycled through a major dealer. An armed raid by officers on one of these boats led to the deaths of three crew members. The subsequent murder investigation led to the arrest of fifteen officers and eventually to the apprehension of some 80 officers (*Miami Herald* 2001).

In another case concerning an elite anti-drug unit of sheriffs in Los Angeles, there developed a pattern of stealing money and drugs from dealers.[32] Of interest is that the enforcement priorities altered when there was managerial pressure to confiscate money that could contribute to the department's budget through asset forfeiture. Arrests were no longer deemed important and this emphasis on money alone apparently encouraged 'skimming off' a portion of the confiscated money. The shift in organisational priorities presumably generated the motive that if the money was going to the department anyway why not take some as 'expenses'.

In fact the FBI came to see drugs and drugs money together as the number one threat to integrity in law enforcement; of the corruption cases they were then tracking 59 per cent were drug-related (GAO Report 1998: 35). The ripping off of dealers became especially the case with South American dealers, with whom there was generally an adversarial relationship; coming from abroad they conducted a 'cash-and-carry' trade with drugs and money on them. Drug enforcement also encourages cooperation with an active informant who can provide information on drug transactions and who can 'recycle' drugs confiscated or stolen by the police. The shift to small, aggressive 'crews' as portrayed by Mollen is reflected in the pattern of predatory and sometimes violent gangs of cops in corrupt drug enforcement.

Mollen had moreover introduced the relationship between corruption and brutality. This may always have been present but it was not previously made explicit in reports or analyses of corruption. Certainly with Dowd and his associates and especially in the unfortunately named CRASH, there is a strong element of macho violence tied to 'process corruption' in relation to false charges and perjury, partly as a gambit to cover up the violence. There may have been a notion of rough justice and noble cause but it appears more like the random exercise of power, the control of territory, the exultation in violence which was at times gratuitous if not sadistic, with celebrations of violent behaviour and pleasure in putting sometimes innocent people away on false charges (Skolnick 2002; Collins 2008). The greed, hedonism, ruthlessness, lack of conscience, lack of compassion for the victim and contempt for the law, mirrors the attitudes and behaviour of criminals. Like the criminals described by Katz (1988) they seemed to be seduced by the buzz and thrill of committing crime just for the sake of it. Indeed, they often copied the culture and style of the crooks and gangs they were meant to be combating and on occasion even joined them. There was an element that when policing 'badasses' the cops had to become tougher and nastier in response.

Reform and good departments

It should be stated that, alongside this gloomy picture above, the US has witnessed constant waves of reform in relation to civic government and policing. There was a period of police reform in the 1930s when several leading departments fought to remove political control over the police; in the late 1960s and early 1970s in the wake of the President's Commission with its *Task Force Report: The Police* (1967); and later in the 1990s after the series of revelations about police misconduct (Gaffigan and McDonald 1997: 80). Indeed, the early reform movement and 'professional' model in policing of Vollmer in Berkeley, Parker in Los Angeles and O. W. Wilson in Chicago was aimed not only at enhancing the status of the profession but also at gaining more control over officers with the specific aim of reducing corruption (Carte and Carte 1975). There is, then, a spectrum from awful and unlawful to admirable in both city administration and police departments. In policing, for example, the US has been a major source of innovation for police forces in many countries and for many decades (Punch 2007).

There have also been significant changes in policing in recent years that present a less sombre picture. For instance, when the NYPD was reeling from the Mollen Inquiry, there was a fresh mayor, Rudolph Giuliani, who appointed a new police chief, Bill Bratton. Between them they became associated with 'zero tolerance policing' (Punch 2007). Briefly, the two men inherited a demoralised police department yet managed to galvanise it by restoring confidence and morale through strong leadership, an expansion in personnel and an assertive enforcement strategy. The revamped NYPD had ostensibly brought down crime and many foreign officials and police chiefs flocked to the New York 'miracle' (Bowling 1999). Part of this 're-engineering' was exercising more managerial and operational control throughout the organisation and this was clearly allied to tackling corruption. This determination is evidenced in Giuliani and Bratton's *Police Strategy No. 7: Rooting out Corruption: Building Organisational Integrity in the New York Police Department* (1995). And it does appear as if certain forms of corruption have more or less disappeared since the Giuliani/Bratton regime. Doubtless this is related to the offences' relative visibility to assertive control, partly with the help of technology, to integrity testing and to managerial pressures for performance. This does not mean that deviance has gone away, but rather that it has taken on other forms.

Furthermore, corruption may appear to be near ubiquitous but there are examples of forces in the US that enjoy an excellent reputation for integrity and professionalism. These tend to be in so-called 'large' forces of 400 or more officers[33] with an enlightened and energetic chief of long tenure having full support from the mayor. These departments are further characterised by the recruitment of high-quality, well-paid officers from several states, no union, excellent resources and a strong ethos of professionalism and integrity. They are usually in relatively affluent middle-sized towns with not too much serious crime; recent examples would be St Petersburgh (Florida), Charlotte-Mecklenburgh (North Carolina) and Charleston (South Carolina). Leadership, political support, resources, professionalism, selective recruitment, élan and an ethic of integrity espoused by the chief are the key factors (Klockars *et al.* 2004).

Conclusion

A perusal of police corruption in the US leads to the conclusion that it is virtually endemic, pervasive, resilient, cyclical, shifting in form over time and often systemic. What is apparent, moreover, is that the form corruption takes fluctuates and is even shaped by the nature of the control system. To a degree corruption and control are symbiotic. When certain opportunities are blocked or strong control is exercised then cops are creative at lying low and shifting to other practices. Traditionally graft in America was geared to gambling and 'vice' and liquor while there was engrained grass-eating. Much of this was consensual, based on stable agreements and close relations with organised crime figures; this could shift to meat-eating with the cops in the driving seat extorting money from criminals and others. Drugs brought in a new element when there was a change in definition of drugs from dirty to 'clean'.

One explanation for this backcloth is that politics and civic life in many cities have been characterised by widespread corruption with the police under the control of the mayor and developing close relationships with organised crime. From the 1960s onwards it was often the case, moreover, that mayors became highly dependent on the police for their own political success in relation to rising crime, moral panics in the media and periodic urban unrest. There was general reluctance among mayors to criticise the police; and when facing up to scandal proved inescapable, there was often resort to the rhetoric of the few bad apples and the gallant majority officers. When *Life* magazine in 1957 was calling the Chicago PD the worst police department in the country the mayor was praising its officers as 'the finest in the nation' (Rokyo 1971: 107). However, a rolling scandal which cannot be contained can damage the mayor's record and reputation and then there is a tendency to appoint a committee of inquiry, to replace the chief and to demand swift house-cleaning with a high turnover of senior officers.

Historically in America, policing required few qualifications and hence was ideal for dispensing patronage by offering a job with the police. One legacy is that American cops were often seen as poorly qualified and of low status. In some cities the politicians, the Mob and the police had an intertwined relationship and ran the town together; official positions, and justice, could be purchased. Indeed, Serpico and Leuci both made the point that it was not just the police that were rampantly corrupt in New York; so was the rest of the justice system including lawyers, district attorneys and even judges. Everything was up for sale, they lamented, including a murder charge. Cases had a price and 'it was never too late to do business', with bribes being offered in the courtroom (Maas 1974: 135). This gave the police a feeling that they were scapegoats for, and victims of, wider corruption which somehow always evaded the attention of special investigations (Alex 1976). This was reinforced when a former member of the Knapp Commission was convicted of corruption, as was a Queen's County District Attorney (DA) (Sherman 1974b: 25).

Indeed, despite a constant stream of reform efforts in governance and innovation in policing there have been recurrent scandals in many of the major cities. This can only lead to the conclusion that corruption is a permanent and recurring feature of policing in America; but it is not universal. There are umpteen examples of periodic exposures of systemic corruption that led to subsequent efforts to 'clean up' the department with commissions of inquiry, investigations and trials, a turnover of senior personnel and structural change. Such efforts often prove not to bring about permanent improvement and there is eventually recidivism; this lends a cyclical nature to the dynamic of 'scandal and reform' (Sherman 1978). It is clear from the comparison between the diagnoses made of corruption and organisational responses to it in New York by Knapp and Mollen, for instance, that the reforms of Commissioner Murphy had been blunted if not reversed by the time of Mollen. Murphy states that as Commissioner he could only move senior personnel because captains and the ranks below were protected by civil service status, and an assertive union. In addition Manning and Van Maanen (1978: viii) write of 'massive resistance to change' from cops and their unions in the US in the 1970s.

The research of Klockars *et al.* (2004) might be taken to indicate that when reform is successful it tends to be in medium-sized, affluent towns and hence reinforcing the image that corruption is typically a problem of large urban police forces. As was said earlier, we can never ascertain the real extent of corruption so we simply do not know if this is correct. For example, the majority of the 18,000 police departments in the US are tiny, often with under ten officers, and this can easily lead to a lack of training, expertise and professionalism and also to being inbred and open to local influence. The example of Sea Girt reveals that small departments have their own peculiar problems of deviancy and control. However, the multiple and large-scale problems of urban deprivation, the high crime rates, levels of violence and racial tensions make policing the large cities a stressful and hazardous enterprise. In parts of some cities the police are perceived as an army of occupation and in response there is often a sour, acerbic, anomic tone to the reflections of officers on their predicament. Perhaps this sense of alienation, coupled with a feeling of low status, helps drive some officers to corruption. Yet Moskos (2008: 77) asserts that in fourteen months' patrol in a tough ghetto in Baltimore he witnessed sloth, disillusion and ritualism, but not corruption and brutality – 'there was no slope'. There must be other factors that make some alienated officers turn to corruption while others do not.

One factor might be the opportunity structure and the availability of graft, drugs and drugs money. This may further be tied to the materialism of US society where a steady untaxed income from graft is enticing to pay for an improved lifestyle. Some groups of officers may be more receptive to accepting money than others. At times the search for, and dependence on, graft is almost obsessive if not addictive and has a rapacious quality; Perez of CRASH spoke of an 'orgy' of corruption. There is also sometimes a sense of deviancy amplification in which bent cops revel in their badness with an identity derived from a special unit, rubbing shoulders with 'hoods', tattoos, body language with an assertive style and outside-of-work celebrations of deviant activity.

Furthermore, officers often have amicable if not intimate relationships with contacts or 'cousins' in the underworld; but there can also be a highly exploitive element to the corrupt arrangements with others. This exploitive and manipulative style can also extend to the police organisation itself where officers put in minimal effort, cut corners, ignore orders and poach 'collars' off those lesser in the hierarchy. That they are allowed to do this is related to the quality of the organisation, poor leadership, weak supervision, security of tenure (in unionised forces), resistance to change from the unions, but also the structure of work.[34] The report on the Rampart affair, for example, is replete with the shortcomings of the organisation (LAPD 2000: 13): 'Essentially, many of the problems found by this BOI [Board of Inquiry] boil down to people failing to do their jobs with a high level of consistency and integrity. Unfortunately, we found this to be true at all levels of the organisation, including top managers, first-line supervisors and line personnel'.

And it was as plain as a pikestaff that in the NYPD at certain times the leaders did not lead, the supervisors did not supervise, the controllers did not control and the workers (if they could be found in the workplace) did not work. The official paradigm was a façade; behind it was a world of sloth, graft and deception in which no one could be trusted and all indicators of work could be manipulated. Nothing was what it seemed. The NYPD of the 1960s was like some old-style Soviet factory where production data were fiction and everyone existed in a collectively constructed reality of surface conformity that masked indolence, low productivity, pilfering, mediocre if not defective products and cooking the books.

At times the NYPD was out of control. There was a dynamic of periodically trying to drag it back to its formal task and back under control. Yet the covert code and informal system managed to reassert and reimpose themselves after a period following reform. This constellation of institutional shortcomings exposed during the major corruption scandals in American policing has been amply and repeatedly documented. Corruption in US policing is near endemic, resilient and shifting in its forms and the police organisation proves often incapable of tackling it, while it may covertly or overtly collude in it. This patent neglect to anticipate and control corruption frequently amounts to no less than repetitive 'system failure'.

Notes

1 President Ford granted Nixon a pardon for crimes he may have committed in office including tax offences, phone-tapping, accepting illicit campaign contributions and complicity in the cover-up of the Watergate break-in.

2 Rokyo's (1971) portrait of Mayor Richard J. Daley of Chicago, provides an excellent description of machine politics. Daley ran the city between 1955 and 1976 as an extension of the Democratic Party; the Police

Chief's office was in City Hall and he was incumbent on the Mayor's favour.

3 Entry requirements to policing were minimal when politics determined hiring; applicants in the 1890s were 'overweight, undersize, and overage; others were illiterate, alcoholic, and syphilitic; others had outstanding debts and criminal records', while a Kansas patrolman had a wooden leg (Fogelson 1977: 8).

4 Skogan (2008) gives recent examples of police chiefs swiftly thrust aside by a mayor facing a media panic on crime. The average tenure of a police chief in the US is around two years.

5 In the relatively recent scandal surrounding the highly popular Mayor Cianci in Providence (Rhode Island) there was still systemic deviance on machine politics lines in the 1980s and 1990s. There was cronyism with jobs for his supporters (some involving no work and no attendance), kickbacks for contracts, bid-rigging, covert surveillance on rivals, illegal campaign contributions to his re-election fund and law enforcement was tailored to his whims while cases could be rigged. Cianci was sentenced to five years in jail in 2002; the judge spoke of 'corruption at all levels' and that he had operated the city 'as a criminal enterprise to line his own pockets' (Stanton 2003: 387).

6 Whyte (1955) in his classic study of 'Cornerville' in Boston details how graft from gambling was routine and institutionalised; payments were graded by rank with senior officers taking the precaution of 'parking' the money with a subordinate who could expect protection from above in any investigation. A gambling 'racketeer' explained, 'of course this business is against the law, but still it's honest, and we aren't bothering nobody' (Whyte 1955: 131).

7 There had been two previous major investigations in New York in 1884 and 1890.

8 This may be exaggeration and self-promotion by the author, as we do not know if there were cases elsewhere in the US up to the time of writing but which hadn't drawn media attention.

9 The NYPD was and is by far the largest police department in the US and by the early 1970s it employed some 30,000 officers.

10 In background and style Durk was different from most NYPD cops of the time; he came from a professional background, graduated from the elite Amherst College and began a law degree at Columbia before joining the police (Maas 1974: 108).

11 Later there were questions as to why Durk's information on corrupt practices passed to a contact in the Mayor's Office received no response. Knapp was asked how he was going to handle the Mayor; 'How, blurted Knapp back, can you investigate the man who appointed you?' (Maas 1974: 250).

12 There are doubtless many reasons why workers decide to take their complaints to the higher echelons of the organisation or even outside;

one can be a pre-emptive defence against measures to sanction them (Anechiarico and Jacobs 1996). They can be the ideal workers who are genuinely concerned about manifest failures within the company; what turns them into full-blown whistle-blowers is when their pleas are ignored or the firm hits back at them. Then a sense of moral indignation at not being listened to after years of loyal service and commitment, as well as being unfairly treated, leads them to go outside the organisation. And they can become involved in an acrimonious battle against the institution which can prove destructive for them (Gobert and Punch 2000). Institutions are repeat players in conflicts and have resources to fight such battles, and can wear down the whistle-blower who has to make a considerable psychological if not material investment in the struggle.

13 Burnham had spent a year talking to hundreds of New Yorkers about their experiences with police corruption and had built a picture of its forms and extent; yet he had trouble persuading an editor to take an interest in the story partly because of the hostile reaction expected from politicians and the police; fellow reporters were sceptical about the newsworthiness of 'yet another story' on police corruption. It was only *after* he had warned the Mayor that the articles were published (Burnham 1976).

14 The book on his life by Maas (1974) was an international bestseller and was made into a movie by Sidney Lumet with Al Pacino as Serpico.

15 Opposition to special investigations by police representatives is standard in the US; this may be a ritual of disapproval and a delaying tactic but in a litigious society it's to be expected; in fact the Civil Liberties Union came to their defence and criticised the Commission's methods (Alex 1976: 94).

16 The most widespread form of grass-eating was the free meal, usually in the local diner, but some cops preferred fashionable restaurants: two officers in a patrol car would pull up behind an expensive establishment where a waiter would appear with a tray of food – right under the windows of the Knapp Commission's office! (Knapp Commission 1972: 173).

17 His story is told in *Prince of the City* (Daley 1979) and in the film of the same name which was directed by Sidney Lumet, who earlier filmed *Serpico*.

18 'Not even a "bad cop" would have accepted narcotics-related money' (Pennsylvania Crime Commission 1974: 225). But as officers explained to the Knapp Commission (1972: 101), stealing from a drug-dealer was 'clean' because it didn't harm anyone and because 'he didn't deserve no rights' as he was selling drugs.

19 Some 185 pounds of heroin and 31 pounds of cocaine, mostly from the so-called 'French Connection' haul – to cops the Tuminaro case – was stolen from the Property Clerk's Office; every time it was taken to be

used in court as evidence some of it disappeared and was replaced with flour; the signatures of fellow officers were falsified – so much for solidarity (Murphy and Plate 1977: 244).

20 As we shall see later (Chapter 6), it took over 30 years for integrity testing to cross the Atlantic to be adopted by the Met in London.

21 Later in the 1980s there was the 'Buddy-Boys' scandal in the 77th Precinct; the group was involved in opportunistic theft, getting pay-offs from street-dealers to continue unmolested and raiding drug-dealers. They sound like the predecessors of the 'crews' described by Mollen; the nickname came from spending so much time on duty hanging out drinking and taking drugs that work was more like a club (Dombrink 1988; Kappeler *et al.* 1994).

22 The gang of cops might also stop a suspicious car but finding nothing incriminating plant a firearm, make a false arrest on the basis of finding a gun, rough up the driver and then charge him with assault on an officer. This might be done towards the end of a tour of duty to generate overtime pay; the officers would go on to perjure themselves.

23 Officer Cabeza gained entry behind a plexiglass barrier in a liquor store by displaying his police badge; he was then followed by civilian accomplices and during the robbery he killed the owner by shooting him in the back while the man was lying on the floor.

24 The so-called 'Gray Wolves' on the City Council were rapacious in their appetite for bribes (Rokyo 1971: 18).

25 He is the son of Richard J. Daley and like his father is a long-serving mayor, having first been elected in 1989.

26 From US Department of Justice, Chicago.

27 Following the arrest of Perez officers found photos of him dressed in red and making Blood gang signs; in prison Mack joined the Bloods and wore as much red clothing as possible.

28 This was written at the request of the main rank-and-file LAPD union.

29 He was sodomised with the handle of a toilet-brush, which was then brandished in the presence of other officers including a supervisor and a union representative. Several officers decided after an initial silence to talk and they implicated the main culprit who confessed and received a long sentence.

30 Collins (2008: 44) analyses the Dillao case focusing on the confusion and mixed perceptions accompanying police shootings.

31 A major scandal emerged from the beatings by Los Angeles sheriff deputies of suspected illegal immigrants in 1996 near the Mexican border and after a long chase which, like the Rodney King incident, was caught on camera, this time by a news helicopter (Weitzer 2002; Collins 2008: 83).

32 The sums encountered at a 'bust' ranged from $500,000 to $4 million; some sheriffs began to 'skim off' some of the money and there were luxurious lifestyles among bent officers.

33 American cops refer to forces of 400 plus as 'large' forces, which are in fact not large by standards in other countries; in the UK that would be an undersized police district.

34 As in other undemanding bureaucracies the standards for performance in New York were so pathetically low that it encouraged sloth and allowed ample time to run the pad. When Serpico worked the anti-prostitution assignment the quota for arrests was four per month; some officers could do that in one night while after completing the arrest and paperwork the officer was free to go home (Maas 1974: 185).

Chapter 4

The Netherlands: Amsterdam and the 'IRT' affair

Police work is dominated by fear and distrust. Everyone distrusts everyone else. It's the same all over in this force.
(Detective in Amsterdam, cited in Punch 1985: 122)

In general the patterns of corruption in Western Europe differ considerably from those reported in the United States. Fosdick (1915) commented on the absence in European forces of a corrupt 'system' as found in American forces. The reasons given for this revolve around the centralised nature of many police systems in Europe with national standards and central inspectorates, the absence of civic corruption in some societies, the patterns of police recruitment, selection and discipline, an ethic of public service, the low emphasis given to enforcing legislation on morals and vice and the less systemic nature of organised crime than in America. This historical background does not mean that there has been little or no police corruption in Europe, while much has changed in policing and crime patterns in recent decades. Perhaps certain forces have proved successful at covering up their misconduct and have had powerful allies both within the system and within government to protect them. The internal corruption that has emerged in Europe, moreover, has tended to be confined to particular segments of the organisation rather than being widespread and institutionalised. Some cases have been driven more by 'noble cause' or the desire for results through 'process corruption' than being primarily mercenary in intent. Violence has often been an issue both in the past and in recent major public order situations.[1] But there has been the occasional exposure of systematic arrangements

93

with organised crime while the deviant practices evident in drug enforcement in the US have also emerged across the Atlantic.

Amsterdam

> When I joined up an old copper said to me, 'In this job you've always got one leg pointing to the sack and the other to the cell'. We used to say, 'You've got two enemies. The first is the public and the second is the police force itself; because if you get into trouble then they'll try and destroy you.
> (Veteran constable in Amsterdam, cited in Punch 1985: 152)

The Netherlands and the Amsterdam Police

When I moved to the Netherlands in 1975 to live and work – with the prospect of conducting research with the police in Amsterdam – I had no intention of studying police corruption. I was aware of the US material on policing and familiar with the New York scandal. But there was almost no record of corruption in Dutch policing history. Systematic arrangements with organised crime and entire units 'on the take' were unknown. This background does not necessarily mean that there has been little or no police corruption or deviance. For instance, Dutch and other European police forces faced a highly corruptive environment which Anglo-American police have never encountered, which is occupation by a totalitarian power (except in the British Channel Islands). The Germans in World War Two restructured the police forces of occupied countries to further the ideology and aims of the Nazi regime. In the Netherlands, for instance, special units of the police hunted Jewish people and their reward for arrests was a premium and/or extra rations (Moore 1997). Under these exceptional circumstances we can observe patterns of police behaviour that were imposed and encouraged by a repressive external authority and were judged then and later by others to be highly deviant, morally reprehensible and illegal.

In 1975, however, Dutch society enjoyed the reputation of being largely corruption-free (Blanken 1976).[2] Rather like a number of other Northern European countries there was not much evidence of civic and political corruption. And when I commenced fieldwork with the Amsterdam Police there was initially an absence of visible grass-eating. The context was a busy inner-city station called the Warmoesstraat (an all-male station). The dominant focus of the police district was the square mile of the red light district, with prostitution, brothels, sex-shows, pornography shops, bars, discos, gambling halls, cafés and restaurants (Punch 1979). There was already a sizeable Chinese community but there had been a recent influx of illegal Chinese immigrants, some of whom were involved in drug-dealing, illicit gambling and opium dens. There was also a thriving street culture of drug-dealing; the 'flower-power' period of Amsterdam as a haven for soft drugs was changing rapidly as heroin came on the market.

Of importance is that much of the activity and many establishments in the inner city were formally illegal. But this was the era of unbridled 'tolerance' in Dutch society and of turning a blind eye to much that was illegal (Brants 1999); this had a major impact on enforcement policies in Amsterdam. Some commentators praised the enlightened criminal justice system in the Netherlands fostered by these progressive values (Downes 1988). But among the long-haired cops in the Warmoesstraat it elicited a nonchalant, laid-back style of non-enforcement; as one officer said to me, 'I'm just the zoo keeper'.

The Amsterdam City Police, then with around 3,000 officers, was the largest force in the Netherlands[3]. On the surface it had bent to the tolerant wind but underneath it was still a fairly old-fashioned bureaucracy. My research was initially with the uniformed branch in the Warmoesstraat and was aimed at studying police – public interaction; but this theme broadened to a wider focus on policing the inner-city area. I was in the field for about eighteen months and was preparing to leave when a senior officer mentioned 'corruption'. Like Moskos (2008) in Baltimore I had not witnessed brutality and corruption in day-to-day policing. I never heard anyone even mention corruption. Overt control and supervision were minimal and discipline was lax. Gradually the patrol team I was attached to became used to my presence and there emerged mild deviance such as sheltering from the rain in a sex club, paying 'police prices' for takeaway food (and sometimes spiking the owners' parking tickets in return) and drinking in the area when off duty (which was strictly forbidden but was typically done in sight of the station).[4]

There was also a plain-clothes squad and a group of detectives in the station with whom at that early stage I had little contact. These claimed certain establishments as their territory and tried to keep the beat cops out of them but some street cops would ignore this and take me along. On entering Chinese establishments the owner would routinely offer us food, drink and cigars. Invariably this was turned down in my presence; the uniformed cops would say that no one could be trusted in the area and it was self-interest to play it straight. Plainly other officers thought differently about this.

The presence of organised crime – particularly the Chinese triads importing heroin – coupled with the almost unlimited tolerance for illegality, which meant low levels of enforcement, should have alerted me to the potential for corruption. But I was absorbed with the routine of my patrol group and had but a snail's eye view of wider developments. This was my first extensive observation of policing, and in a new society, so it took time to become familiar with the context. I was unaware, then, that corruption was going on around me. But it was not visible; the corrupt officers were obviously not going to invite me along and some cops who knew about it kept it from me at first. This was perhaps a blessing as direct knowledge of deviant activities would have presented a serious ethical dilemma with possible consequences for continuing my research (Punch 1986).

Fortunately, when the corruption scandal broke I was granted permission by the Police Commissioner to continue in the Warmoesstraat and study the nature and impact of corruption. This presented the unique opportunity to conduct research inside a police force in the throes of a major scandal. I had access to leading officers in the force, to key documents on the cases (but not all) and also to a number of 'corrupt' officers. The latter were sanctioned by a court for minor offences but had not been formally convicted of corruption.

What this analysis conveys is that when a police agency comes under critical scrutiny and external investigation it is not a neutral, surgical exercise of fellow professionals dispassionately conducting business. For four years the Amsterdam Police was a cauldron of emotions, rumour, infighting, vendettas and guerrilla activity. The scandal created considerable turbulence within the organisation; the supposed solidarity of policing fractured into warring factions; in particular the lower ranks put up a concerted resistance to being labelled and to scapegoating; and two of the police defendants became both institutional victims and cultural heroes.

Drawing on that research my argument is that the context was corruption-conducive and in not seeing that, and in not taking adequate measures to deal with it, the organisation was largely culpable due to a combination of blindness, negligence and implicit collusion.

The cases unfold

Why a corruption scandal unfolded in Amsterdam at that particular moment was serendipitous; there might just as well never have been an affair. The organisation had truly pitiful resources for tackling corruption and these were reactive; and the force leadership was largely into denial on its existence. Research conducted after the scandal, moreover, revealed that many officers could still not agree on what was meant by corruption and what was not acceptable (van Laere and Geerts 1984: 19).[5] The main force hierarchy represented a 'clean-up' party of rule-bound formalists espousing the official paradigm; they were shocked by the exposure of deviance and keen to have it excised rapidly. The minority 'play-it-dirty' party was formed by entrepreneurs who revelled in rule-bending in the new environment of international organised crime and hard drugs – until it was politic to dive for cover. But next to these 'clean' and 'dirty' parties there was another faction; these *'jonge honden'* (literally 'young dogs' but equivalent to 'Young Turks') represented the fresh generation of officers recruited in the 1960s, oriented to change and coming up against the old guard. They opposed both parties in the hierarchy; one for being too rigid and the other for being too 'creative'.

In the Warmoesstraat station two 'young dogs', new chief inspectors, arrived together. These two officers were alarmed by the indulgent style of policing they encountered. And when the first signals of corruption reached them from sources in the area they took them seriously and undertook surveillance themselves (such as lying on roofs with binoculars to watch the movements of suspected officers). They told me later that the traditional way of dealing with deviance was to transfer the miscreants and cover up the matter. By bringing it into the open they were making waves and risked being sidelined for promotion; in fact they both made it to high office.

Unwittingly they unleashed a great deal of turbulence because the investigation not only uncovered several layers of deviance but also started to point up the hierarchy. The main cases unfolded initially at three levels.

First, there were two officers for licensing premises who had accepted kickbacks; later two officers from the Aliens Department who controlled residence permits in the Chinese community were also accused of accepting kickbacks. Second, information started to come in about the activities of the Plain Clothes Squad (PCS) from the Warmoesstraat station (eight men and a sergeant). The PCS was set up to combat street crime but changed its task largely to the drugs area, determined its own hours with the supervisor working only days, never functioned as a team and defined its own priorities. There was supposed to be regular rotation of personnel but some had been members for years, one for fourteen years. An inspector said of the PCS, 'You could never find them; they were always messing about somewhere. They were like grains of drift-sand' (Punch 1985: 64).

The PCS began to focus increasingly on street drug-dealing and two members, 'Bert' and 'Jan', developed a particularly close relationship with a cooperative drug-dealer and also with a suspected Chinese dealer, 'Freddy'. Bert and his wife had apparently been on vacation to Paris with Freddy and his wife; it was rumoured that they returned with some 'merchandise'. These two cops were streetwise, cocky, constantly active, brought in many arrests and large amounts of drugs and had received commendations for their work from police chiefs in three forces.

The third level related to two highly respected detectives from Headquarters who were tasked with building a relationship with the leading Chinese figures in the city centre (these cops became known as the 'Chinese experts'). Much of the illegal activity in the criminal Chinese community was in the hands of the triads with several powerful leaders, and these two cops got to know them well.

Three investigations were mounted. There was the initial improvised inquiry by the two chief inspectors in the Warmoesstraat. There was an internal inquiry from Headquarters which was not very impressive given the lack of resources. And there was an external investigation by members of the National Detective Agency (NDA).[6] The NDA detectives are directed by the Public Prosecution Service and they investigate crimes by government officials. If serious offences are suspected among police officers then the NDA conducts the inquiry. These three investigations began to unearth information and evidence indicating that some detectives were on the payroll of Chinese establishments and had received copious presents in return for favours.

An important feature of the affair was that it was fully played out in the press. Amsterdam is the main centre of the printed press and this was a sensational story; moreover in the Netherlands almost everything is leaked. For example, the prosecution's dossier on the case with the interrogations and witness statements was leaked to the press;[7] and a journalist gave me a copy. There was also a 'whistle-blower' – the so-called 'Serpico of the Low Countries' – and for the first time a cop was openly expanding to the press on deviance in the force. But his motive was money, to help a move abroad having left the force, while his own reputation was not exactly lily-white (*Nieuwe Revue* 1977). The key elements in the allegations were intimate relationships between the police and criminals: cops were entertained by prostitutes paid for by the owner of a Chinese gambling house; Chinese dealers were forewarned about police raids; confiscated heroin was not reported but was used to pay informants who were cooperating with the cops; and money was stolen from suspects and drinks and goods were stolen at the scene of burglaries. What attracted considerable attention was the accusation that Chung Mon, so-called 'godfather' of the illegal Chinese community, had sent gifts of fruit baskets and turkey, and envelopes holding sums of money to police officers and to prosecutors (2,000–3,000 guilders was mentioned, equivalent then to about $5,300–8,000; Punch 1985: 51). These revelations reflected what was in the case dossier and what was widely rumoured; they remained the main thread of the prosecution.

This Amsterdam corruption scandal was unprecedented for the Netherlands. But then two further developments shifted the focus to other levels. First, while the 'clean' party in the hierarchy seemed paralysed by disbelief and denial, it emerged that there was also a 'dirty' party engaged in enthusiastic rule-bending. The press focus moved from the Warmoesstraat station to Headquarters, the Drug Squad and the head of the Central Detective Branch. That not only 'small fry' but senior officers were probably involved was major news. Much of this was speculation but it raised the stakes by also suggesting that some cops were involved in planting drugs, possessing and trading in illegal weapons and drug-dealing (a policeman was said to have driven to Antwerp in a Chinese dealer's car to fetch drugs for him; *Haagse Post* 1977).

Second, serendipity again played a role. By chance I was with some detectives who invited me to join them the following day on an 'exercise'. When I turned up it became evident that this was the American DEA (Drug Enforcement Agency) teaching the Amsterdam Police how to run 'buy and bust' operations. The DEA would set up the deal and pose as the buyers of drugs; but at the moment that the dealers were about to hand over the drugs the police would conveniently move in and arrest them. The DEA had no legal authority outside of US jurisdiction and was dependent on the local police for operational support (Nadelmann 1993). But the problem was that this method was illegal under Dutch law, which forbade entrapment.

Later, detectives told me about having to construct statements on the basis of fictive 'anonymous informants'; also a phrase spoke of 'confusion' allowing the buyers to disappear with the money from the scene. The detectives' concern in falsifying statements was not ethical but more prosaic; if this all came out in the open, who would carry the can? Indeed, much of the inter-rank animosity that arose came from the lower ranks 'taking the rap' for bosses who emerged unscathed.

Trial and tribulations

In April 1977 eight policemen were arrested – the two detectives known as the 'Chinese experts' from Headquarters, two detectives from the Aliens Department and four officers from the PCS in the Warmoesstraat. The trial was held a year later against six of the eight; there was insufficient evidence against the two Chinese experts for taking them to court. Freddy emerged at the trial as the key character in the affair. The main elements of the case revolved around fruit baskets, Chinese paydays and 'lucky money'. Freddy was on good terms with some officers. The evidence alleged that the Chinese cash book of his gambling hall recorded regular payments to the police; that he sent bulging fruit baskets with turkey, champagne and envelopes of money to cops at New Year; that he paid out sums to cops on the two paydays for shareholders in his gambling hall; and that cops accepted 'lucky money' from winners at the gambling table and went on to gamble with it.

The Public Prosecutor demanded prison sentences. The difficulty for the prosecution was in trying to get corroboration, as many Chinese witnesses had been expelled from the country or were not willing to testify; the 'bookkeeper' who recorded payments to the police, for example, may simply have kept the money for himself but was not available to the court. And to prove 'corruption' – the term is not formally defined in Dutch law – meant presenting evidence that the cops not only accepted money or goods but understood the intention of the briber and reciprocated with favours in conflict with their duty. The judges were not convinced of this intent tied to reciprocation and proved mild in sentencing. Ironically the police were always bitterly complaining about judicial laxity. One officer was found not guilty and five were fined for accepting gifts and small amounts of money. Two of the six retired on health grounds and the other four eventually returned to work in lowly functions. This was an anti-climax after all the rumours and speculation.

But of central significance are the reactions of the police and the rationalisations they gave. Furthermore, this became a scandal that could not be laid to rest but kept rumbling on. For a prison sentence, even a suspended one, would have meant automatic dismissal for the officers but now the Police Department had to decide which disciplinary measures it was going to recommend for the officers. Some senior officers were in favour of dismissal but the final say was with the Mayor; he decided not to take the cases to the Civil Service Tribunal, which was notoriously difficult to convince on dismissal. This prolonged process meant that the cops were suspended and insecure about their future; and on return they were moved to lowly, 'safe' functions while some complained that they faced hostility and harassment from bosses who had wanted them removed. It was during this limbo period that they decided to talk to the press. This prolonged the scandal and kept it in the public eye.

In the initial phase of the affair there was a widespread emotional upsurge from cops for their beleaguered colleagues in the Warmoesstraat. Officers were incensed by the negative media and some 2,000 officers from across the country protested about this in Amsterdam. Street cops in the Warmoesstraat refused to go out on patrol. The two chief inspectors who had begun the internal investigation were looked at askance; they became the object of ostracism, threats and counter-surveillance; apparently their telephones were tapped and at night cops would break into their offices to track appointments in their diaries. One officer who had been interviewed by NDA investigators later died of a heart attack; but it was rumoured he had committed suicide with his pistol. His son who was also a policeman aggressively accused the two chief inspectors of being responsible for his death: 'According to some our handling of the issue was responsible for his death and we drove him into his grave. We weren't allowed to attend the funeral. Now his son could shoot us dead. Some people really hate us. They say we destroyed people's careers. We've become almost untouchables' (Punch 1985: 158). Anyone involved in the investigations was roundly disparaged. The NDA investigators were despised, especially if they had originally served in Amsterdam as cops before transferring to the NDA. An investigating officer at Headquarters met a 'solid wall of incomprehension' when he lectured trainee detectives on his function: 'Police see themselves as different from civilians and cannot accept the idea that their own colleagues can be subject to investigation. When I mentioned the NDA detectives there was a completely irrational response ... I was seen as someone who screwed his own mates, and people stopped acknowledging me in the corridor'. (Punch 1985: 158).

There was, then, an almost blindly irrational response to the idea of police investigating police despite the fact that some of the defendants were hardly paragons of virtue. Professional law enforcers became instantly defensive when faced with sustained scrutiny from outside; this 'us versus them' mentality applied to anyone who was suspected of supplying information. Rumours were rife and reputations could be besmirched simply by making a critical remark about the defendants; an officer said a reputation for 'screwing your mates' pursued you through the organisation and took years to live down, if at all. Gossip and talk of conspiracies, plots and intrigue abounded and there was a stream of adverse propaganda against investigators and senior officers. When a second officer died of a heart attack, having been moved from his post in relation to the cases, it was again rumoured that he too had committed suicide.

Much of this emotion and turbulence was geared to presenting the officers under scrutiny as victims of a failing organisation and as scapegoats for pressure from, and deviance in, the higher ranks. In particular the two Chinese experts were viewed as dedicated officers who were formally requested to build a relationship with the leading members of the Chinese illegal community. If they took an egg-roll, a cognac or a jade Buddha then it was purely a means of lubricating the relationships. This was unavoidable and essential in that environment; how, it was argued, could they have refused? But they were investigated, arrested, suspended for over two years and then removed from serious detective work to lowly administrative jobs.

If there were 'victims' then the role of villains was for the higher ranks but also the organisation itself. The organisation was reified as the cause of much of the difficulties; first by indolence and indifference – ignoring the warning signals – but when the cases emerged it became heartless and vindictive in trying to swiftly remove a few sacrificial bad apples while ignoring the rotten pumpkins higher up. In their interviews with me the four members of the PCS who had been sanctioned launched a diatribe on the defects of the organisation as if it was their natural enemy. They spoke as if they were involved in their own righteous enterprise divorced from the police organisation which only hindered them in their mission.

My study revealed the Amsterdam police not as a harmonious, integrated institution but rather as a deeply divided organisation which endeavoured to confine an exposure of deviance to the lower ranks – the 'bad apples' strategy – except the bad apples fought back. The force was confronted with resistance from below with a counter-strategy of pushing the label back up the hierarchy. Of course, this theme of victimisation and blaming the organisation was the key strand in the cop's self-justification and their legal defence. And it was precisely the laxity in the organisation and the tolerant enforcement that had allowed them the freedom to become bent largely undisturbed in the first place. One of the most deviant miscreants of the PCS rather hypocritically claimed, 'There was just no leadership, no coordination, no control, there was nothing. Nobody ever said anything like "when are you going home?" or "when are you coming back?" Nobody asked you anything. You just messed around as much as you wanted. We used to be frightened of the bosses, but now you don't give a shit about them' (Punch 1985: 64). Particular venom was, then, directed at the senior ranks for being either inept or else collusive in encouraging rule-bending while evading responsibility. Bosses were variously seen as lazy, incompetent, mercenary, careerist, manipulative, vain, vindictive and keen to poach cases and good officers from elsewhere to enhance their personal status. Tales abounded of senior officers who were inadequate, womanisers, alcoholics (who had been caught driving under the influence but it had been covered up) or who had been involved in domestic violence. These were recounted with great authenticity about the shortcomings of individuals concerned but probably contained occupational myths.

Such negative stereotypes of leaders abound in many organisations. In Dutch policing, moreover, there was a caste-like two-tier system of entry and training for senior officers and lower ranks where there was little chance of promotion from below. The lower ranks typically portrayed themselves as practitioners who had 'done the business', while their disparaging imagery of the higher ranks was of desk-bound theoreticians who had never got their boots muddied. And Dutch society generally had witnessed many attacks in diverse institutions on people in authority since the late 1960s. In Amsterdam these critical feelings about members of the hierarchy were exacerbated by the reimposition of control following a long indulgency pattern. This downward focus was seen as unacceptable scapegoating.

One response to this was censoriousness about the leading officers. The main bone of contention was that some senior officers were also said to have received presents (the notorious baskets of fruit, champagne, turkey and brown envelopes), were deeply deviant themselves and, above all, encouraged the rule-bending. Some stimulated risk-taking, did not accept responsibility and disowned the risk-takers lower down when the heat was on. In the new environment of drug-dealing there was clearly a lot of 'creative' policing going on at the margins of the law. Several senior officers of the new generation had entered this grey area eagerly but the 'Young Turks' faction played it formally as the new realists willing to bend the rules for results but always in agreement with others, including cooperative prosecutors. But one officer in particular attracted a great deal of animosity both from this new guard and from the lower ranks for his personal style of bravado and rule-bending.

The Head of the Detective Branch, Jansen, had plunged into the new world of drug enforcement, Chinese criminals, informants and DEA operatives with gusto. When I interviewed him he rubbed his hands together vigorously and said: 'I go to work like this every day. What with the Caransa case [kidnapping of a wealthy businessman] and the RAF business [German terrorists] I've been putting in a hundred hours overtime a month. I'm on the go Saturdays and Sundays and I tell my men to call me out at any time of the night or day, whether I'm at home or at a party' (Punch 1985: 74). He encouraged his detectives to bring in arrests and drugs, gave the assignment to the two Chinese experts from the CID (Criminal Intelligence Department) to develop relationships with Chinese community leaders and became personally close to those key figures himself. His prime motive appears to have been results and personal status while the results were more important than rules; he reputedly had taken money but he predictably swept this accusation aside. My feeling is that what was important to him was the buzz of intrigue and being the central link in a range of murky operations. He was the stereotypical, old-style detective boss, unlike many of his duller and more formal colleagues whom he openly disparaged; he was a vain, dominating wheeler-dealer type who would have been at home in Scotland Yard in the 1970s. Indeed, he can be compared to Kelaher of the Met who also came unstuck through creative enforcement in the drugs area (see Chapter 5).

There was then a context with a clash of personalities, generations and working styles but also inter-departmental rivalry as well as friction between the lower and upper ranks. Within that there were growing suspicions that Jansen's relationships with leading members of the illegal Chinese community had become too intimate and that he was manipulating informants in relation to the drugs trade. While he was on vacation – vacations are precarious times for the deviant – his safe was opened and out tumbled incriminating evidence. This was said to have included money, drugs and the passports of Chinese informants who could not leave the country without his say (Punch 1985: 173).

I was told by leading and reliable officers that Jansen was deeply and indisputably deviant. But they added that it was unthinkable that an officer of his rank could be prosecuted for a crime as it would have brought shame on the entire Dutch police.[8] He was never prosecuted but as a disciplinary sanction was moved from leading the Central Detective Branch to be head of a police district, which was a huge humiliation for him. But for others he was the rule-breaker at the top, championing deviance in subordinates yet never having to face arrest or trial; above all he disowned the two Chinese experts and did nothing to rescue them. To the lower ranks his case represented the great betrayal; the subordinates had taken the risks, some had faced sanctioning in court, but the big fish had got away with it. Even among the supervisory ranks there was sympathy for this view; a chief inspector at Headquarters said: 'In a way, in my heart, I agree with Smit [member of PCS]. There should also have been bosses standing next to him in the dock. Too few questions were asked and bosses neglected to set clear guidelines. The end justified the means. Only the result mattered and that is still the golden rule for most governors' (Punch 1985: 78). But Jansen could not stick to his dull role as district chief. On vacation – again a holiday proved fatal – he spent two days in Karachi where he met a Pakistani drug-dealer and former informant who paid the hotel bill and other expenses for Jansen and his wife (Middelburg 1993: 38). This was the last straw and he was relieved of his post and given some obscure administrative task, but he soon took early retirement.

Rationalisations

Initially during my fieldwork corruption was a taboo subject but later, with the trials and publicity, officers began talking about it. Generally they did not perceive these cases to involve 'corruption'; for them that meant something large-scale, systematic and involving substantial sums of money and that was definitely pernicious. But these practices were inherent in policing, and were seen as forms of cadging and mooching involving the universal pitfalls of drink, females, gifts and money. Furthermore, not to accept anything – which was the formal rule – was seen not only as unrealistic but also as offensive to the giver. A reasonable level of grass-eating was acceptable and harmless but systematic, financially based transactions with favours in return for crooks were seen as completely unacceptable.

I was able to interview four of the defendants after the trial. I knew all four from the Warmoesstraat but I never achieved access with the other defendants at Headquarters. They had all been well drilled by the defence to reject in court any question of reciprocation in order to avoid a conviction for corruption; and they certainly were not going to admit anything serious to me. But it was obvious that all of those involved had taken presents and in some cases sexual favours and money. One officer admitted to me that he and his partner were taking kickbacks from establishments in the inner city. Also one suspect had drugs in his possession when arrested; another had drugs in his house (and a photograph of a naked prostitute taken in the station); and another suspect had an extensive collection of weapons, ammunition and drug attributes in his flat. There were, too, persistent rumours of close relations with drug-dealers and informants, allowing dealers to continue in business in exchange for arrests, transporting drugs, dealing in firearms, retaining confiscated drugs and stealing from suspects. There was, as often in such cases, a question as to who was running who; were some of the cops exploiting their relationships or had they been effectively co-opted to work for the dealers? A Dutch 'bouncer' at Freddy's gambling hall claimed, for instance, that Freddy was too soft and two officers in particular would take money off Freddy and gamble with it, turn up on the two paydays in the month for shareholders in his casino and go out on the town at his expense; the cops 'milked Freddy completely dry' (Punch 1985: 106).

But putting together what they were prepared to tell me and material from the media and other interviews, how did the police officers justify and rationalise their conduct? Their accounts (Lyman and Scott 1970) and vocabularies of motive (Sykes and Matza 1957) were replete with crude, even coprophiliac imagery of disease, pollution, swamps and contamination (shit, mud, dirt, blood and cancer).

You can't play dirty without getting dirty. A detective said of Jansen reportedly having dirty hands: 'But if you ask a gynaecologist to make a caesarean cut then his hands will be covered in blood. Who can dig out a cess-pit without tools and yet not get his hands dirty?' (*Extra* 1978). An investigator said he could start stirring in a pot of shit but some of it would doubtless stick to his hands; a detective spoke of anyone walking in a swamp in patent leather shoes would emerge with dirty feet. The theme was that a cop could not do certain police work without getting contaminated in some way; and that this occupational predicament should be taken into account when judging him.

Everyone was doing it. This was the suggestion that some of the 'grass-eating' deviance was widespread and accepted both within the force, including senior officers, but also outside of it (for example among prosecutors, but this was never substantiated). One suspect said that if you stood next to the gambling table in an illegal Chinese casino then anyone who had won would give 'luck money' to everyone around the table; 'we were standing there too so we took it as well'. One of the defendants with drugs on him at the time of arrest intimated that everyone in the station had something illegal in their locker and that senior officers in the Warmoesstraat had also accepted gifts; he pointed upwards, indicating upstairs where the officers worked and said, 'they have all had them', meaning fruit baskets.

We could not refuse. A central bulwark in the policemen's defence was that they were obliged to accept small sums of money, gifts and food because they could not refuse these without offending their contacts. An officer, asked in court how he interpreted these gifts, answered: 'I saw this as an expression of esteem for the work we performed ... we were rewarded for this work as an Eastern token of gratitude' (Case Dossier: statement, 26 April 1977).[9]

Relationships were part and parcel of the job. An extension of the above was that the cop had to build a relationship with criminals and informants as essential to fulfilling one's task. To glean information you had to spend time in the Chinese casinos. As one of the suspects said; 'Of course I took something. But Chinese people will only agree to talk to you if you eat and drink together and they pay the bill. And the whole point was to build up a relationship with them'. (Punch 1985: 146).

We didn't do it for ourselves. A strong theme was a form of 'noble cause'. They did not accept things from a base, mercenary motive; if anything they acted from a form of altruism. They were doing it to get a result, achieve convictions and see justice done. Indeed, several suspects and especially the two Chinese experts emphasised the sacrifices they had made and the energy they had expended without thought of personal gain. The imagery was of devoted, dedicated detectives, neglecting their family and social life in order to pursue criminals relentlessly and incidentally taking a meal or a gift as a means to achieving a higher end. They lived for their work and would have done nothing to betray it.

We were victims – of the work and the bosses. An important feature in their justifications and rationalisations was positioning themselves as victims of the nature of the working situation with exposure to illicit opportunities; in this regard they were practically all 'slippery slopers' who gradually slid into deviance. A key factor in the work environment pushing them down the slope was pressure or encouragement from above. The argument was that there were new rules of the game with hard drugs taking over the market and this had brought about rivalry and competition among the main players. Two of the PCS officers, a 'golden couple', felt that they were first ignored but then when they became successful they were encouraged to bring in drugs and arrests by those from above, with no one questioning their methods until the wheel came off. And the two Chinese experts clearly felt that they had been instructed by a senior officer to build a close relationship with the leading members of the illicit Chinese community in order to gain information. It was also suggested that they may have been set up because they were getting too much information and some Chinese criminals wanted them out of the way.

Then there was a theme of *we were not treated properly.* This is not an excuse but more an ironic by-product; the defendants and other police suspects complained about how they were treated by investigating officers or by the detectives of the NDA. Also graphic stories circulated of inhumane treatment – arrests in the night, long interrogations, lack of sleep and refreshments – that pressurised officers to confess. In this they echoed the typical complaints of civilians and suspects of police misbehaviour. Several defendants complained to me that they were not arrested or searched 'properly' following the legal procedure; but as one admitted they never kept to the procedure either during arrests. They had been processed as suspects, stigmatised in the press, held in custody (one for 38 days), suspended on a reduced salary, given house detention and been forbidden to visit police stations and meet with other cops (inevitably this was ignored). When I met the four defendants they were no longer the self-assured cops who strutted through the inner city; they were rather forlorn, had variously problems with drink, finance or their spouses and faced an uncertain future. Above all they felt banished like pariahs; as one cop said, the Amsterdam Police had acted like some medieval town 'casting the people out, and closing the gates behind them'. One of the Chinese experts explained what it was like to be arrested – 'we were treated like pigs' – whereas Jansen had 'VIP treatment' because he was a commissioner. This detective spoke further of his utter dedication to the job, seven days a week, always on call. Even when his wife went into hospital for a serious operation he left her bedside to respond to a call. Yet he would probably do it all over again, he said, because 'being a cop is a bit like having an incurable disease' (*Extra* 1978).

Comment

The Amsterdam scandal provides a number of insights into both the genesis of corruption and how a police organisation reacts to external scrutiny and labelling. The organisation was not well run or coordinated at that time and it devoted no attention or resources to the risk of corruption, which was a taboo subject. There was an element of ignorance – this was a new experience in Dutch policing – and even of denial. The Police Commissioner admitted that he and other senior officers had failed: 'I had enormous confidence, almost a blind faith, in my men. But now it seems that things existed about which the leadership remained blind ... the police organisation is an after-the-incident, reacting, reactive concern. We only do something when things get out of hand. We've been completely swamped by this whole business' (Punch 1985: 79).

There was a strong indulgency pattern within the organisation; formal control and supervision were weak. Also there was a broader context of tolerance towards much of the illegal activity in the inner city; as a result some officers felt stymied in tackling crime in the area. This could lead to indifference, frustration, to becoming 'cowboys' who became involved in the delights of the area or to corruption. For instance, the low internal control allied to the tolerance of illegal activity opened rich opportunities for some entrepreneurial arrangements with drug-dealers. Officers could also use their discretion to exert favours or kickbacks from vulnerable groups such as prostitutes or Chinese immigrants who were in the country illegally. They could threaten them with sanctioning or expulsion or promise to help them avoid these when they knew full well that this was most unlikely.

The scandal was played out in the press over a period of four years. The tone of the reporting was ambivalent. On the one hand there were juicy revelations of sex, bribes and trips abroad but on the other hand there was a portrait of devoted law enforcers fighting crime with a weak police organisation run by vain incompetents while being hampered by a mild justice system. The main right-wing daily paper and several of the more sensational weekly magazines had discovered law and order and used the stories of the disgruntled detectives to attack the 'tolerance' that attracted foreign criminals to the Netherlands. This tied an alien conspiracy theory to seeing the cops as Dutch Dirty Harrys who bent rules to achieve results; their contacts in the media helped present them as admirable, fearless crime-fighters.

What strongly emerged was antagonism between the ranks. The lower orders were vitriolic about the shortcomings of senior officers. There simply was no solidarity here. Rather there was animosity about absentee bosses, bosses who encouraged rule-breaking in subordinates but then ran for cover when trouble was on the horizon, and bosses who were themselves bent but got away with it. There was a powerful sense of betrayal about senior officers who stimulated rule-breaking in subordinates but abandoned them when the heat was on. Some cops clearly felt used and then left to be the 'fall guy'. The view from below was that bosses could play around but always got away with it; one cop remarked that in his 35 years on the force senior officers 'have never done anything wrong. That's unthinkable. And it holds for higher-ups too, like public prosecutors, who can do no wrong' (Punch 1985: 87)

There was an upsurge of sympathy and support from all over the country for the officers in the Warmoesstraat. This was emotional and irrational given that several of the suspects were clearly deviant and probably accepted food, gifts, sex, money and drugs from criminals in the inner city. Several may have even have been involved in drug-dealing. These were hardly role models for the Dutch police. The two Chinese experts, however, could be seen both as institutional heroes – well-liked, dedicated, dyed-in-the-wool detectives – and as corporate victims, as they were seen to have done their work in an exemplary way only to become scapegoats, accepting trifling presents while others who were really bent got away with it.

Great hostility was shown to anyone involved in investigating a colleague. This almost blind rage applied to the two chief inspectors in the Warmoesstraat, to internal investigators at Headquarters, to the members of the NDA and to any cop who was thought to have given information – or even just raised justified suspicions – about a colleague. There were threats, physical intimidation, ostracism, counter-surveillance, telephone tapping, adverse propaganda and covert support for the suspended officers.

The cases brought about a snowball effect. They began with kickbacks in licensing, moved to close relationships with drug-dealers among members of the PCS, started to focus on senior officers and specialised units at Headquarters and began to open up the role of the DEA. It is an illusion to think that we will ever know the full story of went on within the Amsterdam Police at that time, as well as in the prosecution service. There were so many intrigues, so much rumour and such a proliferation of conspiracy theories that it was impossible to unravel fact from fiction. As a researcher I felt that there were too many levels, too much manipulation, too many people either refusing to meet me or trying to sell me their version of the story and too many interests at stake to get closer to the truth. I had been involved with the Amsterdam Police for six years and had to move on (Punch 1989).

Finally, the Amsterdam scandal is of value for three main reasons. First, it revealed the unwillingness of the lower ranks to accept a negative label from above and outside and their power to mount a sustained campaign of resistance with the media as an ally. The conflict was almost a form of prolonged industrial dispute, as if workers accused of pilfering rejected blame and guilt and enthusiastically pointed upwards to the more rapacious villains at the top. The view from below was that during the scandal the lower orders, including the majority of straight cops, were likely to be double losers both from external labelling and from the fallout from the factional battles within the elite. For, second, the Amsterdam Police was not a coherent, coordinated law enforcement agency with a unanimous strategy and a culture of comforting solidarity. Rather it was a cauldron of conflicting egos, bickering blood groups and almost infantile rivalry; the turbulence caused by the scandal opened the fissures between the layers and factions and the organisation imploded into many warring factions. It was rather like a dysfunctional family. Of course, this may also be true of other organisations under stress. But third and finally, perhaps police organisations are more likely to be segmented and factional than many other organisations. For Van Maanen (1978c: 322) states: 'In many respects, police organisations represent a hodge-podge of cliques, cabals, and conspiracies. Since members often do not trust each other ... deceit, evasiveness, duplicity, innuendo, secrecy, double-talk, and triple-talk mark many of the interactions'.[10]

Perhaps, then, we have to revise our views on solidarity in policing. In Amsterdam any presumed solidarity became fractured and fragmented in the segmental solidarity of generational cliques, within ranks, inside departmental factions, between warring operational units and even at the micro-level of specific couples. At times it was a Hobbesian war of all against all.

The 'IRT' affair

A significant feature of the Amsterdam scandal was that, although it remained a media item for several years, it stayed confined to the Amsterdam force, did not spread to prosecutors or politicians, did not become a national issue and did not generate a major house-cleaning. The latter is partly related to the difficulty of removing police officers with civil service tenure in the Netherlands. But also the Dutch style of reacting to crisis was far less the dynamic of scandal and reform as it was in the US. The Dutch reaction was typically more oriented to shoring up the system, with serious reflection postponed until later. Yet the Amsterdam scandal undoubtedly had a long-term influence in changing the organisation, but that did not manifest itself with a commission of inquiry or replacement of senior personnel.

In comparison, the IRT affair two decades after the Amsterdam scandal attracted enormous publicity in the Netherlands and had a powerful impact on the image and the functioning of the criminal justice system (Sheptycki 1999). There were several commissions set up including two parliamentary inquiries and these fostered significant changes in police procedure. There were two main reasons for the attention paid to the affair. One was that the accusations and revelations came from within the system and from highly placed officials. And the other was that the media had become far more assertive and television was especially influential in bringing the events and personalities involved to a wide public.

The affair focused on police responses to the growth of serious organised crime and in particular the drugs trade (Sheptycki 2000a). The strategic position of the country, with the large harbour of Rotterdam, had made the Netherlands a major centre for the import and distribution of drugs and a stamping ground for new-style criminal gangs (Dutch Report 1994). There was, too, a growing sense that the authorities (police, justice, customs and tax) had been lax in tracing this development and were poorly equipped to deal with it. Policing, for example, was primarily locally focused with few regional or national squads (Punch 1997). This period coincided with a major reorganisation of the police when in 1994 the two separate agencies (the National Police and the Municipal Police) were integrated into 25 regional forces and one central force. In anticipation of this reorganisation a number of 'inter-regional' crime teams (IRTs)[11] had already been formed to tackle major investigations that overlapped the new regional boundaries (Klerks 1995).

One of these was the IRT for the two Provinces of North-Holland and Utrecht, which was operational from 1989, drew on personnel from six forces and was located in Amsterdam. Just trying to set up the team was a typical Dutch circus of consultation, delay, bureaucracy, infighting, jealousy, squabbles about leadership and friction between the 'provincial' members and the Amsterdam contingent. In some circles there was great frustration at this institutional failure to take tackling organised crime seriously and growing impatience to take on the gangs (Middelburg 1993: 176). Then in 1994 this IRT was suddenly disbanded, with a great deal of bad blood between the forces involved and between the Amsterdam Police and the Public Prosecution Service (PPS) in particular.[12] Rumours surfaced about 'dubious' methods of investigation and, most unusually for the Netherlands, one police chief spoke publicly of 'corruption'. The turmoil resulted in the first of several commissions of inquiry (Wierenga Commission 1994). The Wierenga Report brought to the surface much friction, tension, squabbling and rivalry between the chiefs involved, members of their forces, and particularly between police and prosecutors.

Amid all this the key question was; had the IRT used 'unacceptable' methods in tackling organised crime? Wierenga stated in his report that the method employed was acceptable; but the part of his report detailing this was confidential and this initially confused the issue as all the evidence was not publicly available. The 'method' in question was promoted by two industrious and innovative detectives in the IRT squad. They formed what was known as a 'golden' or 'royal couple', were widely respected and had been rewarded for their earlier efforts in enforcement. They believed in high-level infiltration within the drug trade, of providing the active infiltrator with a company as a front, and, above all, in the method of 'controlled delivery'. The whole point was to reach as high as possible in the criminal organisation and this meant allowing the active informant to commit crimes. To establish the credentials of their agent they provided him with large sums of money (some 4 million guilders or about 9 million US dollars) and permitted him to import large quantities of drugs from Colombia with a company as front. The idea was to let a number of the containers full of drugs to pass the customs, to follow them to their destination, to allow some to enter the market to establish the infiltrator's credentials, trace who were at the top of the criminal organisation and then move in for arrests and confiscation following a substantial shipment (Besse and Kuys 1997; Langendoen and

Vierboom 1998). Although the two detectives personally promoted this method in the Netherlands there had also been a long-standing relationship with the DEA which since the 1970s had enthusiastically endeavoured to teach European police forces new tricks of the trade (as mentioned above; Nadelmann 1995). Given the central position of the Netherlands in drugs distribution the DEA has been particularly active in the country; generally these activities are clouded in secrecy. It is not known if the DEA played an active role in this case but given that it involved large amounts of cocaine from South America the agency was almost certainly present in the background. But DEA officers pleaded diplomatic immunity and refused to testify before the commissions (Punch 1989; Nadelmann 1993).

This creative idea of the 'golden couple' had a major stumbling block; it was bending Dutch law to the limits if not actually breaking it. It is difficult to trace the intricacies of what went on in this case but some of the elements were: manipulating evidence that went to authorities and the courts; not fully informing senior officers in one's own force of the unit's activities; throwing up a veil of secrecy around the activities of the IRT; generating illicit funds to set up the infiltrator and finance parts of the investigation; misleading the customs authorities; forming an alliance with 'innovative' prosecutors and allowing the import of large amounts of drugs.[13] Behind this was a shift to a more assertive and proactive enforcement stance. A senior officer in another squad for tackling organised crime summarised this approach: 'Creative thinking is the key phrase. You must not allow yourself to be tied to the law books: nothing is too extreme for us. We have to be exhaustively concerned with the search for alternatives' (Naeyé 1995: 11). It is likely that there were diverse groups within the team with varying opinions about the strategy to be followed; also that there was frustration at the delays and infighting and determination among some to 'search exhaustively' for those creative alternatives. The 'creative' cops were apparently disparaging about the so-called 'check-list' or 'follow-the-scenario' cops on the squad (Haenen and Meeus 1996: 91)

This deep and complex type of operation depended on a lot of variables to make it work; a central one was that the 'controlled' delivery of drugs would be traced and that much would be confiscated before reaching the market. The idea was to focus on soft drugs, allow some on the market and then strike on a large delivery. Unfortunately, the surveillance of the containers by the IRT was not perfect, so quantities of drugs, including hard drugs, did get on the market without being traced and the infiltrator even kept some of the proceeds of this illegal operation by playing a double-game. It is also possible that the authorities were being conned by so-called 'parallel imports' which the informant had concealed. It was estimated that the IRT was responsible for the import of 230,000 kilos of soft drugs (over 200 tons) and 40,000 kilos of hard drugs; later it was also suggested in a subsequent inquiry that some 15,000 kilos of cocaine had reached the market illegally because of corrupt cops and custom officials (de Volkskrant, 1998d, 1999). In effect, the PPS and police had been held hostage by a single infiltrator and the Dutch government had become the largest importer of drugs into the Netherlands!

This case has to be seen in the light of a Dutch criminal justice system that was trying to fight organised crime while the legal rules and procedures remained, in the eyes of the more innovative officers who put opportunism and results before strict legality, antiquated and restrictive. Various proactive methods were forbidden under Dutch law while the courts were traditionally tough on entrapment and on anonymous witnesses who had taken part in crimes. But a new generation of 'creative' cops and 'innovative' prosecutors were engaging in rule-bending; and, importantly, the courts were not proving overly inquisitive. Formally the police are under the direction of the PPS but in reality they often have high operational autonomy. Also, in the Continental European 'inquisitorial' system, as opposed to the Anglo-American 'adversary' system (Rose 1996), the prosecutor sees himself (or increasingly herself) as allied to the judiciary in the search for truth. Traditionally the 'Officers of Justice' were legalistic, 'clean hands' officials far from the reality of crime enforcement but in recent decades some had become explicitly 'crime-fighters'. The innovative 'golden duo' in the IRT case were insulating their case and protecting their participating informant by being economical with the truth towards their superiors and police chief; they had struck up an alliance with cooperative prosecutors who in turn did not fully inform their superiors within the PPS. The five highest officials of the PPS, the Procurators General, claimed to have no knowledge of the controlled delivery method (de Volkskrant 1995). There were clearly layers of actors within the system with diverse channels of information related to those 'in the know' and those kept out of the frame.

In effect, segments of the justice system were innovating and the checks and balances were being stymied, side-stepped or overlooked. Naeyé (1995: 30) states that the focus on covering up creative investigative methods and protecting sources of information had become so prominent that 'investigators operate within a legal grey

area of unwritten law where everything seems to be permissible'.
Part of the genesis of this deviance lies in the structural changes
to detective work. New-style cases had become geared to carefully
tracing the contours of the criminal organisation, investing in long-
term intelligence gathering – with surveillance, telephone taps, data
collection and searches – in trying to reach the top of the criminal
hierarchy. The emphasis was more on disrupting the machine,
confiscation and asset-stripping than on early and low-level arrests.
This meant a considerable investment of time before reaching the
executive stage of an operation; roughly 70 per cent was spent on
gaining intelligence and the rest went on arrests and then rounding
off the paperwork (Naeyé 1995).

It also encouraged the use of participating informants to get close
to the leading players. These informants had to be given considerable
resources to establish their front – and also later in protection
programmes – while they were also allowed to take part in crimes.
There is, then, always the issue in such operations of how far to go
in supporting the infiltrator's front and allowing him to take part in
crime. This in turn relates to the question of who is running who,
as he can dictate terms from his position of power as he gets deeper
and higher in the criminal organisation and closer to the climax of
moving in for the 'kill'. Once under way it was difficult to change
course in these operations as the investment is high, the preparation
long and the all-essential egg is in one vulnerable basket. This was all
a new game in the Netherlands. The structure, style, aims and tempo
of investigations had altered; it is conceivable that some detectives
brought up on a more traditional culture of short-cycle operations,
a 'break-down-the-door' style and early arrests, experienced some
difficulty in adjusting.

An insight into what this new-style intelligence orientation could
mean for operational police work was given by an investigation into
an elite detective team in South Limburg (an 'OT' – *Opsporingsteam*,
or 'investigative team'). The NDA was called in to investigate 42
incidents of dubious methods relating to thirteen detectives in the
squad. The OT members were accused of fabricating crime reports;
these reported fictitious observations of criminals; and the signatures
on documents had been falsified. A female infiltrator dropped off
drugs in Germany but it was falsely reported that this 'unknown
courier' had 'escaped' when in fact the whole operation had been
shadowed by Dutch and German officers. The OT team was also
illegally breaking into property. One detective was described as a
'highly motivated policeman' who, because of his devotion to work,

'had completely lost the ability to draw the line'. He had trained in Germany as a 'key specialist', meaning in practice he had become an expert burglar. Dutch law forbids police breaking into property in order to investigate possible criminal activity unless formal permission by an investigating magistrate has been given and a formal report is made up afterwards.

To avoid this, detectives practised so-called 'key-hole' operations which involved breaking into property without permission and then, obviously, not reporting it. Generally this went smoothly but one day a door was forced open which could not be shut properly. The detectives tried a cover-up, with an anonymous call to the local police about a break-in; but the call was tapped by a another squad and when it emerged that other officers had made the anonymous call and misled their colleagues 'there was a fair old shindig' (de Volkskrant 1997).

In brief, this insight into how police in a specialised unit were operating indicates that they were continually and routinely breaking the law, failing to report incidents, fabricating informants, distorting the truth, carrying out illegal break-ins, and falsifying signatures. This case emerged after the IRT affair but was held to be indicative of the 'Wild West' behaviour of some officers before the post-Van Traa reforms (see below) these were determined to book results in their personal 'war on crime' (according to the prosecution service; de Volkskrant 1997). A number of potential crimes were uncovered but finally no one was prosecuted, with the PPS proving mild by not pressing charges. There is a wider pattern in several societies of not robustly sanctioning cops caught in 'bent for job' offences; but this was doubtless enhanced here by the fact that in the Netherlands the PPS is formally in charge of police investigations and had to take some responsibility for the police failings.

Furthermore, this OT squad in South Limburg was an elite unit of highly motivated officers; they were the cream of the crop. The deviance, with potentially criminal offences, was generated primarily by a determination to achieve results. The unit had invested much psychic energy in investigations and when these were proving fallow they turned to rule-bending by fabricating material which conveyed positive results. The deviance was, then, self-induced and in a way self-defeating as the real situation of low progress was bound to emerge eventually; but the detectives blinded themselves to the consequences.[14] There are institutional issues here about how much autonomy, control and supervision the unit was permitted. Indeed the squad's deviance had only emerged from two amateur blunders.

But it was precisely this sort of 'Wild West' behaviour, according to the spokesperson of the PPS, that later gave rise to the controversy on police methods of investigating organised crime in the IRT case.

The initial debate on acceptable methods was, then, greatly amplified by the IRT scandal. This led to critical questioning in Parliament where an initial working party was followed by a full parliamentary commission of inquiry (both chaired by the Member of Parliament, Maarten Van Traa). This full-blown commission attracted considerable attention because many prominent figures in the criminal justice arena had to testify to the commission – under oath, in public and before the cameras – about police methods. Some witnesses tried to plead secrecy, appeared in disguise (and had their voices distorted), and some faced critical questioning. A number of seasoned detectives had an 'attack of the carmens'; which is Australian police slang for repeatedly saying, 'I do not recall' (Voyez 1999). Before the inquiry started there had been public fights between police chiefs, battles between police and prosecutors, and two ministers had resigned. It is rare for ministers to resign in the Netherlands and unprecedented that two should resign together; but they had not adequately informed Parliament on the IRT affair. This already made it an untypical Dutch scandal.

The Van Traa Commission (1996) had high visibility and a profound impact. In comparison the earlier Amsterdam scandal was a local sideshow. But since the 1970s the media had changed and could broadcast extensively the public sittings where ministers, policy-makers, academics, prosecutors, senior police officers and detectives were in the spotlight. There emerged a picture of senior officials who were not in control of their organisations, of rivalry and disputes among leading figures, and of specialised crime squads that bent and broke the rules and that colluded with criminal informants to allow substantial shipments of drugs to enter the Dutch market (and markets in other countries: Sheptycki, 1999).

A full parliamentary commission is rare in the Netherlands and is employed only for the most serious of issues; hence this one became daily news. It powerfully reinforced the public feeling that there were serious defects within the criminal justice world. For quite a time afterwards there were reverberations related to spin-off investigations, possible criminal prosecutions, police chiefs being moved around (as it was almost impossible to dismiss them), and new legislation in the area of police methods of investigating organised crime. The cumulative impacts of these reports, amplified by the accompanying media coverage, meant that the criminal justice system had been placed under the microscope.

The commission's report, for instance, spoke of a crisis at three levels. First, on standards there was confusion about what was acceptable and what was not in investigations. Second, there were problems organisationally of coordination between the many agencies involved in the investigation and the prosecution of serious offences. And, third, with regard to authority, there existed friction between the police and the PPS which proved disruptive and led to disputes about who was really in charge of investigations. As a result the two detectives at the centre of the controversial method were prosecuted for perjury, several chiefs retired early or were transferred, a procurator general (one of the top five officials of the PPS) resigned and there was new legislation tightening control in investigations.

In effect, the police had bent and broken rules, some prosecutors had gone along with them, and some judges had not probed vigorously. 'Innovative' police methods had contaminated other segments of the system. Senior officers had failed, as had public prosecutors, checks and balances did not work or were sidestepped, judges failed to probe and ministers failed to inform Parliament properly. Dubious working practices in specialised squads had implicated others in the system and brought about a major scandal in criminal justice.

In short, the *system* had failed. This multiple failure was echoed in the conclusion of the Van Traa Commission (1996: 433). It stated that until the IRT commotion police chiefs had displayed little interest in investigatory methods or in their own CID units (Criminal *Intelligence* Squads; Klerks 1995); the Ministry of Justice was poorly informed on this area; and Parliament never imposed serious control of such activities. In effect, new-style police work had simply not been managed adequately at diverse levels; and some organised criminal gangs were having a field day. It started with something of a moral panic about organised crime, followed by political pressure to do something about it (Dutch Report 1994). This led to new-style, inter-regional units with high autonomy and secrecy; these were established at the moment that policing was experiencing a major overhaul and most chiefs were absorbed and distracted by this reorganisation; they paid little attention to these squads floating outside the boundaries of their region.

For IRTs were unlike traditional units in that the focus was primarily on collecting intelligence to reach high up the criminal organisation; consequently much time and effort was expended before reaching the operational phase (Naeyé 1995). This could also mean that there was institutional pressure for results with internal determination to justify their existence and these two forces encouraged creativity, innovation and rule-bending. These IRTs were new elite units striving to establish themselves and show results. The 'golden couple' in the IRT case, for instance, had earlier been praised and rewarded for their efforts and were widely seen as highly motivated if not ideal officers. They sought no direct personal gain and presented themselves as motivated, selfless detectives for whom police work came before their families, and at times the restrictions of the law. Like the two Chinese experts in Amsterdam earlier they positioned themselves as dedicated cops, devoted to their job in which informants came first and who bent the rules occasionally to get the job done (Langendoen and Vierboom 1998). They continually insisted they did nothing wrong but were victims of inter-institutional rivalry and squabbling bosses in a war of superegos. (Haenen and Meeus 1996).

With new challenges, new organisational forms, low supervision, and probably with encouragement from the DEA, the innovators had gone outside the already blurred boundaries. An unintended conspiracy of factors gave the rule-benders the opportunity, which they grabbed with enthusiasm. But their individual motivation has to be placed in the specific context of policing in the Netherlands in the early 1990s with external and internal pressure for results, the setting up of new units outside of the traditional hierarchy and force control structures, a willingness to push the rules to the extreme among some prosecutors and leniency among the judiciary. All the actors protested in various ways that they were lily-white and were simply motivated to catch crooks. But the institutional, managerial and political failure to manage the processes surrounding these developments – and to protect and implement the checks and balances – elicited the largest scandal in Dutch criminal justice since World War Two (Punch 1985).

Conclusion

In general there is still a relatively low level of public corruption in the Netherlands; and this also holds true for policing (Lamboo 2005). There have been a number of sizeable scandals related to deviance in business with links to local corruption among officials; but these are hardly ever related to national politics.[15] Police corruption is usually either small-scale – one or two officers accepting kickbacks or leaking information – or confined to special units with rule-bending to gain results. But there have never been whole units linked to organised crime or to systematic payoffs as in the US. There are a number of explanations for this.

First, Dutch policing came late to dealing with serious organised crime and to 'creative' methods; it took the DEA to introduce them to murky methods in the 1970s. Second there is, at least on the surface, a strong formal accountability structure, with police answering to the mayor and chief public prosecutor, while key parts of an investigation are directed by an investigating magistrate (*Rechter Commissaris* in Dutch; c.f. Tak 2003). Third, the courts have generally remained fairly conservative with regard to new methods of investigation and anything smacking of entrapment, while there are no conspiracy laws in the Netherlands. It is clear, however, that some prosecutors had become highly 'innovative' and some judges were prepared to be indulgent. Indeed, it was the Amsterdam Police that protested to the PPS that the controversial method was not kosher (even if their motives for this were mixed). Finally, the Dutch police has become more professional and managerially oriented in recent years, with more attention to control and discipline.

It has also started to pay serious attention to issues of ethics and integrity; this was stimulated by the Minister of Home Affairs, Mrs Dales, which led in 2001 to a national initiative reaching all 50,000 officers throughout the country (Punch 2002). One can, of course, be sceptical about the impact that this has had on enforcement practice in the Netherlands. Almost certainly a fair amount of wheeling and dealing and of 'creativity' continues to surround enforcement against organised crime and particularly with regard to drugs, which remain major law enforcement's main challenge with gang warfare, a series of public, Chicago-style assassinations and very few convictions of leading criminals and their 'hit-men' in recent years (Middelburg and Vugts 2006).

But in general there is little evidence of widespread or systematic corruption in Dutch policing and when it occurs it tends to be small-scale, tinged by 'noble cause' and some of its exponents are motivated and well-regarded officers who push boundaries too far in the search for results. Both cases examined here occurred at moments of significant change both in the criminal environment and in the wider social-cultural environment. In the Amsterdam case the scandal exposed shortcomings within the Amsterdam Police while the

IRT affair revealed deficiencies within the police justice system. The turbulence of the former was related more towards organisational defects and institutional politics and of the latter more towards bitter inter-agency rivalry and turf wars with divisions on investigative methods as the *casus belli*.

There are two broader strands running through the two cases. The first is that Dutch society was and is relatively tolerant and liberal in the criminal justice area compared to many other societies (Downes 1988). This has produced what many see as enlightened policies, but the downside has been a measure of indifference if not denial of problems with a near rigid ideological belief in tolerant policies while ignoring the side effects. This *gedoogbeleid* or tolerance policy was rife in the inner city of Amsterdam in the 1970s and it functioned to localise and contain the so-called 'victimless crimes' of prostitution, gambling and drug use (Brants 1999). But the arrival of the Chinese triads importing hard drugs changed everything. It increased the risk of corruption and also exposed the weakness of tolerance with the authorities proving irresolute. There has been a continual struggle since then between the more hard-line law enforcers and that progressive socio-political style (Punch 2007).

This in turn is related to the second strand. From the 1970s onwards the Netherlands became the centre for the Europe drug trade and witnessed the growth of organised criminal gangs. The justice system has, however, remained relatively old-fashioned and restricted, legally and in resources. Already in the 1970s and later in the 1990s' case we can see 'creative' methods stimulated by the DEA. There is, then, an evident and continual search for the boundaries of what is acceptable. This had been very much a matter of individual forces, particular units, specific prosecutors and certain courts willing to permit new methods or overlook 'creative' operations. To a degree the organised criminals have continually outsmarted the authorities and there is a sense that this in turn has stimulated much 'creativity' in law enforcement. When this surfaces it tends to be noble cause or combative corruption to gain results.

Scandal opens up a window into these mostly submerged processes. It reveals a constant negotiation if not battle between practitioners exploring the boundaries of the operational code – for some 'bent for self', for others 'bent for job' – and the formalist guardians retreating behind the official paradigm. But the full story is rarely told; in Amsterdam in the 1970s it was in no one's interest to pursue the cases because inquiries would have exposed grave deficiencies in the organisation and led to the dangerous territory of deals between police, prosecutors and the DEA. In a sense, then, the IRT affair forms the Amsterdam case for slow learners because some ingredients of murky deals with drugs, informants, creative cops and innovative prosecutors in the first affair reappear on a grander scale in the second.[16]

But a police organisation can only take so much external scrutiny and internal turmoil generated by investigations. The Amsterdam Police almost tore itself apart dealing with just a handful of cases; it would have imploded if the investigations had reached further. To a degree the Amsterdam scandal was a ritual house-cleaning with a downward focus aimed at expunging a few scapegoats for wider failings. The 'victims' of this were low in the organisation and to defend themselves they appealed to two sources. One was to the police occupational community; that they were solid, motivated cops getting their hands dirty and their boots muddy in the core business of catching crooks; this elicited wide support from the lower ranks from across the country. The other was that they were simply adhering to an occupational code that was not only SOP but also approved by others, including senior officers.

The Chinese experts, for example, were by all accounts dedicated professionals, deeply committed to policing. But to defend themselves they accused fellow cops and senior officers of theft, cover-up, falsifying documents, amateurism, stealing from suspects, fraudulently obtaining money, incompetence, endangering the lives of informants, rancorous and vindictive intrigue against subordinates, using dubious methods and manipulation in internal investigations, invading the privacy of people's homes, personal jealousy and rivalry that handicapped investigations and a fixation on publicity and personal reputations (Punch 1985: 185). In resorting to this defence they, as dedicated officers of long experience with inside knowledge, served to strongly confirm the most negative criticism of outsiders – that cops otherwise routinely disparage – that the police persistently bend and break the law.

Notes

1 There have been major public order disturbances in Europe in recent years around international meetings with diverse accusations of excessive police force including at Genoa in 2005 when one demonstrator died.

2 This may have been true when Blanken wrote, although it may also reflect the fairly deferential press of the time and a traditional willingness

to sweep matters under the carpet, but since then there have been a series of scandals in corporations and politics (Punch 1996).

3 There were over 100 city forces, some with under 100 officers. In these forces the mayor was head of the police and the chief public prosecutor was formally responsible for criminal investigations (Punch 1979).

4 Other forms of deviance that emerged later were driving out to the coast during night duty with prostitutes, stealing confiscated clothes and stripping parts from confiscated vehicles; more serious were the theft of money from the safe in Headquarters and assisting in a burglary. Two detectives were cooperating with criminals to divide the insurance reward for information leading to the return of stolen property which the criminals themselves had stolen on the basis of information from the officers (Punch 1985: 55).

5 Interviews revealed that there was no consensus among cops on what was acceptable and very little was specified and defined in writing available to everyone. The Amsterdam Police Chief seemed bewildered by what was going on around him and asked me to write a paper for him about corruption.

6 In Dutch, *Rijksrecherche*.

7 In fact it was an offence to possess it but no one took steps against the journalists; there are no jury trials in the Netherlands and *sub judice* rules as in the UK scarcely exist.

8 Officers in the rank of Commissioner are formally appointed by the Queen (in reality by the Minister) and it is almost impossible to remove one from office.

9 This refers to the Public Prosecution's 300-page dossier with interrogations and witness statements which was leaked to the press and passed on to me.

10 One incident in particular conveyed the distrust and bad faith in the Amsterdam organisation. Smit from the PCS was on suspension and asked for a confidential 'clear-the-air' talk with Bos, of the 'young dogs'/clean-up faction, which was arranged late one evening via an intermediary, Deelman. Smit was suspicious and hung around the hotel afterwards; he saw Bos depart later with two men whom Smit believed had placed a bug to secretly record the conversation. Smit confronted them and Bos jumped in his car and reversed wildly down the road. Smit, who had had too much to drink, drove after Bos but following a wild pursuit lost him. Smit drove to Deelman's house, (it was now deep in the night), who immediately phoned Bos who gave his word that there was no recording. A few months later I was sitting in a car on a stake-out with one of the 'young dogs' (a chief inspector) and ostensibly one of the 'good guys' faction, who started telling me about the recording; he suddenly realised what he had revealed, saying, 'I've talked too much, don't write this down.' Of course I wrote it down.

11 *Interregionale Recherche Teams*.

12 The IRT comprised several forces and there were 'blood groups' from diverse backgrounds with a measure of tribal warfare; the Amsterdam Police was keen to dominate but had initially to cede leadership of the IRT to another force; it was when leadership later passed to Amsterdam that it exerted its dominance by disputing the method in a fashion that has still left emotional scars on some of the leading actors.

13 It would be interesting to research customs in this period; sometimes customs officers were illegally involved in the import of drugs, sometimes they were asked not to control containers in the interests of a police operation and sometimes they were kept in the dark about what was taking place. Indeed, customs is an under-researched area in law enforcement.

14 Cf. Punch (1996: 85 – 95) for a similar collective blindness, but with near fatal consequences, in the Goodrich Brake Scandal.

15 As with corruption of local officials and regulators by the construction industry (Meeus and Schoorl 2002).

16 It is nigh impossible to convey the Byzantine rumblings and reverberations in the aftermath of the IRT scandal with various investigations taking place but achieving little and many allegations and accusations; what emerges is a picture of long-standing institutional vendettas, intense personal animosities and of investigating teams on poor terms with one another, with rivalry and failures in coordination. Behind this were deep fissures in the police and justice systems about the strategy of enforcement to be followed and the methods to be employed (van de Bunt *et al.* 2001).

Chapter 5

The UK: London, miscarriages of justice and Northern Ireland

> There you are, my old darling. Carrying an offensive weapon can get you two years.
>
> (Allegedly said by Detective Sergeant Challenor when planting a brick on a demonstrator in London in 1963; cited in Christie 2004: 94)[1]

In this the chapter I examine police deviance and corruption in Great Britain and Northern Ireland and how they have contributed to change and reform in policing. In particular the exposure of corrupt police practices in the UK reveals deviance at three levels. First, where it is contained within the policing arena; second, where it is related to defects in the wider criminal justice system; and third, when there are suggestions of state encouragement or collusion. From the earliest years of policing in Britain there have been continual debates about police powers and accountability and these have escalated in recent decades with scandals, *causes célèbres*, commissions and new legislation (Reiner 2000). Of special interest has been the founding in this century of independent, external oversight agencies to investigate the police in the UK.

London: the Met, Mark and investigations

When the New Police of the Metropolis (hereafter the Met) commenced patrol in 1829 in London the institution was shaped by Home Secretary Peel to achieve two main aims. First, he wanted the

'Bobbies' to replace the patchwork of often inefficient if not corrupt private enforcement agencies with a disciplined and accountable force. Second, he was determined to avoid any sense of the state mobilising a force to 'spy' on the public, as associated with the despised French police (Critchley 1978). Hence, there were no criminal investigators at first and when later the handful of detectives was expanded to form the Criminal Investigation Branch (later the Criminal Investigation Department CID) this was viewed with suspicion and 'entirely foreign to the habits and feelings of the nation' (Allason 1983: 1). The detectives were, moreover, forbidden to associate with criminals. The most prominent form of deviance was drunkenness on duty and many constables were dismissed in the early years. But Peel and the first commissioners of the Met, Rowan and Mayne, moulded a police force that gained the reputation for being low-key in its operating style, unarmed and unmilitary, dependable, courteous, close to the citizenry and nigh incorruptible (Miller 1977).

However, that reputation was severely dented when the first major scandal hit the Met in 1877. In the 'Turf Frauds' case it emerged that the elite CID had become highly corrupt. Three of the four chief inspectors running the department were arrested and convicted in relation to a fraudulent betting ring run from France with two civilian accomplices. Suspicions of the fraudulent scheme led to investigations but these were hampered by the fact that an Inspector Meiklejohn had been bribed to undermine the investigation. But on arrest the accomplices implicated the detectives; all four were arrested and three convicted for perverting the course of justice. The case elicited great consternation and there followed a reorganisation of the CID to gain tighter control of it but also to professionalise detective work (Allason 1983: 2–3). This had the unintended consequence of creating a near autonomous 'empire' within the Met, which would cause severe problems later.

For instance, the historian of the Met, Ascoli (1979: 198), maintains that by the early 1920s the CID had become 'a thoroughly venal private army' but that successive commissioners had refrained from grasping the thorny nettle of reforming it.[2] Some of the deviant practices were revealed in the Goddard case of 1928. Goddard was a detective sergeant who was held to have arranged protection on a grand scale for the flourishing vice establishments of the West End of London. He was fortunate to have been sentenced to only eighteen months for perverting the course of justice (Sherman 1974b: 29), for there were implications surrounding this case of wider perjury, ill treatment of suspects and of large sums of money reaching police hands. The level of organisation in all this hinted at a much wider involvement than this single sergeant. In retrospect, this was seen as a missed opportunity to bring the CID under tighter supervision with better integration with the rest of the force.

In the post-war period there were a number of scandals in Britain affecting particularly chief constables. Incidents in Cardiganshire, Worcester, Nottingham, Southend and Brighton led to resignations, dismissals and even the occasional prison sentence. It was held that police chiefs enjoyed too much independence with low accountability and this had led to patterns of institutional incestuousness with misuse of office and of funds. There was also growing dissatisfaction with the police in the late 1950s and early 1960s, which was amplified by the turbulence of the mid-1960s. There was an unrelenting wave of criticism of the police; the critical spotlight, aided by an increasingly assertive media, focused on the handling of public order situations, racism, interrogations, violence during arrest and with prisoners in custody, drugs enforcement, pornography and civil rights (Bowes 1968; Young 1971; Bunyan 1977; Hain *et al.* 1979).

In London, for example, there were persistent rumours of officers routinely planting evidence – as with Challenor's infamous brick – committing perjury and 'verballing' suspects (Rose 1996: 22). The latter meant constructing statements or confessions that the suspect was alleged to have said.[3] These suspicions came to a head in 1969 when the prestigious daily newspaper *The Times* printed a devastating exposure of corruption in the Met.[4]

Firm within a firm

Don't forget always to let me know straight away if you need anything, because I know people everywhere. Because I'm in a little firm within a firm. Don't matter where, anywhere in London I can get onto the phone to someone I know I can trust, that talks the same as me. And if he's not the right person who can do it, he'll know the person that can. All right? If you are nicked anywhere in London ... I can get onto the blower to someone in my firm who can get something done.

(A Met detective talking to a criminal; recorded by journalists from *The Times*; Cox *et al.* 1977: 15–16)

The revelations of corruption by *The Times* were a bombshell. The newspaper was not only reputable and reliable but could convincingly back up its story with photographs and tape recordings. This sparked off a chain reaction which fundamentally altered the positive image of London policing, enhanced the pressure for change and subjected the Met to a series of lengthy and painful inquiries and subsequent trials. Crucial in this setting was the rise of sophisticated criminal gangs. Their lawyers began to counter-attack any police investigation or prosecution involving them with accusations of 'lying, bribery, fabricating and planting evidence, perjury, theft, threatening witnesses, assault and drunkenness' (Ball *et al.* 1979: 159).[5] In this context of rumour, accusation, denial and disclaimer there was suddenly the unambiguous material from *The Times*. It detailed accusations about police officers planting evidence, committing perjury to obtain a false conviction, taking money from criminals in return for favours, urging a criminal to act as an *agent provocateur* and selling 'licences' to continue in criminal activity without fear of arrest (Cox *et al.* 1977).

The deviant practices covered conventional corruption with arrangements for payments from organised crime but also a large dose of 'process' corruption related to planting evidence, verballing suspects and perjury. This could be simply to get an easy conviction in a routine case but also be a form of predatory strategic corruption. For example, criminals could be exploited by being 'set up' and then recruited as an informant or be made to pay for police leniency. They could also be drawn into almost avuncular relationships where the cop and crook worked together on criminal activities with the cop instructing his 'partner' and protecting him even at the moment he was committing the offence. The threat was that if they did not comply they would be prosecuted. Indeed, it was this predatory police behaviour that had brought about *The Times'* attention. One criminal faced years in prison on the basis of false evidence: he had shaken hands with a detective who had gelignite concealed in his hand; the officer could use the man's fingerprints to implicate him in crime. It was only when this criminal approached *The Times* that the journalists mounted their investigation.

The 'firm within a firm' motif – in police underworld slang a firm refers to a criminal gang – indicated the existence of systematic police deviance covering the London area. Senior officers were devastated that such accusations could be raised against the 'world's greatest police force' and reacted with stubborn disbelief while launching an attack on the integrity of the journalists (Cox *et al.* 1977: 28). This inadequate response signalled a protracted battle within the Met, notably between the CID and the uniformed force hierarchy, and externally with the media, the Home Office and politicians. Furthermore, the provincial police forces were generally hostile to the tolerance of deviance in the Met and to its arrogance and were also resentful of the reputational damage done to British policing by the scandal. Provincial distrust of the Met was widespread (Parker 1981: 15); an officer from a provincial force said to me in 1980, 'Nobody trusts the Met. In twenty-one years of service I've encountered nothing but total mistrust of the Met. I'll coordinate readily with a provincial force but not with the Met and I speak from bitter experience. I could tell you horror stories about them; but, really, I wouldn't give them the time of day' (Punch 1985: 32).[6]

One bone of contention was that provincial forces were open to external investigation by another force and in serious cases of possible crimes by provincial officers this usually meant by the Met. In contrast the Met fell uniquely under the authority of the Home Secretary and not under a local police authority. Moreover since the structural reform in the wake of the Turf Frauds scandal the CID had been responsible for investigating *all* allegations against Met officers, both uniformed and detective.[7] It was said that the CID had developed 'the special loyalties and codes of a closed and introverted society' and yet here it was being asked to investigate itself (Cox *et al.* 1977: 37). The result was a predictable and blatant failure. For instance, an investigating officer was removed from the investigation by Commander Virgo and replaced by Detective Chief Superintendent (DCS) Moody;[8] but both Virgo and Moody later faced prosecution and conviction (1977: 188). Then Frank Williamson of Her Majesty's Inspectorate of Constabulary (HMIC) became the first outsider to be asked to advise the Met on the investigation of possible crimes. He became so disgusted with resistance that he gave up and also resigned prematurely from the police service remarking, 'I was very conscious of one fact ... You mustn't talk about police misbehaviour because half of the officers would be foaming at the mouth' (*Sunday Times Magazine* 1977). He also asserted there were only three sorts of detective in the Met; those who were corrupt, those who knew others were corrupt but did nothing about it, and those 'who were too stupid to notice what was going on around them' (Cox *et al.* 1977: 69). At the trial arising from *The Times'* allegations, two detectives were sentenced to six and seven years respectively for offences involving bribes, blackmail and conspiracy. But this was just the beginning; there followed two other investigations related to drugs, vice and close involvement with criminals and these in turn resulted in five trials. And after those there was the 'Countryman' investigation.

The Drug Squad

In this and the following section I deal first with the Drug Squad in the Met and then with the 'Porn Squad' – officially the Obscene Publications Crime Squad or OPS (known in the Met as the 'Dirty Squad'). The two portraits provide a contrast between combative and predatory corruption.

The Met Drug Squad under Detective Chief Inspector (DCI) Kelaher in the late 1960s and early 1970s had started to employ some unorthodox methods, having enthusiastically imported them from the USA. There were also close and even intimate relationships between cops, crooks and informants. The style and methods brought the Squad into conflict with some powerful stakeholders including liberal opinion-makers, the Home Office, the Foreign Office, some provincial forces and, above all, Her Majesty's Customs. Indeed, the 'turf war' between the Met Drug Squad and Customs, which was also involved in drug investigations, became one of 'total animosity'. There were accusations of Met officers planting drugs, of granting immunity to a favoured group of dealers in return for arrests and then rewarding them with part of the haul and of actively instigating deals in the American 'buy and bust' style. On occasion this was with the assistance of the American Bureau for Narcotics and Dangerous Drugs (BNDD, the forerunner of the DEA). Kelaher even defended a dealer in court, whom he said was one of his informants, and the man's defence was that he had been working as a police informant. But Kelaher's intervention for the defence proved unsuccessful and when the dealer was sentenced to seven years it destroyed the officer's credibility. It also raised serious questions about the Squad's working style.

This became a turning point in the relations between the Met and the outside world. For the first time, a full external inquiry was mounted and this was conducted by officers from the Lancashire Constabulary. And importantly an outsider, Robert Mark, was appointed Assistant Commissioner, Deputy Commissioner and then Commissioner (1972–77). Mark was a provincial officer with no experience in London and a largely uniformed career outside the CID; in the Met he was viewed as an outsider and not a 'real' copper. Apparently his appointment saved the Met from a parliamentary inquiry (Honeycombe 1974: 269).[9] As for Kelaher, he was fortunate to get away with a medical discharge, but of the six other officers who went to trial three were convicted.[10]

It does seem, however, that the members of the Drug Squad were primarily motivated by making arrests and did not seek financial profit.[11] Its unorthodox style developed under near complete autonomy and it forms a good example of combative strategic corruption conducted mainly to achieve formal goals. But the demise of the squad was yet another element in the pressure building up for the Met to do something substantial to put its house in order. As Cox *et al.* (1977: 129–130) comment:

> First, London's detective force had by the late 1960s clearly been corrupted by almost absolute power. They had become a law unto themselves ... Secondly, the Drug Squad's basic reliance on a very close relationship with criminal informants led to a dangerous system of law enforcement. London's drug dealers were effectively divided into two classes: those who operated with the blessing of the Drug Squad, and those who did not ... the arrogance of the Yard[12] displayed in the Drug Squad affair did not pay off, because it forced the government to take action against the old regime.

The Obscene Publications Squad (OPS)

One of the interlocking events of that period was a photo in the *Sunday People* in 1972 that showed Commander Drury, one of the Met's leading detectives, enjoying a holiday on Cyprus with the Soho pornographer James Humphreys. Drury was with his wife and he signed the hotel register with his police rank and gave 'Scotland Yard' as his address (Cox *et al.* 1977: 188).

The somewhat unglamorous world of the 'Porn Squad' or OPS functioned in ripe conditions for straightforward conventional corruption. Soho was the red-light district of West London, where 'vice', including pornography, was concentrated. Enforcement and prosecution were haphazard given the state of the law on pornography at a time of rapidly changing values and this gave the police the opportunity to informally 'licence' some premises while shutting down their competitors; this also conveniently provided arrests. The arrangements were designed to keep the businesses running with a minimum of interference; for the owners this meant prudently taking precautions by investing in 'bent' cops. And *The Sunday Times* (1977) said, DCS Moody 'liked things to be done systematically. It was Moody's intention to bring a measure of organization into the corruption of Scotland Yard's Obscene Publications Squad. To put it on a business footing as it were.'

While it was agreeable for both parties to amicably regulate the trade, there was also a measure of predatory corruption because those who were not in on the deal were preyed upon. There is little doubt that the leading members of the OPS were entrepreneurial meat-eaters; they set out to organise the graft. Large sums of money were involved, there were regular payments, and payouts were graded according to rank. This was very similar to the 'pad' in New York. There was a great deal of socialising between cops and the vice entrepreneurs, with meals, gifts, entertainment, drink sessions at a pub in Soho, common membership of a Freemasons' Lodge and attendance at CID Christmas parties (Cox *et al.* 1977: 186).[13] One pornography dealer wearing a CID tie was allowed into the basement of Holborn police station to view confiscated pornography and what he selected was 'recycled' to him. New members of the Squad were initiated with money thrust into their pockets and assurances that 'It's the easiest money you will ever make. It's safe money. You have nothing to worry about' (*Sunday Times*, 26 November 1976).

Commissioner Mark's reforms

Robert Mark was a prototype reforming chief, determined and at times ruthless. And as Goldstein (1977: 37) observes, reforming chiefs are usually hated by their men (*sic*). The challenge he faced was that many London detectives had developed close if not intimate relations with criminals, that serious rule-bending had become the SOP for conducting cases and achieving convictions and, above all, the Detective Branch had become a near autonomous bastion of 3,000 officers within the organisation. Crucially, the CID had not only become a law unto itself but it also policed itself.

As Commissioner from 1972 to 1977 Mark set out to tackle corruption, to break the power of the CID and to re-establish the supremacy of the force hierarchy and the uniformed branch. To a degree his reforms mirror those of Commissioner Murphy in New York but in London Mark did not have the advantage of a Knapp Commission, a special prosecutor or a supportive mayor; but he doubtless enjoyed political support from the Home Office.

In brief, Mark established a new department, A10, to investigate *all* complaints, of both a disciplinary and a criminal nature, and against all officers including detectives.[14] In his assault on the Detective Branch he placed a uniformed officer in charge of the CID (unthinkable in the past and an insult for detectives), placed all divisional detectives under their local uniformed superiors, moved a number of detectives back into uniform and rotated CID personnel in sensitive areas. Mark conveyed his views to representatives of the CID at what must have been one of the frostiest meetings in the history of the Met: 'I told them simply that they represented what had long been *the most routinely corrupt organisation in London,* that nothing and no one would prevent me from putting an end to it and that if necessary I would put the whole of the CID back into uniform and make a fresh start ... I left them in no doubt that I thought bent detectives were a cancer in society, worse even than the criminals' (Mark 1978: 130, my emphasis).

During his five years as Commissioner almost 500 officers left the force (Hobbs 1988: 69). The majority left voluntarily rather than face procedures against them and some were offered early retirement deals based on 'ill health'. A central plank in Mark's strategy to exorcise the 'cancer' was to back up criminal investigations and prosecutions – which were time-consuming and often resulted in a low conviction rate – with a determined application of the force's internal disciplinary regulations which carried a variety of sanctions including dismissal. He wanted to rid the Met of bent cops. For instance, he used the Serious Crime Squad from outside of Scotland Yard to mount a determined, three-year investigation arising from the Porn Squad's activities and the corrupt relationships with the Soho pornographer Humphreys whose diaries meticulously detailed the bribes and entertainment doled out to officers. As a result of that investigation there were three trials involving fourteen officers; twelve were convicted, including ex-Commander Virgo and DCS Moody, who both received twelve years, and Drury was sentenced to eight years (Hobbs 1988: 75).[15]

In a sense Mark *needed* the corruption cases and success against them as the catalyst for change in the same way that Murphy had needed the scandal in New York in order to push through reforms. Indeed, by showing the outside world that the police on their own could handle corruption and effect change he helped preserve the autonomy of the police and shielded the institution from external interference (Laurie 1972; Mark 1977). It could be argued, though, that Mark's courageous determination to root out corruption in London had a hidden, essentially conservative agenda of defending police independence and keeping external oversight at bay (Hobbs 1988). Indeed, he was virulently opposed to the new Police Act 1976, and stepped down early: 'I feel conscientiously unable to surrender the ultimate responsibility for police discipline to political nominees' (Mark 1978: 228). All 43 police chiefs in the Association of Chief Police Officers (ACPO) were also opposed to this part of the Act; and it was rare for them to be unanimous on anything.

The issue was, however, that people might have confidence in a courageous individual chief like Mark in an individual force to tackle corruption; but this was not a structural solution to the problem of controllers controlling themselves. After all, this was still the police policing the police; and it would take another 30 years to bring about independent oversight. And, as we have seen in the chapter on the US, reforms in policing tend be of short durability while corruption proves to be resilient and adaptable.

The Countryman investigation

Within just a year of Mark's retirement it transpired that his scalpel had not removed all the 'cancer'. In May 1978 an armed gang held up a delivery of money to a newspaper company and a security guard was shot dead. The *New Statesman* (1980) referred to this as a cold-blooded murder resulting from a 'carefully organised and ruthlessly executed crime'; but added that an 'equally organised group of policemen were involved in the circumstances surrounding his killing'. The allegations that emerged from this and other cases were shocking. There was predatory corruption but also 'police crime'; as one robber lamented, 'At the finish all you was doing was working for the police to give them a lion's share of what you were getting' (*Economist* 1982: 19–20). But there was also police involvement in organised, violent robbery. The 1970s had seen the emergence of a number of 'super-grasses' who were informants on a grand scale and who 'shopped' large numbers of their colleagues in serious crime but especially for armed robbery.[16] But in interrogations they also started to implicate London police officers in some of the crimes.

As a result 'Operation Countryman' was set up to investigate these allegations.[17] The lead was taken by the Dorset Police with a team of 80 officers from provincial forces. The name 'Countryman' was provocative because Met officers disdain provincial cops as bucolic 'swedes' and the provincials were returning the compliment. Countryman became a four-year investigation which scrutinised the conduct of over 200 officers including several senior officers. The allegations focused on Met detectives from elite units, along with officers from the neighbouring City of London Police,[18] with accusations that the police had helped to set up robberies, to deflect attention away from the raids, to help some criminals evade investigation but to frame others and to receiving handsome pay-offs (*New Statesman* 1980). It was claimed that a City detective had masterminded the newspaper raid; 'he helped pinpoint the target: recruited an underworld "draughtsman" or detailed planner; and later subcontracted the job out to a gang of armed robbers with whom he was already corruptly involved' (*Sunday Times* 1979).

From the beginning there were rumours that the Countryman team had been obstructed, and the ex-chief of Dorset later spoke of 'sabotage'. Team members complained that Met officers were leaking information to criminals about their investigation; then on surveillance Countryman officers would encounter counter-surveillance from Met detectives or else a patrol car would inconveniently appear to alert those under observation (*Observer* 1982). The Met also counter-attacked with adverse propaganda about the quality and integrity of the Countryman investigation. The successor to Mark, Commissioner McNee (1983), strongly denied any obstruction and insisted that the Met would have achieved far more success than Countryman if the inquiry had been conducted internally. One can hardly expect him to have said anything else and this sort of mutual mud-slinging is par for the course when cops investigate other cops. No one anywhere likes external investigators but this was particularly true of what were seen as arrogant Londoners facing scrutiny by provincial colleagues.

But, again, a commissioner of the Met missed the vital point that however professional and successful that internal investigation might have been by the highest of objective standards, a police agency with a long record of corruption would have been investigating itself. Under such circumstances there simply has to be an independent, external institution to investigate the police. Indeed, a minority of the members on the Royal Commission, leading to the Police Act 1964, had proposed this on the principle 'no man (*sic*) should be a judge of his own cause. But they were forty years ahead of the times' (Cox *et al.* 1977: 30). If this principle needed any corroboration it came from two sources; one was from a series of miscarriages of justice in Britain and the other came from Northern Ireland.

Miscarriages of justice

> The officers must have been lied.
> (Lord Chief Justice Lane at the Central Criminal Courts
> in London on 19 October 1989 at the successful appeal
> of the Guildford Four, cited in Rose 1996: 1)

Allegations of corruption had, then, dogged the Met in the 1970s and 1980s while the force had also faced several major investigations. But the scandals had been contained to the capital city and to the police domain. The 'miscarriages of justice' cases, in contrast, raised critical issues not just about police practices in several forces but also about the deficiencies in the wider criminal justice system. There were a range of cases but those catching most attention concerned people suspected of Irish Republican Army (IRA) terrorist activity in the 1970s. But the broader revelations concerned miscarriages in a range of cases completely unrelated to terrorism.

The British criminal justice system has traditionally presented itself to the outside world as highly accountable and professional. Robert Mark espoused the formal paradigm (1978: 149): 'The fact that the British police are answerable to the law, that we act on behalf of the community and not under the mantle of government, makes us the least powerful, the most accountable and therefore the most acceptable police in the world'.[19] Yet in the cases concerning people suspected of IRA terrorist activity the victims of the miscarriages had spent years in jail on the basis of dubious evidence and/or false confessions before being released (Walker and Starmer 1999). In the hierarchy of harm and victimisation associated with police deviance, illegally depriving innocent people of their freedom for many years must surely rank high. The importance of these 'IRA' cases is that they displayed that it was not just the police who bent the rules but also that other members of the criminal justice fraternity colluded in various ways in sustaining the convictions (Justice Report 1989).

In the early 1970s the IRA began a bombing campaign on the British mainland. There were explosions particularly in and around the Midlands and London. In Birmingham in November 1972 two explosions in pubs, frequented largely by young people, resulted in 21 deaths. A bus with army personnel and their families on board was blown up on the M12 motorway with twelve fatalities; and in two pubs in Guildford frequented by army personnel there was a bombing that left several dead. There was another explosion in Woolwich in 1974.

The indiscriminate nature of the bombings – without warning and in public places leading to many deaths and severe casualties – led to national outrage. There was clearly unprecedented pressure on the police to secure arrests and gain convictions. Later, the doubts about the convictions focused primarily on the following four 'IRA' cases (Reiner 2000: 65):

- The Birmingham Six (for explosions in Birmingham)
- The Guildford Four (for explosions in Guildford and Woolwich)
- Judith Ward (for involvement in several explosions, including the one on the army bus)
- The Maguire Seven (for possession of explosives)

Following the explosions a number of suspects were arrested; they nearly all were Irish or of Irish background and/or were held to have some link or sympathy for the Republican cause in Ireland. Some were assaulted by the police, intimidated with further threats of severe violence and were beaten by prison officers following transfer to jail. All were relentlessly questioned and bullied into answering. Some confessed and some allegedly confessed. A confession was then considered a vital piece of evidence within the British legal system where a jury tended to be convinced by a confession; it was seen as a trump-card in the hands of the prosecution. There was also forensic evidence that seemingly supported the handling of explosives and circumstantial evidence. At the trials the suspects – two of whom were teenagers aged fourteen and seventeen years – in these four cases all received prison sentences with some being given life imprisonment with recommendations by the judge of up to 35 years before release.

Within a few years, however, doubts arose about the convictions, and families, friends, politicians and people in public life began to take up the causes of those incarcerated. In Britain there is no automatic right of appeal against the trial and/or sentencing, as in some Continental European jurisdictions and the appeal process has to go through the Attorney General who is the senior legal advisor to the government. The Home Secretary also plays a role with regard to those prisoners serving life sentences. In effect this was a political-judicial decision that would have been discussed in Cabinet. For almost 20 years from 1979 there was a Conservative Government in Britain and it was most unlikely that an appeal on behalf of convicted terrorists would have found support in the Cabinet.[20] Several requests for appeals were rejected. For example, the original appeal shortly after the trial of the Guildford Four was rejected; this was even after an IRA unit had been captured and tried in Britain who had claimed responsibility for the Guildford attacks. Yet the members of that unit were not prosecuted for the bombings and the Four remained in prison for another *twelve* years. Another request for an appeal was turned down in 1987. It was only after a police officer from another force reviewed the case materials and discovered discrepancies in the original investigators' notes that a successful appeal took place in 1989 (Royakkers 1997: 133).

Nevertheless the campaigners persisted and they included the journalist and later Labour MP Chris Mullin, who dedicated himself to helping the Birmingham Six who were from his constituency. His book (Mullin 1990), and a television documentary, were vital in attracting media and public attention and in pushing the appeal process. Eventually all the cases were successfully appealed. The Guildford Four were released in 1989, the Maguire Seven in 1990 and the release of the Birmingham Six[21] from prison in 1991 was a highly emotional event and a major news item broadcast live on international TV. Judith Ward's conviction was also quashed (Reiner 2000: 66).

In the aftermath of the releases the following facts emerged. All the suspects had been physically and/or mentally pressurised using lack of sleep, persistent questioning and threats. They all confessed or signed confessions that they had supposedly made. These confessions were mostly fabricated by the investigating officers. Forensic evidence (Esda analysis) indicated that so-called verbatim notes of interrogations had been amended and the wording rehearsed by the officers. Judith Ward, moreover, had a background of psychiatric problems and was apparently prepared to confess to almost anything.

Important information was withheld from the courts, for example on Ward's mental record, and on negative results in the forensic testing (Walker and Starmer 1993: 8–12). The forensic evidence itself, particularly in relation to the handling of explosives, proved highly questionable. Tests conducted by the expert for the Home Office, Dr Skuse, which were said to prove with high reliability that there were traces of explosives on the hands of suspects, were found to be unreliable as similar results could be had from handling several household products (including playing cards, and the Birmingham suspects had been playing cards prior to their arrest).[22]

At the judicial level judges were not always impartial and the appeal procedure had not functioned well.

Typically miscarriages are composed of a number of elements related to fabrication of evidence, unreliable identification, expert testimony, confessions, non-disclosure of information, conduct of the trial, the portrayal and presentation of the accused in the media and especially in court, appeals and failure of state agencies (Justice Report 1989; Walker and Starmer 1993). The intense pressure generated by the fact that these were high-profile terrorist cases enhanced deviance between a disparate range of actors and this cumulatively led to the collective failure in the system.

The impact of these cases was immense but attention to the issue of miscarriages had already been gathering a head of steam. In fact the concern following the quashing of the convictions of three teenagers in the Confait murder case in 1972 led to the Fisher Report (1977), which itemised how the youths' rights had been persistently neglected by the police. This in turn brought the Home Secretary of the time to announce a Royal Commission on Criminal Procedure (1981) which was 'eventually transmuted' into the Police and Criminal Evidence Act or PACE of 1984 (Reiner 2000: 176–83). Legislation was endeavouring to specify the limits of police powers, to set guidelines for investigations (as with the recording of interviews) and to lay out the rights of suspects. PACE was viewed as a watershed in regulating police powers.[23] Yet the Cardiff Three miscarriage occurred after PACE.[24] When the tapes of the police interviews with the suspects were played in court they revealed aggressive interviewing by the police even in the presence of a solicitor; the appeal court moved swiftly to quash the convictions (Reiner 2000: 65).

But in that series of supposedly IRA cases there was no graft, no external corruptor and no direct material gain. Rather this was a case where intense political, media and institutional pressure distorted the processes of investigation and prosecution and provided the investigators with motive and with rationalisations. The 'corrupter' was in a sense the pressure for a conviction and if one can speak of 'gain' then it was acclaim for cracking the case. For the key to the miscarriages is the concept of 'noble cause' corruption. The cases were extreme and the police were under persistent pressure to get convictions; the detectives presumably convinced themselves of the suspects' guilt and felt the ends justified the means. As these were defined as crimes falling under the new Prevention of Terrorism Acts (1974–1989), their investigation probably took place in a different institutional climate with increased powers, secrecy and autonomy than in conventional detective work. Rather than for gain or gratification this was deviance 'for the organisation' and it could be viewed by those involved almost as a moral obligation.

One can perhaps understand, if not condone, the strength of the motivation to get convictions in these extreme cases with many innocent deaths. But this justification is not valid for many other cases. These were typically with vulnerable suspects who had been pressurised into a confession; some were young and of a low mental age; and these suspects had nothing whatsoever to do with terrorism (Walker and Starmer 1999). At the heart of these cases was police abuse of powers and manipulation of the rules. There were the four men convicted in 1979 of the murder of Carl Bridgewater, the Cardiff Three (1990) and Stefan Kisko (1976), who were all imprisoned because of police falsifying confessions or withholding information from the court. Kisko had spent sixteen years in jail before it emerged that evidence indicating his innocence had been withheld at the original trial (Reiner 2000: 66). If the police knew Kisko was innocent then what was 'noble' about the cause? It used to be reasoned that only 'good villains' who had committed an offence were 'stitched up'; and 'verbals' were seen as a 'moral service to the community' (Rose 1996: 23). Perhaps the officers involved either convinced themselves he was guilty or else it was simply a 'good result'. Indeed, some officers and parts of the media argued that getting off on appeal did not necessarily mean that those released were not involved. In fact no police officer was ever convicted for offences arising from the miscarriage cases. When officers did go to trial and were acquitted there were press articles that their prosecution was the 'real' miscarriage and perhaps the original suspects were guilty after all (e.g. regarding the 'IRA' cases; Rose 1996: 297). The trial of Surrey officers involved in the Guildford Four case was turned almost into a retrial of the Four themselves (Bennett 1993).

In fact there had been a line of police chiefs, officials and politicians who had argued for years that trials were weighted in favour of the defence and that many serious criminals were getting off on technicalities. This may well have been interpreted lower down that if you stick to the rules you lose; and that to ensure a conviction in court rule-bending was 'essential'. A leading chief constable admitted, 'Everyone knew it happened liked that, judges, magistrates, the whole criminal justice system had a sort of conspiracy … If you didn't do it that way, you couldn't actually convict guilty people and that needed to be done' (Rose 1996: 12).

This raised two fundamental issues. One was the psychological propensity of some people to confess to crimes that they did not commit. Indeed, what impact does the whole physical and social-psychological context facing suspects under police interrogation have on them (Ofshe and Leo 1997: Leo and Ofshe 1998)? The other was the way the detectives went about 'constructing' a case (Goldschmidt 2008). In other words, the techniques that were *routinely* used in run-of-the-mill cases to intimidate suspects, to manipulate witnesses, to reformulate statements, to present doctored material to senior officers and prosecutors, and to withhold evidence in court that might weaken a case or might work in the defendant's favour. In this light these miscarriage cases uncovered three fundamental features of the system.

First, some police officers routinely deviated from rules and regulations in order to secure convictions; in effect, to achieve formal organisational goals. There is a wealth of material from many sources including senior officers that cops 'have to' bend or break the rules in order to enforce the law (Reiner 1978: 77–81; Holdaway 1983: 101). We cannot know if these practices were engaged in universally in the UK but in certain units at certain times the operational code was geared to manipulation, intimidation and falsehood leading to the imprisonment of the innocent. Indeed, in 1989 the entire Serious Crime Squad of the West Midlands Police was disbanded because of persistent complaints about the methods it employed; these also related to suspects of terrorism with an appeal judge even speaking of 'torture' (Kaye 1991; Royakkers 1997: 143). These practices were not simply related to the qualities of individuals, but to the organisational context, the institutional dilemmas, and the pressures *to get the work done*. They impact on the daily working habits of some detectives motivated to achieve results by routine recourse to rule-bending. One feature is the reversal of the assumption of innocence and, convinced that they have the 'right suspect,' the locking into a form of 'tunnel vision' that filters out disconfirming evidence. Clearly intense pressure can amplify this process almost to a form of cognitive dissonance. For instance, during the Broadwater Farm riots in north London in 1985 PC Blakelock was hacked to death; three young black men were arrested and convicted of his murder. This was a major investigation for the Met involving the horrendous death of a fellow officer. Yet all three men were released on appeal because of irregularities during custody and/or during police interviews leading to a 'confession' (Reiner 2000: 69).[25] Most unusual for the time, there was an apology from the Court of Criminal Appeal: 'In allowing these appeals we wish to express our profound regret that they [Tottenham Three] have suffered as a result of the shortcomings of the criminal process. No system of trials is proof against perjury, but this will be of little consequence to its victims' (Rose 1992: 220).

Second, there are checks and balances within the system. What raised the miscarriages of justice to the 'system' level was the collusion of other actors in the system – supervisors who did not intervene when violence occurred; senior officers who uncritically signed 'dodgy' statements from detectives; forensic specialists who worked unprofessionally; prosecutors who did not probe into the police material given to them; judges who turned a blind eye to discrepancies in evidence and were blatantly biased against defendants; and the government, which forestalled an appeal for so long. (Walker and Starmer 1999).[26]

Third, and crucially, the system investigated itself. There was no external agency in Britain that could investigate deviance within the police; the police conducted the investigations themselves. There was no truly independent institution to conduct what needs to be accepted as a totally impartial inquiry. The MP Chris Mullin perceived this point to be pivotal with regard to the lessons from the miscarriages of justice cases (Royakkers 1997: 256; cf. McConville and Bridges 1994).[27]

Everyone concerned in these cases retained an individual responsibility and could have been held accountable for their individual conduct. But they all worked in a social context with inbuilt assumptions about how cases were typically constructed. As the cases moved up the hierarchy of the criminal justice system – from investigation, to prosecution, and on to trial – it was almost as if the 'system' invested more and more in the presumption that these were the real, 'guilty' terrorists. This made it increasingly difficult to raise doubts from within the system. It was, then, more than an individual or group failure, for it was the 'system' that failed. This can also be said of police deviance and the lack of accountability in Northern Ireland, which has been largely neglected by British criminologists.

Northern Ireland

The bombing campaign by the IRA in Britain, which was fundamental to generating the four 'IRA' miscarriages, was related to the near civil war that afflicted another part of the United Kingdom. 'The Troubles' in Northern Ireland led to the deaths of over 3,500 people during 30 years (1969–99). This extreme situation not only generated serious deviance in the police and security services but also raised suggestions that the British state was implicated in stimulating and colluding in covert activities. These involved the deaths of innocent UK citizens and the deaths of suspected terrorists under highly suspect circumstances (Ingram and Harkin 2004: 12).

The three issues covered here relate to the so-called 'shoot-to-kill' incidents involving the police; to police resistance to external inquiries; and to wider support and collusion from state agencies. This section portrays police deviance that is generated partly by the reaction to extreme, almost 'warlike' circumstances and partly by external actors.

Northern Ireland was and is a constituent part of the UK but it forms a separate jurisdiction from Great Britain with a form of devolved government. It had been policed since 1922 by the Royal Ulster Constabulary (RUC) which was an armed, paramilitary organisation.[28] The governmental administration and the police were predominantly Protestant and many of the Catholic majority felt that there was discrimination against them in several areas but particularly by the police. For a number of reasons the political and security situation in Northern Ireland deteriorated in the second half of the 1960s with severe inter-community violence, with the Provisional IRA becoming highly active and with the British government sending in troops to restore order.[29] There was a further deterioration leading to 30 years of violence during which some 300 police officers and over 600 military personnel were killed and many injured.[30] Effectively the IRA was 'at war' with the British state (Mulcahy 2006).

During those turbulent years the RUC was in the front line and constantly under attack and threat. Critics saw the RUC as a biased, repressive force that had overreacted in a number of public order situations; had on occasion used excessive violence against Catholics; and had mistreated prisoners in custody under suspicion of IRA involvement. But in the 1980s the most serious suspicions related to a number of so-called 'shoot-to-kill' incidents which in turn led to further accusations of obstruction of an external inquiry.

Shoot to kill

The Troubles fostered an intricate and creative range of murky deeds by the security services in Northern Ireland in response to IRA violence (Dillon 1991). For example, there is much evidence that during the Troubles the police and military shot suspected IRA and republican activists in highly suspicious circumstances (Urban 1993).[31] I shall focus here on the RUC and three shootings in particular in the 1980s.

In November 1982 three RUC officers were blown up in their car by a landmine near Lurgan; they were victims of a hoax call. Then, within a few weeks, three shootings took place near Lurgan in which six suspected republican activists died and one was seriously injured. One interpretation, and the one held by the external investigator from Britain (Stalker, see below), was that these were revenge killings mounted by the RUC in retaliation for the deaths of their colleagues.

In two of the incidents ostensibly ordinary RUC officers manning a routine roadblock opened fire when cars drove through, and in the other a 'patrol' stumbled by chance on two young men handling firearms in a hayshed.[32] In none of these incidents were shots fired at the police; in the two involving vehicles the suspects were unarmed; and in one of the latter the police fired 108 rounds.

Later it emerged that these were not, as claimed, ordinary officers on routine patrol. They all belonged to the same special RUC unit, the undercover Headquarters Mobile Support Unit (HMSU), which had been specially trained for covert operations. Several of the victims were suspected of the Lurgan bombing and it is thought an informant passed on details about their movements. The incidents were made to sound like chance encounters with an element of danger to the officers. But the nature of the incidents – prior intelligence, covert surveillance, an ambush, no warning and the large number of rounds fired – had the hallmarks of a military-style combat operation as used by Special Forces. Then after the incidents the officers and their vehicles were taken from the crime scene before an investigation could take place. With senior officers from Special Branch present they were coached on giving versions that constructed an element of danger for them in the encounters; vehicle logs for that evening were altered; and the HMSU officers were then meant to perjure themselves.

In short, police officers within the UK were apparently involved in a conspiracy to murder, in covering up a crime and hindering a criminal investigation, in falsifying official documents and in lying under oath. Although the situation in Northern Ireland was extreme, with a serious security situation and with a number of emergency measures taken, this was still part of the UK and the rule of law still applied; martial law had not been declared and with regard to fatal force the officers concerned were under the same legal strictures as on mainland Britain.

After investigating two of the 'Lurgan' incidents – evidence from the third was incomplete – the external investigator, Stalker, and his team came to the conclusion that:

> Special Branch officers planned, directed and effectively controlled the official accounts given ... The Special Branch targeted the suspected terrorists, they briefed the officers, and after the shootings they removed the men, cars and guns for a private de-briefing before the CID officers were to be allowed to commence the official investigation of what had occurred. The Special Branch interpreted the information and decided what was and was not evidence. (Stalker 1988: 56)

Investigation of the crime scene by CID officers was hampered and the HMSU officers, weapons and vehicles had been removed from the scene before CID could inspect them; access to the scene was also delayed for security reasons. Officers engaged in the incidents were told to lie to protect an informant and assured that they would be shielded by the Official Secrets Act. The latter was not the case and when several officers were charged with murder relating to one of the incidents one of the officers divulged in court that he had been told to lie in his statements to protect the operation: 'It became clear that investigating CID officers, the Director of Public Prosecutions, and finally the courts themselves, all had been quite deliberately misled in order to protect police procedures and systems' (1988: 13). The officers were cleared and returned to duty.

External inquiry: Stalker

The formal paradigm in policing maintains that police deviancy and crimes will be properly investigated and that institutions and individuals will be held fully to account. But in the *cause célèbre* of the Stalker affair there are strong indications of obstruction of an external inquiry from two sources. In 1984 the Deputy Chief Constable of the Greater Manchester Police, John Stalker, was asked by the Chief Constable of the RUC (Hermon) to investigate allegations against RUC officers of murder and conspiracy to pervert the course of justice in the three Lurgan shootings. The RUC was, however, a police force under siege which had already faced much hostile scrutiny; and within the force there was often provincial antagonism to outsiders from the mainland.

Stalker maintains that he and his investigatory team not only faced obstruction in Northern Ireland but that he personally faced a dirty tricks campaign on the mainland. During a crucial phase of his investigation he was not only removed from it but also controversially suspended from his post in Manchester. He faced an inquiry into alleged misconduct in his own force; although nothing of substance emerged from this and he was reinstated, Stalker resigned from the police (Stalker 1988). He is convinced that the allegations were timed to coincide with his imminent presentation of a highly critical interim report on the shootings and of his intended return to Northern Ireland to complete the investigation with the questioning of very senior officers.

In Northern Ireland, the clash of codes and styles in this affair came about because Stalker was a representative of the official paradigm, based on the dedicated and impartial pursuit of truth, arriving from another part of the UK after just a brief plane trip but almost to another world in a 'war' situation. There was an expectation that officers from outside would display solidarity and make allowances for this. In a combat zone of constant threat and dirty tricks by all parties, but especially the IRA – who targeted RUC officers, often when off duty and with their families – the neat, formal, legal rules no longer applied, it was argued. But Stalker was a motivated, highly professional investigator determined to lift stones and he clashed with an RUC on the defensive. Stalker and his team were treated with suspicion and disdain; there was outright obstruction, personal hostility, calculated insults and blatant failures to keep appointments; and there were also point-blank refusals to hand over evidence. Stalker was warned anonymously that his offices were bugged, and a fire broke out in the team's offices. He and his team were not provided with certain files (with denials of their existence, only for them to turn up later), were kept in the dark about informants and had information from surveillance devices withheld (Stalker 1988: 35). Stalker wanted the recording and the transcript from the 'bug' in the hayshed as evidence but was refused access on security grounds. A constable who had listened to the tape was interviewed but refused to cooperate by saying what was on it unless he was instructed to do so by his senior officers, he was in effect obstructing a murder inquiry (1988: 69). But the team had no legal authority in Northern Ireland and could take no steps against the non-compliant constable.

Stalker never did get to hear the tape or see the transcript. He was obstructed in his investigation in Northern Ireland and removed from the inquiry on dubious grounds by developments in his home force. The conduct of the RUC and its hierarchy in terms of accountability and transparency was highly dubious. But there were doubtless other actors within Northern Ireland and the British government who had an interest in Stalker not completing his investigation at a time when the RUC was in the forefront of the battle against the IRA. As Stalker recognised, he was sacrificed as a matter of political expediency. His unfinished inquiry was completed by another British officer and, although it has not been published, it is believed to have supported Stalker's interim findings. The Department of Public Prosecutions (DPP) in Northern Ireland then declined to take action against any RUC officers arising from the report.

There are four features arising from these incidents that I wish to emphasise. Firstly the RUC was constantly involved in a range of deviance throughout the Troubles. Clearly it was also a force under constant threat and taking many casualties. Its supporters focus on this and speak of sacrifice, courage and of the many brave and professional men and women in the force (Mulcahy 2006). This may well be true but the evidence is that the deviance was persistent; and for several decades Special Branch was pivotal in using the mantras of 'security' and 'protecting informants' to justify a range of dirty tricks. For example, another area of grave deviance that followed the controversy about the Lurgan shootings was that of collusion between the police and the loyalist paramilitaries. Officers were passing on classified information to the loyalist paramilitaries about people suspected of involvement in IRA or republican activities who were then threatened, attacked and in some cases murdered (Barker 2004; Mulcahy 2006).

Second, a senior police officer from the mainland, Stalker, had been obstructed in an external investigation. And it is rare for someone of his standing to reveal the inside details of an investigation. He was said to have been an abrasive person who antagonised RUC members, as if character was the problem; but any senior investigating officer from the mainland worth his salt would have behaved identically and would have met the same barriers. Indeed, several years later there was yet another senior officer from the mainland, John Stevens (who later became Commissioner of the Met), and he conducted three investigations into the RUC covering a period of fourteen years.[33] And like Stalker, Stevens faced not only obstruction but also had a fire in his offices, which he called 'arson' but which an RUC investigation termed 'an accident' (Ryder 2000: 377). From his three reports it is plain that what had emerged from his inquiries was police conduct that was indisputably in abeyance of the rule of law. Only a brief summary of the interim report on the third investigation has been published, in which Stevens (2003) states that his inquiries had highlighted collusion in many ways with 'the wilful failure to keep records, the absence of accountability, the withholding of intelligence and evidence, through to the extreme of agents being involved in murder'. The failure to keep records could be taken as a technique of concealment; the lack of accountability meant that misconduct went unchecked; and withholding information hampered investigation of wrongdoing. Finally, Stevens stated that the unlawful involvement of agents in murder implies that 'the security services sanction killings'.[34]

Third, this pattern of serious deviance followed by hostility to external investigation could not be maintained indefinitely and there was a mounting groundswell of opinion for reform and for enhanced accountability. This was especially the case from the early 1990s with the prospect of peace and of a future when the RUC would have to become a conventional police service. This was greatly amplified by the fact that a large proportion of the population viewed the RUC as a deviant organisation with little or no legitimacy and a disturbingly poor record of dealing with complaints (Weitzer 1995). In fact, accountability of the police became one of the key factors in the peace process.

Fourth and finally, there can be no doubt that the situation of near civil war in Northern Ireland elicited a range of murky deeds from the police, army and intelligence services. Such activities are sometimes referred to as 'enforcement terrorism' (Brodeur 1981: 157).

This has clearly emerged from the interviews and memoirs of participants and from a raft of popular and academic publications on the Troubles. Furthermore, there were formal channels in Northern Ireland for collating the information from these agencies and coordinating activities against the IRA and that information was regularly funnelled to London for review at higher levels. This included the Joint Intelligence Committee (JIC) chaired by the Prime Minister, which raises the issue of state encouragement if not collusion. It is in the nature of decision-making at that level that there is typically no audit trail direct to operational decision-making. But when in the early 1980s the RUC set up its own covert anti-terrorist units it was part of a formal policy of 'police primacy' to remove responsibility for security in Northern Ireland from the army and return it to the RUC; furthermore to train those new RUC units requiring expert training from Special Forces and the intelligence services (Urban 1993).

This major policy shift can only have been decided at a high level. I am suggesting – but there may never be convincing evidence to confirm this, given the cloak of 'national interest' – that Northern Ireland was a case where the British state was complicit in police deviance of the gravest sort (Davies 1999). Stevens had unequivocally displayed collusion by Special Branch with the Protestant paramilitaries leading effectively to assassination by proxy by the British state. Yet collusion continued after his investigations, after the arrests and sanctioning of officers and even after the end of hostilities.

Independent oversight: OPONI

In the UK in the 1990s there was then a growing call for independent oversight of the police, drawing on the miscarriages of justice and other affairs in Britain, such as the Stephen Lawrence murder, and on the deviant activities by the RUC in Northern Ireland. There were four main strands to this development.

First, the perennial debate about the police policing themselves was amplified by growing dissatisfaction about the police complaints system. Second, there was a stream of legislation and directives about police powers and police accountability (Reiner 2000). Third, the police themselves began to display an interest in issues of integrity and in adopting more robust anti-corruption strategies. There was the HMIC Thematic Report of 1999 on 'Police Integrity' and an ACPO Presidential Task Force on Corruption (1998). Also, proactive 'Professional Standards Units' were set up which went after bent cops using assertive methods, including integrity testing, with the intention of getting convictions in court. And fourth, discussion and debate began to converge on the need for an independent oversight agency to investigate police wrongdoing.

I shall return to three of those themes later in Chapter 7 in relation to mainland Britain but here I focus on one in particular and that is the founding of the Office of the Police Ombudsman for Northern Ireland (OPONI). It was the first independent oversight agency in the UK and it emerged from a volatile situation with a long legacy of police deviance, resistance to external investigation and a conflict situation where a large proportion of the public had no faith in the police complaints system. This makes it a valuable test case as to the role and functioning of oversight in policing.

OPONI was established as part of the peace process and became operational in 2000 under the Police (Northern Ireland) Act 1999.[35] Its work has, then, taken place since the cessation of hostilities and in part after the transformation of the RUC into the Police Service for Northern Ireland (PSNI) in 2001; the PSNI came under new leadership with Sir Hugh Orde as Chief Constable from 2002.[36] OPONI had to start from scratch with no premises and no personnel but commenced work towards the end of 2000. OPONI was given a broad mandate: no less than uniquely taking responsibility for *all* complaints against the RUC. Complaints could lead to informal resolution or be returned to the police for investigation. Following an investigation by OPONI the Ombudsman could recommend prosecution to the DPP; recommend to the chief constable disciplinary proceedings against an officer, and in case of dispute, insist on this; and recommend compensation for those disadvantaged by police misconduct.

OPONI attracted strong leadership in the person of Nuala O'Loan.[37] It recruited highly experienced investigators from the mainland and other countries, all of whom had the status of constable, giving them the powers of a law-enforcement officer; and they worked on a 24/7 basis for referral to critical incidents. Its main task was to respond to complaints against the police but it could independently and retrospectively open an inquiry in the public interest. And this small society of 1.7 million people had had 3,363 murders within 33 years, of which about half remained unsolved. The Ombudsman invested in publicity about the complaints system and how to make a complaint; she and her personnel held public forums about their work with members of the two communities and with RUC officers; and OPONI mounted seminars, with officers from the Irish Republic invited, and an international conference in 2003.

It is in the nature of new oversight agencies that they have to establish and assert themselves and this was a tough assignment in a sometimes hostile environment. Northern Ireland is something of a tribal society and the mutual antagonism between the two communities makes all change politically charged while fostering a robust rhetoric of discrediting mud-slinging. For instance, unionists tended to see the RUC as 'their' police force which had to be defended against any criticism, which was routinely dismissed as biased. There have, then, been attacks on the Ombudsman, attempts to discredit her and the institution and calls for her resignation. But by most accounts OPONI has established itself as an important factor in criminal justice in Northern Ireland and has attracted worldwide attention. Surveys indicate that most people from both communities believe in its impartiality; most RUC officers who have been investigated by OPONI report that they were fairly treated; and a House of Commons Committee praised the Ombudsman's performance.[38] Early on there was suspicion and resistance among some RUC officers and the answer to that – apart from forcefully asserting the right to require evidence and to interview officers involved in incidents – was the sound professional competence of the investigators and the complete impartiality of the findings. For example, in a number of cases of baton-round use (also known as 'plastic bullets'), a highly controversial issue in Northern Ireland, OPONI concluded that their use was often justified, which waylaid the claim of fundamental bias against the police. In an overview of the first seven years' functioning of OPONI the Ombudsman reported that the office had received roughly 20,597 complaints containing 30,283 allegations; there had been a decrease early on (2001/02–2004/05) but since 2004/05 there had been an increase; there had been a shift in the main category from 'oppressive behaviour' to 'failure in duty'; roughly 50 per cent of complaints had been dealt with by OPONI and some 954 cases had been referred to the DPP with recommendations for prosecution in 61 of these (OPONI: 2007a).

Furthermore all regulatory agencies have to build a relationship with those they regulate and in negotiating that there is a balance to be made between an unproductive adversarial relationship and the pitfall of co-optation or capture (Hawkins 2002). Since its inception the RUC has been a disputed organisation and at the beginning of this century it was also under threat of disbandment. There was undoubtedly friction between the two agencies and in 2003 the Police Federation for Northern Ireland was still claiming that the Ombudsman did not enjoy the confidence of many officers that the Federation represented. This tension came to a head following the investigation into the Omagh bombing.[39]

In 1998 the largest number of deaths during the Troubles occurred in the busy market town of Omagh when a car bomb exploded killing 29 people, seriously wounding many and causing extensive damage. For quite some time no one was prosecuted for this offence and it has proved difficult to get convictions. The Ombudsman decided in the public interest to open an investigation into the bombing and concluded that information had reached the RUC in advance about the operation and that if utilised properly this could have possibly altered the chain of events (OPONI 2001). This was a clear criticism of the police use of intelligence and of police leadership, while O'Loan added that officers had been uncooperative and defensive to the inquiry. The then Chief Constable, Sir Ronnie Flanagan, was furious and wrote a long rebuttal; Sir Ronnie and the Police Association (representing all police ranks) contemplated taking legal action against the Ombudsman; and she was vilified by unionists and loyalist spokespersons and their supporters in the media.

But the key point was that the victims' families, the survivors and the public have a right to know. The sensitivities of the police are not unimportant but are not of primary significance. And, effectively, the Ombudsman was putting out the message that she was prepared to take on any investigation without favour but also certainly without fear. This was an important signal that no area of policing was sacred and no one would be spared criticism, whatever their rank. At the time of her departure the *Belfast Telegraph* (2007) called the report 'a watershed in police accountability' and said it had broken the 'taboo around criticism of police in Northern Ireland'.

There was perhaps the danger of a damaging adversarial relationship developing between the two agencies, except that the police *needed* the Ombudsman. When there is no legitimacy there is no credibility; and this was a post-conflict situation where significant change was being demanded of the police. In the manoeuvring around power-sharing in the new Northern Ireland Assembly, for instance, the republican *Sinn Fein* party was advising people not to cooperate with the PSNI. The PSNI, moreover, had begun with new leadership espousing a policing paradigm based on human rights, a new accountability structure and oversight by a bevy of agencies. Indeed, the new chief constable announced that he was the most accountable police chief in Europe (Orde 2003). The proof of the pudding was that any deviation from this official paradigm could be tested by an impartial agency. Effective oversight was an essential condition of reform, legitimacy, credibility and acceptance for the new force. And the need for effective oversight in Northern Ireland can be no better illustrated than by another OPONI investigation, known as the 'Ballast Report' (OPONI 2007b).

The Ballast report

Stevens (2003) had unequivocally displayed collusion by Special Branch (SB) with the protestant paramilitaries during the Troubles, leading to the deaths of innocent people. The significance of the Ballast Report is that it documents a pattern of systematic 'fudging' and serious rule-bending within SB which was perpetuated well *after* the armed struggle had been abandoned. The report examines the circumstances surrounding the death of an individual but at the same time provides a penetrating spotlight not only into collusion between SB and a loyalist informer but also into SB's working style, particularly with regard to informant handling. The context is that some groups of paramilitaries on both sides had since the end of hostilities moved towards organised crime activities including drug-dealing.

'Informant 1', who was a member of the loyalist Ulster Volunteer Force (UVF), plays a key role in the inquiry.[40] He had become a police informant, working for both the CID and SB but latterly only for SB. Yet he was never registered as an informant by either unit although he was paid around £80,000 between 1991 and 2003. He had a long criminal career including murder and attempted murder and intelligence linked him to 72 different crimes including punishment attacks, bombings and drug-dealing between 1989 and 2002. This relationship of SB with Informant 1 was replicated with other informants who were also members of the UVF and associated with him. The Ombudsman concludes that there was a 'major failure to ensure the proper management of Informant 1 and other informants' (OPONI 2007b: 36). A major difficulty was the 'generally poor standard of record-keeping' which made retrieval difficult. Documents on key SB decisions were routinely destroyed; financial management of funds to informants was 'totally inadequate'; and many important documents were missing.

The investigation focused particularly on the relationship between SB and Informant 1, who was suspected of involvement in ten murders, including that of the individual (Raymond McCord Junior), and a number of other serious criminal activities. The report maintains that little or no police action was taken with regard to these offences. This led the Ombudsman to conclude that there were grave concerns about certain police practices. These included:

- The failure to arrest informants for crimes they had allegedly confessed to or to treat them as suspects.
- Concealing intelligence about informants' involvement in murder and other crimes.
- Arresting suspects to murder, holding sham interviews and releasing them without charge to provide them with a cover.
- Creating deliberately misleading interview notes, failure to record and retain original interview notes.
- Withholding intelligence, including the names of suspects, that could have been used to detect or prevent crimes.
- Blocking searches of an informant's home and of an alleged UVF arms cache.
- Providing misleading and inaccurate information for the Court with the effect of protecting an informant.
- Destroying or losing forensic exhibits; not complying with Home Office and ACPO guidelines or with legislation on the handling of informants although the Regulation of Investigatory Powers Act (RIPA) had come into force in 2000.

The report concludes this amounted to 'collusion by certain police officers with identified UVF informants' (2007b: 13).

In essence, SB officers were employing informants from the UVF who were deeply involved in serious crime, including murder, in a completely irregular and illicit manner and were protecting them from investigation and prosecution while blocking inquiries on them by the CID. Interviews with suspects were not recorded, evidence was manipulated and documents disappeared to the advantage of informants. There was a pattern of informants providing information about activities they were involved in themselves, enabling them to collect reward money; but their involvement was omitted from reports.[41] It looks very much as if SB attached so much importance to Informant 1 and his associates that it was being manipulated by him; indeed, some officers referred to him as a 'protected species'. For example, Informant 1 sometimes supplied SB with information about other drug-dealers, including some of his own associates, but it appears 'that his motivation in supplying this information was to incriminate rival drug-dealers, in order to protect his own interests and maintain control over the drugs trade in his area' (2007b: 111).

A central feature of the inquiry is the attention paid to failings in the supervision and management of informants. Home Office guidelines for the handling of informants were supposed to have been implemented in the RUC but an exception was made for SB following a decision at chief officer level. There were multiple failures within SB to comply with new legislation in relation to the handling of Informant 1 (2007b: 129). In brief, this OPONI Report maintains that there was RUC collusion in the cases it examined. Indeed, the Ombudsman concludes that the conduct regarding Informant 1 indicates 'systemic' failures (2007b: 133–7).

There was a culture of 'subservience' to SB within the RUC that can be traced to chief officer level. The lower level deviance was related to 'knowledge and support at the highest levels' of the organisation: 'Chief Officers should have been aware of the processes used. The most serious failings are at Chief Officer level, particularly those officers who were responsible for Special Branch, since they are responsible for ensuring that training and systems are put in place to meet legal and policy requirements.' She adds a comment on the dominant role of SB and how that distorted other areas of policing:

> Officers in the rest of the RUC have articulated quite clearly that Special Branch maintained control over those normal ethical policing activities which effect either Special Branch informants or Special Branch operations. The consequence of this was that, in the absence of effective Chief Officer management of Special Branch, *it acquired domination over the rest of the organization which inhibited some normal policing activities.* (2007b: 143, my emphasis)

Reflecting on this, the Ombudsman sums up by stating: 'This investigation demonstrates graphically the dangers of a separated and effectively unaccountable specialist intelligence department with extensive and uncontrolled powers' (2007b: 145). Of interest is that Stalker had said something almost identical about SB 20 years earlier: 'I had never experienced, nor had any of my team, such an influence over an entire police force by one small section' (Stalker 1988: 56). His interim report has never been published, whereas here is a public report from an independent agency. The patterns of deviance including collusion were effectively routine and systemic and persisted through changes of RUC leadership and through changes in policy, procedure and legislation; they persisted after the official end of terrorist activity, during the peace process and during concerted efforts to reform the RUC/PSNI; it also continued when it was clear that some activities were related to serious crime rather than offences related to the security situation. Yet the mantra of 'national security' and 'protecting informants' was still being bandied about; it helped protect a long-standing culture of exclusiveness that masked embedded deviousness which in turn justified shoddy work.[42]

This strong, resilient and persistent culture of deviant practices and collusion fostered poor record-keeping, interference with evidence, destroying documents, conducting 'sham' interviews with suspects, manipulation of reward money, pressurising officers not to take notes or to falsify notes, evasion of legislative guidelines and carrying out arrests on informants to provide them with a cover story. The evidence indicates that one part of the RUC, Special Branch, had a disproportionate influence on the rest of the organisation; that its culture and practice of giving primacy to intelligence from active informants made the organisation dependent on those informants; and that the organisation ended up allowing them to be involved in crimes of violence and drug-dealing.

This overwhelming emphasis on the special status of active informants carried with it the 'capture' of the organisation by the informants; informants were at times virtually handling the handlers. The final responsibility and accountability for this long, resilient and systemic deviance had to rest with the force leadership. The evidence about SB in the OPONI report indisputably conveys that this was *organisational deviance*.

But of especial interest is the section containing the Ombudsman's recommendations. Following every recommendation is a comment from the PSNI about its level of compliance with the measures proposed. This designates a dramatic paradigm shift compared to the days when Stalker arriving for a prearranged meeting with the chief constable in the 1980s and was told that he was not available; or his being given the run-around on the notorious missing tape recording. The current chief constable, Sir Hugh Orde, has also issued a public apology for the wrongdoing of his officers as revealed in the so-called 'Ballast Report' (OPONI 2007): 'While I appreciate that it cannot redress some of the tragic consequences visited upon the families of those touched by the incidents investigated in this report, I offer a whole-hearted apology for anything done or left undone.'

Conclusion

This chapter first examined forms of police deviance and corruption in London that were located primarily within the police organisation. There were diverse arrangements and varying relations with criminals; some were amicable and some adversarial if not predatory; on a number of occasions police were cooperating in, if not directing, serious and even violent crime. Second, attention was paid to cases where the motivation was ostensibly 'noble cause'. The targets, and victims, of police deviance were in a number of cases considered to be highly dangerous terrorists who were a danger to society and to the state; the dominating motivation was to gain a conviction by almost any means. But it also emerged that noble cause could be used as an excuse for gaining easy convictions against vulnerable people whose rights, and freedom, were seriously abused. The significance of the subsequent exposure of the miscarriages of justice which had condemned innocent people to long jail sentences is that the blame and critical focus extended beyond the police to defects in the wider criminal justice system. Legal elites and the judiciary in Britain are particularly loathe to admitting mistakes as it would tarnish their caste-like impregnability and undermine the aura of infallibility around adjudication in court. But this system characteristic did mean that innocent people spent more time incarcerated than if the system had displayed more flexibility and self-reflection.

The patterns of corruption have altered in the UK. The almost 'pad' style activities of London in the 1970s have disappeared as they were too visible and vulnerable to control; in the 1990s there was a shift towards the safer method of leaking information to criminals (Miller 2003). Certainly in the last fifteen years there have been efforts to exert more managerial control within the police organisation and to employ assertive, proactive internal control measures. Generally corruption in Great Britain has, compared to the US, tended to be more sporadic, less highly organised, confined to small 'crew-style' groups or special units such as the West Midlands Serious Crime Squad and frequently tinged with the 'noble cause' rationale.

Northern Ireland was a special case where the security situation stimulated particular forms of police deviance and traditional forms of conventional corruption were largely absent. The context was one both of armed conflict and of a range of covert practices by a number of state agencies raising the issue of state collusion in serious deviance including killings. As Stalker put it, if a police force in the UK could in cold blood 'kill a seventeen-year-old youth with no terrorist or criminal convictions, and then plot to hide the evidence from a senior policeman deputed to investigate it, then the shame belonged to us all. This is the act of a Central American assassination squad – truly of a police force out of control' (Stalker 1988: 67).

There have been a number of corruption cases related to drugs enforcement with a mixed cooperative and predatory style – in Merseyside, West Midlands and in the South East Regional Crime Squad (the latter will be dealt with in Chapter 6). The highly aggressive police 'gangs' encountered in some US forces are not apparent in the UK. Blair (1999), who became responsible for the Complaints Investigation Bureau of the Met in the early 1990s and later became Commissioner, also maintained that excessive violence had not been a major issue in Britain in recent decades and corruption had moved successively from conventional financially based forms to process corruption and into taking drugs and drug money.[43]

And, finally, the landscape of policing in Northern Ireland altered fundamentally with the establishment of an impartial, independent agency to investigate the police. As it was the first in the UK, did the example of OPONI in Northern Ireland provide a model for the first independent police oversight agency in England and Wales – the Independent Police Complaints Commission (IPCC) in 2004?

Notes

1 This was during a protest against the Greek royal couple; Challenor also hit the man several times. Forensic evidence indicated the brick had been planted in a pocket but Challenor evaded trial on grounds of mental illness; he was not only violent and racist but had been behaving strangely for some time before this incident (Morton 1994: 117). He retired with a full pension but three other officers associated with him were sentenced; subsequently 24 people were pardoned regarding related cases (Hobbs 1988: 63).

2 Hobbs (1988) warns that such statements reflect the dominance of the Uniformed Branch which has strongly influenced historical accounts; consequently we know comparatively little about the Detective Branch's history.

3 This term is used as a noun, 'the verbals,' or as a verb 'to verbal'.

4 The Metropolitan Police is responsible for policing over 8 million people and in the 1960s and 1970s it had an official strength of some 25,000 officers; currently it employs around 45,000 people of whom about 30,000 are police officers.

5 In this period before the founding of the CPS (Crown Prosecution Service) in 1986 the police were responsible for preparing cases for prosecutions by solicitors working for the police.

6 Hobbs (1988: 69) describes where two provincial officers attended court in London regarding a suspect arrested in their area by Met officers, only to discover the case had been dropped and the suspect released although formally this requires permission from the Director of Public Prosecutions (DPP).

7 When Robert Mark was appointed Deputy Commissioner of the Met he was responsible for force discipline but this did not apply to allegations of criminal conduct against officers, which remained a matter for the CID (Hobbs 1988: 69).

8 Virgo told the officer, 'You have backed the wrong horse. You have backed Frank Williamson against your own senior officers.' He was sidelined and resigned from the police (Cox *et al.* 1977: 62).

9 When Mark was appointed Assistant Commissioner by the Home Secretary he was told by the Met Commissioner that his appointment was not welcome and the Commissioner even gave him an advert for a job elsewhere; Mark describes his four years as Deputy Commissioner in the Met, waiting in the wings to take over the top job, as the 'most unpleasant years of my life'. He also maintains that the Home Office had been 'desperate to bring the Met under control' for some time and there was even talk of a Royal Commission (Mark 1978: 78, 120).

10 The medical discharge was often used to persuade someone to leave rather than go through formal proceedings while it provided the person with a 'disability' pension.

11 Honeycombe (1974) describes through a 'documentary novel' the detectives in the Drugs Squad as jovial and essentially honest detectives who got mixed up on their notebook and diary entries leading to their prosecution for perjury and conspiracy in relation to a drug trial. Kelaher was a motivated, results-oriented and rule-bending boss, admired by his personnel, who took decisions with little supervision from above; he'd instructed officers to record misleading statements in their notebooks to protect operations and informants. Note-taking was sloppy anyway, often done long after the event with officers copying entries from one another; there was an old saying in policing: 'If they want they can always get you on your diary.'

12 Meaning 'New Scotland Yard', which was Met Police Headquarters from 1875 until the move to new premises also known as New Scotland Yard in 1967; 'the Yard' is also used to refer to the Detective Branch.

13 For many years there has been a debate about the influence of Freemasonry in British policing (Knight 1983).

14 This was established when Mark was still Deputy Commissioner and it reported directly to him; he had the support of the Commissioner, who was to retire shortly afterwards, who announced the move while the

Head of the CID was out of the country (Hobbs 1988: 71). It was the first salvo in Mark's campaign against the CID.

15 Virgo's conviction was later quashed on appeal and Drury's sentence reduced to five years (Ascoli 1979: 322).

16 The trial of the armed robbers 'shopped' by the 'super-grass' Bertie Smalls turned into a concerted attack on the police methods used in the investigation and on their integrity (Ball *et al.* 1979).

17 The Commissioner would approach another force to conduct an inquiry; a team led by that external force would be 'invited' to conduct the investigation and the Home Office would be informed.

18 The City of London Police polices the small area containing the financial centre of London.

19 Mark is quoting from his Dimbleby Lecture given on BBC TV in November 1973.

20 It is also doubtful if a Labour government would have been sympathetic to an appeal at that time.

21 One of the Six had died in prison. A member of the Maguire Seven also died in prison; several members of the Seven, including two boys aged fourteen and seventeen at the time of arrest, had served out their sentences.

22 Logan, solicitor for the Maguire Seven, believed that evidence was planted on the mother, Anne Maguire; forensic tests for nitro-glycerine were negative on her hands at first but positive on gloves which had been in police possession for nine days before a 'doctored' glove was found in her possession (Royakkers 1997: 263).

23 Police powers had long been regulated by the non-statutory 'Judges' Rules' (Reiner 1997).

24 Three young men were convicted of the murder of a woman in 1988 on the basis of 'confessions'. Known as the Cardiff Three they spent four years in prison before it was admitted that they had been the victims of a miscarriage of justice.

25 I was told that one of the Met officers under investigation regarding the Silcott case (one of the Tottenham Three), which turned on a false confession, tried to justify his conduct to investigators as 'noble cause'.

26 Blair (1999: 7) refers to an English judicial culture which, during the 1950s and 1960s, had been 'casual about the rights of suspects to the point of an enthusiastic collusion in unrealistic confessions and ludicrous rules of evidence'. The solicitor for the Guildford Four, Alistair Logan, spoke of the judiciary behaving 'quite outrageously' in relation to appeals; in 1977 the Court of Appeal rejected their appeal with the words, 'We are sure that there has been a cunning and skilful attempt to deceive the Court by putting forward false evidence' (Royakkers 1997: 133).

27 Royakkers (1997: 250–70) interviewed Alistair Logan, Michael Mansfield QC and Chris Mullin MP in 1993 who were involved in varying capacities

in the 'IRA' miscarriage cases (the interviews are reproduced in English); all three were not surprisingly acerbic about police conduct in these cases, the appeals procedure and the police complaints' system.

28 The RUC was formed from the Royal Irish Constabulary (RIC), which had roots in Peel's model for Irish policing (Ryder 2000). The Irish War of Independence (1919–21) was followed by partition of the island in two with a border separating the two states. In Northern Ireland there was a Protestant minority with a one-party administration determined to remain part of the UK; in the South there was a Catholic, nationalist government which continued to hold claim to the North. Also, Irish republicans wanted full independence from Britain and reunification of Ireland. Northern Ireland had a form of autonomous government but during most of the Troubles was ruled directly from London.

29 The Provisional IRA, founded in 1968, was the main proponent of the security services; the armed republican movement has a long history and there were several republican paramilitary organisations involved in the Troubles; by IRA I mean the Provisional IRA. There were also several 'loyalist' paramilitary organisations which supported the 'unionist' and largely Protestant cause for continued union with the UK and were violent towards Catholics and people suspected of IRA or republican involvement, as in the political wing of the IRA, *Sinn Fein* (English 2004).

30 I think everyone will recognise the sacrifice the force experienced during the Troubles; and many ordinary officers were undoubtedly brave and honest – nearly everyone who has known the RUC says this including Stalker (1988) who investigated it for serious offences; but it has a long history of bias and abuse of power while the events portrayed here are amply documented.

31 The incidents sound very much like the 'encounters' in Indian policing (Belur 2007); in Northern Ireland as in Mumbai there was an obscure location, usually no witnesses, much firepower from the police but no returned shots, fatalities among the victims but no injuries to the police and formulaic scenarios in court suggesting danger to the police.

32 In the hayshed case the antiquated guns, which could not be fired and had no ammunition, were presumably planted to suggest an element of danger to the officers. The police were waiting for the men to enter the shed, which was 'bugged' with a listening device; the shed had earlier been used by the IRA to store explosives. The survivor said the police started shooting without warning when he and his companion – a teenager with no association with the IRA or any republican organisation – picked up the rifles. The survivor was associated with the IRA. The two young men were looking after property for an acquaintance and apparently climbed into the shed 'out of curiosity'; but it is also conceivable that an *agent provocateur* informed them about the guns and provoked that curiosity.

33 At one stage his CIO (Chief Investigating Officer) was Hugh Orde from the Met who later became Chief Constable of the Police Service of Northern Ireland (PSNI).

34 By the third inquiry Stevens' mandate had been extended to agents of the army's intelligence service (Davies 1999); unlike Stalker he was able to mobilise the RUC (later the PSNI) to make over 90 arrests on his behalf (officers from Britain have no jurisdiction in Northern Ireland).

35 Maurice Hayes played a key role in developing the model for OPONI (Hayes 1997); he has been a senior civil servant, the governmental Ombudsman in Northern Ireland and is now a politician in the Irish Republic.

36 PSNI had a new uniform and new symbolism to make it acceptable to the republican community and above all it had to downsize in numbers while shifting focus from security to conventional policing.

37 As a Catholic woman from the mainland married to a nationalist politician Mrs (now Dame) O'Loan had four discrediting factors in the eyes of opponents. Dame O'Loan was appointed for a non-renewable term of seven years and completed her term in 2007. She is widely acknowledged as having done an excellent job.

38 The website of OPONI contains data on patterns of complaints and the reports on specific investigations; all this material can be downloaded: www.policeombudsman.org.

39 A splinter republican group, the Real IRA, was held responsible for the attack.

40 Informant 1 has since been identified by the media. The UVF was a loyalist paramilitary organisation with a history of extreme violence against Catholics and republicans during the Troubles.

41 A bizarre incident was when explosives were moved in the car of an assistant chief constable, without his or the driver's knowledge, to a spot where they could later be 'discovered' by the informant.

42 Again Stalker (1988: 263) had earlier said something similar: 'Procedures and processes within some sections of the Force were in a sorry state. Dangerous practices, slackness, loose supervision and fundamental inefficiency ... remained unnoticed.'

43 Mark (1978: 52–3) states that violence against suspects was routine in pre-war Manchester; one 'fairly senior detective' gave prisoners the choice, 'will you talk or be tanned?' Assaulting an officer led to 'first aid rendered', meaning a thrashing for the assailant. In the early 1990s several senior officers admitted in public debate on TV that violence and intimidation had been typical of the policing they had known in the 1960s and 1970s (Rose 1996).

Chapter 6

'Creatures in between': pathways into police deviance and corruption

You hear people say 'the best cops are corrupt because they are out there, they are on top of it; they have to be a bit corrupt.' But they are not cops; they are some form of creature that exists in a dark space between cops and the bad guys.

(Bob Leuci, former corrupt cop, in *Bad Cops*, 1993)

In this chapter I scrutinise several police officers and two units that were deeply deviant and corrupt. They represent the dark side of policing with a wide discrepancy with the official paradigm. The offences in the two units are largely *strategic predatory corruption* with ripping off criminals; but also at times cooperating with some of them. These deviant cops engage in an amalgam of consensual and predatory corruption – with bribery, blackmail, robbery, drug-dealing and in some cases brutality – revealing the unbridled abuse of police power coupled with organised criminal behaviour. This inevitably includes 'process corruption' with lying, falsifying documents, perjury, intimidating witnesses and manipulating or destroying evidence as a cover-up either for their own deviant activity, for money or in deals with criminals.

The focus here is on the actual construction of corruption with specific officers and particular units. This includes rationalisations and implementing social arrangements. The processes of entering deviancy and of becoming highly deviant are similar to those in other groups (Downes and Rock 2007). The difference is that we are dealing with members of a law enforcement agency who are assumed to be on 'the other side of the fence' to many groups defined as deviant or as lawbreakers (Sherman: 1974b). This implies that they have to go through a considerable process of neutralisation, leading to routinisation, in order to engage in the deviance. Later they can face harsh reality if exposed as 'criminals' within a police organisation. The offences have in a sense been against the organisation and occupational community they belong to; and they will be arrested by their own colleagues or other cops. Regarding their moral 'career' the cops have first to become corrupt; some become 'un-corrupt' without detection (say by moving or retiring); some are caught and confess, and these *pentiti* become a 'snitch', 'stool', rat or 'grass'; others enter yet a new career as collaborators.

Given the rule of silence, the emphasis on solidarity and the likelihood of sanctions, this is a considerable step to take. For instance, a key witness for the Wood Royal Commission in Australia was Trevor Haken who went undercover and recorded illegal transactions with fellow New South Wales (NSW) officers. His 'ratting' cost him his job, marriage, friends and his livelihood. Ten years later he still feared reprisals and felt he should not have cooperated but should have stayed with his bent NSW mates: 'Even if I had gone to jail, it would probably have only been for a couple of years and not the life sentence that I've got now' (ABC 2005).[1]

In pursuing this theme – on becoming bent, collectively articulating the 'business' of corruption and deciding to 'step out' of corruption – I refer to two cases in particular. One relates to the 'groovy gang' within the South East Regional Crime Squad (SERCS) in the UK and centred on Detective Constable Neil Putnam, drawing on a BBC Panorama TV documentary and other sources.[2] The other concerns Bob Leuci – 'Prince of the City' – and the Special Investigation Unit (SIU) of the NYPD. I draw on insights from these and other cases to examine the pathways through which police officers enter corruption, become criminals, and also become 'un-corrupt'.

For instance, the account by Leuci is especially valuable because he was at first eager and 'clean'; then he became corrupt; but later he turned to collaboration, going undercover to gain evidence of corruption within the SIU and beyond. This was then a double deviant 'career': one took him into corruption and the other took him out of it. Undetected officers can 'step out' of corruption and take their guilty knowledge with them. There are four categories of cops who decide to talk about corruption. (There is as well a group of steadfast cops who never talk or admit anything after detection.)

First, there are 'whistle-blowers' who talk voluntarily without being involved in corrupt practices (as with Serpico). Second, there are undetected cops who come under suspicion and become 'spontaneous confessors' (without this necessarily leading to a legal admission of guilt, as with Leuci). Third, some are caught and confess to their own crimes; and some of these will also give up other cops, perhaps following a bargain. I call these *pentiti*. Fourth, there are those cops who not only talk but 'roll over' by actively cooperating with the authorities against their colleagues. These I term 'collaborators'.

Bob Leuci, for example, was a 'spontaneous confessor' who became a 'collaborator'. He has spoken and written widely on his experiences; there is a film of the book *Prince of the City* by Daley (1979) and his autobiography (Leuci 2004).[3] After the court cases drawing on his testimony Leuci remained in the NYPD but as he was not permitted to return to operational policing, for understandable reasons, he resigned.

I first deal with the case of Putnam and the SERCS, then turn to Leuci and the SIU and finish with an analysis of the 'pathways' cops take into deviance, corruption and crime.

'Groovy Gang': SERCS and Neil Putnam

A BBC television documentary dealt with corruption in the SERCS in the early 1990s. The six regional crime squads in England and Wales were formed in the 1960s to tackle serious crime in areas covering several police forces. SERCS was the largest, operating in a substantial part of south-east England. The partly dramatised documentary (a BBC *Panorama* programme broadcast in 2000) drew largely on the account given by a *pentito*, Neil Putnam. He was initially a 'good detective' who had earlier worked in the Drug Squad.[4]

Within the SERCS there was a small group, rather like a New York 'crew', centred on the informal leader, Clark, and his 'sidekick', Drury. Putnam drank a lot, had domestic problems and was short of money; Drury also drank heavily and was addicted to drugs. On his first day with this clique Clark told Putnam 'not to worry' about money. This 'groovy gang', as they called themselves, was into heavy drinking and cocaine use and there was, on the surface at least, strong group loyalty. Their 'MO' (*modus operandi*) was to receive tip-offs from informants about drug shipments and locations, arrest the courier or raid the location and confiscate the drugs and money, steal some of the drugs and sell them and keep some or all of the money. Early on, Clark asked Putnam for a holdall which Putnam later realised was used to transport stolen drugs; shortly after Clark gave him £300. He says he was caught, 'on the hop, unawares', had to react in a 'split-second' and 'took the wrong decision'; he realised it was wrong but he just 'couldn't react.' He thought, 'well, if that's the way I've got to succeed here to be accepted, to be part of the team, then I've got to go along with it'.

Their main informant was a woman who was also having an intimate and serious relationship with Clark. She received money for information, could continue dealing and Clark resold stolen drugs via her. Clark had a pattern of conspicuous consumption, saw the woman regularly and even took her to police social gatherings. Some supervisors must have known of this liaison according to Putnam. Putnam was drinking heavily, indulging in marital violence and left home. Clark visited him, asked him to hide some drugs and gave him an envelope saying, 'this should help you out in all your present problems'. Putnam was perturbed, drove to a park and saw that there was £2,000 in the envelope (then worth about $3,000); he reports saying to himself, '"What have you done? You stupid fool." This was a lot; really the first time ... *there was no way out, no one to turn to* ... I couldn't go to senior officers because I didn't trust them' (my emphasis).

Despite his reservations Putnam became an active gang member and the corruption escalated. On raids there was a 'stealing frenzy'. Clark kept most and was also holding back from the rest. The group felt untouchable and were convinced that 'no one would get us'. Things started to unravel when, tipped off by Clark's informant, the team raided the wrong house looking for drugs. They encountered a young couple, stole their money and blackmailed them by taking their recreational drugs and threatening to arrest them if they talked. This was apparently a turning point for Putnam. He viewed these victims as a different moral category from usual, who didn't deserve to be ripped off; he felt 'despicable ... I couldn't get lower ... I hated myself'. Subsequently the plight of the victimised couple reached other officers and the 'groovy gang' came under suspicion.

Sensing this they got together to 'construct lies and deny everything', but the investigation was dropped for lack of evidence. But then their informant was arrested and, facing a long stay in prison, she began to talk in the hope of reducing the sentence. Clark and Drury were arrested but stonewalled. Putnam was now reunited with his wife and he feared a long prison term and perhaps losing his family again. He had reverted to uniformed patrol work and was instructing youngsters on the dangers of drugs (McLaglan 2004: 270). He was frightened and decided to talk, with a spontaneous confession as he had not yet been charged with anything; but he says, 'my world was collapsing; I wanted to tell the truth'. The Putnam family went into witness protection; and he told the full story to investigators and testified in court. Clark was sentenced to twelve years, Drury to eleven, three others to lesser terms, one case was dropped and one officer retired. Putnam was out of prison within two years. He was dubbed a 'super-grass'.

The case's components are as follows. Putnam was a good detective but suffered from the occupational hazards of policing – debt, drink and marital problems. He was clearly targeted and tested by the ringleader. The gang had a strong leader and there was bonding with drinking and drug sessions. Clark was a stereotypical 'hard man' – macho, manipulative and bullying – and boasted of intimidating and even 'selecting' supervisors (recorded through surveillance). His bravado led him to almost flaunting his relationship with a female informant yet apparently he was never challenged on this. This raises the familiar issue: where were the supervisors and what were they doing?

When Putnam decided to talk investigators were staggered by this 'jewel', as he provided an 'inside track' to the corruption. The bent cops were in a specialist squad but low in the rank hierarchy; they networked to get postings together while Clark recruited compliant accomplices. They started small, according to an investigator, with increasingly larger steps into deviance; this 'erosion' could later be traced. Following arrest they were tough opponents and difficult to convict. Clark would never cooperate and maintained an inscrutable, iron-like defence for hours on end, answering 'no comment' to every question.

One thinks of the questions: did no one observe the clique-forming, out-of-work drinking, dominance of Clark – flaunting his female informant – and Putnam's marital problems? Why was there no one to turn to in the organisation? Why did this small group have so much autonomy? The SERCS was operating largely in the notoriously vulnerable and predictable area of drug enforcement and yet no one seemed to be alert to the risk and dangers; where was the risk assessment? And although this was an elite unit Putnam was not impressed with the quality of leadership and control within the Dulwich section he had joined; 'I found that SERCS was fragmented, disorderly and with a lack of discipline. Everything was muddled and people seemed to be going off and doing their own thing. The senior officers seemed disinterested and there was a lack of respect for the sergeants' (McLaglan 2004: 256). This may have some validity

167

but could also be an excuse, which was used by his defence team, to reduce his personal responsibility.

Prince of the City: SIU and Bob Leuci

> Hardly any detective survived SIU with reputation intact. Imagination, fearlessness, a sense of adventure, a disregard for procedure – SIU men had these qualities in abundance. They were great detectives. Of course it was these qualities that got them into trouble. (Daley 1979: 329)

A colleague of Leuci's describes how to make money by 'squeezing' dealers: 'No pad. No specific amount, no regular payments. But let's say we're short, we step in on one of these guys and hit them for a hundred or something.' Leuci comments that this talk led to the 'inevitable sleaze that was yet to come and began my descent into the night of full-blown corruption. All that was once my honor fell from me piece by piece' (Leuci 2004: 173). In 1969 Leuci joined the SIU which was an elite squad of detectives focused on major drug-dealers. Then the early 1970s saw the Knapp Commission scrutinising the NYPD which led to the SIU also coming under suspicion. Indeed, Commissioner Murphy called it 'probably ... the most corrupt single unit in the history of American law enforcement' (Murphy and Plate 1977: 242). Leuci was never caught in corrupt activities but came under suspicion and agreed to cooperate with the authorities.

Leuci is of Italian heritage and joined the NYPD in 1961. Initially he encountered only the customary grass-eating. But Leuci was keen to do 'real' police work and become a top detective; also he was eager, if not desperate, to be accepted by fellow cops. Leuci refers almost romantically to a fraternity with every cop 'your brother' and to the comfort when an old hand aids him during an arrest saying, 'Remember – you belong to the biggest, baddest gang in town. You need help, don't wait – ask.' The intimate relationship with one's police partner he viewed as a form of 'love'; in policing he found what 'I was looking for – acceptance, connection, kinship ... belonging just to belong ... It is a very particular sort of yearning, a curious personality trait that has afflicted me all my life' (Leuci 2004: 2–3). Leuci soon became an active, streetwise cop, rapidly made it to detective and, still relatively young, he reached the prestigious SIU.

Its members were the best of the best; they wore expensive clothing and looked like the 'wise guys' of organised crime they were ostensibly combating. Initially, the SIU was highly motivated and not corrupt. Giuliani (DA, later Mayor of New York) said of its detectives: 'They were the best, brave and tough, and started with the right motivation. They were not corrupt and had a fervent desire to catch crooks; they hated the dealers and their drugs. But they started to take their money and then started to take their drugs and sell them to informants. They used an elaborate web of rationalisations' (*Bad Cops*, 1993). The enforcement was geared to Mafia and South American dealers and the unit was keen to make 'busts' with arrests, seizures of money and of drugs. Leuci's fellow cops were motivated, skilful and highly successful men who committed corrupt acts 'once in a while. It was just something that happened. It was just there one day, and then it grew' (Daley 1979: 311). The unit began to use illegal methods to achieve formal success; this meant tapping phones, picking locks, planting bugging devices and committing burglaries. Later the stealing of money and drugs started.

Leuci is clear that when this gradual 'slide' reached a certain level he knew it was wrong, but he suppressed this. The slide began with frustration and temptation, and then 'you fall prey. You know, evil has a face and you can recognise it straightaway. When someone offers you something a voice in the back of your head says "this is wrong", period. *But you suppress the voice*' (*Bad Cops*, 1993, my emphasis). The SIU graduated to using illegally obtained information to 'score' against the dealers, stealing money and drugs during the busts; they sold some of the drugs to dealers for recycling and kept some of the money (from the South American dealers they would often take everything); they then committed perjury to get convictions.[5]

There were often good relations with Italian-American 'mobsters'[6] and certain practices were aimed at helping them. These included getting a dealer's drugs back from the laboratory marked 'no narcotics'; or predating the registration of a dealer as an informant to avoid prosecution (two lawyers, a DA and a judge were in one deal; Daley 1979: 91, 97). One gangster was in danger of losing his parole; he'd been sentenced for homicide and faced completion of a life sentence. A detective negotiated his release from custody with Leuci and three colleagues for $75,000 plus an informant. SIU detectives would sell tapes from illegal taps, and thus inadmissible in court, to an unsuspecting criminal for $50,000; and would take payment for getting a case 'dropped' while already knowing it was to be shelved. These were the patterns of cooperation, exploitation and manipulation that marked these arrangements which were lubricated by kinship, friendship and, above all, money.

The elite SIU was keen to gain results. They spoke of passing through 'the Door' to fame by making a spectacular arrest and/or bust; the detectives on the so-called 'French Connection' case achieved celebrity status and were swaggering institutional heroes.[7] When Leuci won praise for a major success he felt 'a throbbing rhythm' to his life like 'playing the lead in a rock and roll band' (Leuci 2004: 196). More prosaically, the cops got used to the extra money; Leuci had been strapped for cash but now habitually had several hundred dollars on him. And it was doubtless exciting to reach the headlines following a success. Unfortunately the SIU made the headlines for other reasons.

The SIU's culture was based on close ties between colleagues with particularly intimate relationships with working partners.[8] Leuci became friendly with certain detectives; he looked up to them, and especially to Joe Nunziata whom he admired greatly. Yet he betrayed them. For all the talk of fraternity and 'love' he betrayed his close friends and colleagues. He became another sort of deviant – one who not only 'rats' but also collaborates in an undercover operation against them – and one virulently despised by all cops. I deal with Leuci's double deviant career in the next two sections: 'Pathway in and belonging' and 'Pathway out, betrayal and becoming a collaborator.'

Pathway in and belonging

When Leuci joined the NYPD he was idealistic; he initially encountered almost no corruption but was aware of corrupt segments. He was determined to remain 'straight' and protested about being sent to the Public Morals Division which was reputedly highly corrupt. He was assigned instead to the Narcotics Division. He began to 'slide' through opportunity, temptation and ambition but especially through a strong desire to be accepted. Fitting in led him towards rule-bending, both to be included and to gain results.

The operational code in narcotics was that detectives developed close ties with informants who were usually street dealers and sometimes users. These could continue in business as long as they gave information on someone 'worse than themselves' (Daley 1979: 194). If short of drugs cops would supply them with drugs (which was a felony offence); and if the dealer was arrested then the handler would get them released. Cops were on 24-hour call for their informants. The working environment was, moreover, one where lawyers and bondsmen would pay officers for getting a client off a charge by reducing the offence, mislaying evidence or making mistakes in statements that would lead to dismissal in court. Also, district attorneys and even judges accepted payment to throw a case. Money was an offer on the streets, by dealers for not being arrested or for staying in business, and in the courts; temptation abounded.

This was amplified by the work and lax control. Only arrests counted and a conviction was irrelevant; there were quotas for arrests but these could be completed in an afternoon. This generated an incentive to gain kudos by an arrest but then make money by fixing the case to fail in court. Confiscated drugs were only tested for 'narcotics present' so cops could easily dilute drugs before handing them in or on withdrawing them as evidence. Drugs were periodically destroyed without analysis, which encouraged theft. Between 1969 and 1972 some 400 pounds of heroin and cocaine disappeared in withdrawals from the NYPD property office: 'This quantity represented one-fifth of all narcotics seized by the department since 1961. The value of the stolen narcotics ... was estimated at seventy million dollars, far surpassing any bank or jewelry robbery in American history' (Commissioner Murphy in Leuci 2004: 313). There was then temptation and opportunity within a lax organisation; and the motive for taking the impounded drugs was perhaps a combination of greed and pleasure at bucking the system.

SIU focused on sophisticated drug wholesalers, Italian-Americans and later South Americans. Serious dealers were rarely caught in possession and so detectives resorted to illegal telephone taps and break-ins when they could not get a warrant. The initial motivation may have been to make cases, with the law seen as cumbersome, but the overriding wish to succeed led to the means becoming ends in themselves. There was an adversarial attitude to South American dealers; these were 'cash-and-carry' importers who were likely to have drugs, money, jewellery and weapons with them in the US and in a bust these were typically at the scene. This could mean 'skimming off' money and offers of bribes at the scene or later through a lawyer. And rather than face jail in the US, the South Americans could be persuaded to undertake 'voluntary' deportation for a consideration.

For instance, Leuci (2004: 187–9) describes a case where two suspected Cuban drug dealers from Florida were stopped in a car; the trunk was full of money but there were no drugs or firearms. One feigned surprise and said the money must be false and anyway it wasn't his; if the cops took half and let them go then he'd swear to God they would go back to Miami and never return to New York. The sergeant took the SIU unit aside and said, 'Let's say we confiscate all of it.' They would have to spend hours counting it and registering all the notes' serial numbers; then they would turn it over to the City and it would go the Department of Welfare. 'The Department of Welfare … will hand it to some asshole on welfare. That asshole will go out, buy a gun, and then shoot a cop. I'm not going to be responsible for the shooting of some poor unsuspecting cop.' Having invented a convincing justification that the others shared unanimously – after all, no one wanted to be responsible for killing a cop – the sergeant further reflected that Cubans are very religious people and can surely be trusted if they swear to God never to return; 'that's good enough for me.' They kept half the money and let them go.

In practice SIU was poorly led and hardly supervised. Some officers avoided the office for months, took unannounced vacations and attempts by senior officers to reimpose control were virulently opposed and usually soon abandoned. The unit's autonomy was great if not unlimited. There was friendship and camaraderie but also competition and mistrust. Leuci was warned several times that you could not really trust anyone in this environment. He is explicit on two key features of police corruption. One is entering it by sliding down the 'slide'; and the other is the ability of officers to rationalise.

First, Leuci made a gambling arrest but was unaware the person was on the 'pad' and hence protected from arrest. To get him out of custody, money passed hands and Leuci received $500.[9] He states: 'that was the first time, and I was shocked that I felt no self-disgust, no regret' (Leuci 2004: 151). But the erosion had really begun earlier with a dealer for whom he bought 'junk' (drugs). In drug enforcement he felt he had to break the law to enforce it; and it was 'the beginning of the end of whatever innocence I still possessed'; this 'gave birth to a kind of moral and ethical erosion that would carry me to greater depths than I could ever have imagined' (2004: 123, 136). Again there is with Leuci the constant theme of seeking inclusion: 'I felt a sense of belonging and a sense of betrayal … Something had gone wrong'; he had started as a straight cop but after seven years on the streets 'all that I once believed in had been crushed under the weight of the daily routine of being a narcotic's cop. It was a hard thing to admit, but I knew that *I was capable of doing whatever it took to belong*' (2004: 153, my emphasis). Later in the SIU he started to go 'totally over the edge'; his partner pushed him onto the 'slide' when two informants started to make small payments to them.

Second, he states: 'my own fingerprints were all over my own downfall. I knew it was wrong, seriously wrong, yet I did it willingly, knowing full well how asinine and outrageous such behavior was. And what is truly astonishing, I knew that it would harm me. Still

I was prepared to do it ... No one did a better job on me than me when it came to rationalising what I was doing' (2004: 74). He coped by denial and sensed he was falling even 'deeper into the abyss'. He fought to evade such thoughts which would 'tighten and sour my stomach and make my head spin. My own unspoken rule; *don't think about it'* (2004: 199, my emphasis). He expresses an inability, rather like addicts, to stop the practice despite his gnawing self-doubt: his life was 'a jumble of interconnecting, double-dealing scams, deals and seductions' that made him feel mentally and physically sick. But he could not find the 'resolve, backbone or the means to do anything about it ... I'd stand in front of the mirror ... asking myself, What are you doing? Who are you? ... I had come to feel that all of this was fated. I believed that sooner or later I was bound to go along. *I thought I had no choice. If I wanted to be accepted into a very private club, a group that meant everything to me, I had to conform'* (2004: 233, 238, 243, my emphasis).

But eventually he did step out of one club and into the fold of another one formed by anti-corruption investigators.

Pathway out, betrayal and becoming a collaborator

If I were successful, my actions would be thought of as a betrayal, a betrayal worse than any betrayal. I had been accepted, transported with smiles and hugs into a very special club – I was trusted. It was far, far worse than anything Serpico had done. Serpico was, in reality, an outsider – not one of us, he set out to deceive no-one.

(Leuci 2004: 259)

There is a 'career' of getting out of corruption as well as one of getting into it. Leuci talks of simply deciding to 'step out'.[10] Stepping out can mean transferring to a safe haven elsewhere, leaving policing, deciding to talk when caught (becoming a *pentito*) or actively cooperating in investigations against former colleagues as a 'collaborator'. For some cops it literally meant committing suicide.

Leuci says he began to enter situations where he was frightened and he started to think about getting out. There was, too, disillusionment which was amplified when a new leader of SIU spoke forcefully about cleaning up the unit but later demanded 50 per cent of the take for his new house (Daley 1979: 55). He felt he had landed in 'the theatre of the ridiculous in a world gone insane' (Leuci 2004: 1999). He met Serpico and Durk and discussed his experiences.[11] The Knapp Commission's attention also turned on Leuci as one of SIU's

173

most active members. He was invited to meet the federal prosecutor Scoppetta who was allied to the Knapp investigation. Scoppetta managed to get Leuci talking about his life and career and eventually he opened up on corruption. Finally Leuci agreed to cooperate partly through a desire to expose corruption among lawyers, judges and others and not just cops.

Leuci had not been caught out but he spontaneously admitted to three offences. This was not a formal interrogation but Scoppetta needed to know if Leuci was being open about his own misconduct otherwise he could be disbarred from giving evidence. It is unusual for cops to admit offences if not detected, as the golden rule is 'never cough'. When caught or under strong suspicion officers may be persuaded to talk to save themselves from dismissal and loss of pension or to avoid a prosecution and prison sentence. In the US and some jurisdictions a police suspect can be offered immunity or can plea bargain to get a reduced or suspended sentence, with judge and prosecution taking their cooperation into account.[12]

There is no data on what percentage of police officers decide to talk during investigations. Scoppetta maintained that most cops cooperate: 'In their hearts they want to admit their guilt. That's the way cops are' (Leuci 2004: 286). In Leuci's case he was troubled by his past, felt guilt, remorse, a shame that 'afflicted him like a disease' and displayed a wish to confess (Daley 1979: 32). He saw the prosecutor as a friend and the experience as releasing him from strain; confession he realised usually brings with it a measure of 'self-destruction ... I had already gone too far, said way too much. Oddly, though, it was almost a pleasant unburdening. There was this sense of letting go, a kind of freedom in it' (Leuci 2004: 258). Even the federal agents guarding him advised him not to talk; they warned him that everyone hated him – Internal Affairs, DEA, prosecutors and cops – and they would eventually find a former colleague to implicate him; they advised him only to think of his family (Daley 1979: 301). Leuci hoped to keep his SIU friends out of the investigation although this meant lying in court; but he was going to lie anyway about the extent of his own corruption. It proved impossible to keep his former colleagues out of the spotlight.

Going undercover led to being fitted with a 'wire' on his body – his car and phone were also 'bugged' – and he started to record conversations with crooks, cops, SIU detectives and lawyers that would implicate them. This was dangerous work and at times he found himself in tricky situations when the backup failed to materialise for various logistical reasons.[13] And once the wire started to burn into his skin; he had to rush to the toilet and tear it off his burning flesh. But he proved very persuasive and managed to win people's confidence. Then he betrayed that confidence. This is, of course, what undercover work is essentially about – gaining confidence by playing a convincing role in order to obtain incriminating evidence. And Leuci was good at it.

There was a lot of paranoia at the time with various investigations taking place and some cops and crooks became suspicious of Leuci. He was patted down several times but narrowly managed to evade detection. His undercover role was threatening to unravel. His family moved to an isolated lodge outside the city protected by armed agents. This undercover phase lasted sixteen months and was followed by four years of preparing for court and testifying. Several times he was asked if he wanted to continue with the undercover role as the risk increased, but he insisted on carrying on as if he was driven. In the film *Prince of the City* it is suggested he enjoyed going undercover, revelling in the risky thrills of the 'game'. There followed several years of transcribing some 100 tapes, preparing cases and appearing in court where he faced hostile defence lawyers. There were now several agencies chasing bent cops and investigators from one began to focus on the theft of the French Connection drugs; this brought Leuci and other SIU members under suspicion. During a related undercover 'sting' operation to 'burn' corrupt cops Nunziata accepted a payment and was called in for questioning. Fearing prosecution, he committed suicide. Leuci was devastated by his death; then a former SIU partner of Leuci's also committed suicide. By now Leuci himself was under considerable strain and felt depressed, was on medication, contemplated suicide and made at least one suicide attempt.

He testified in court cases and according to Giuliani Leuci proved of 'immeasurable value' in gaining evidence on corruption.[14] The SIU was disbanded and 52 of its members were indicted; several received stiff sentences. An investigation into wider corruption among lawyers and judges which had originally motivated Leuci to cooperate was shelved when leaks compromised it; Leuci (2004: 302) observes wryly: 'we got sold out'.

Joining and leaving 'the Club'

I never saw myself as a criminal; I was on the other side of the fence.

(Former corrupt officer in *Bad Cops*, 1993)

This book has drawn on cases from the literature and other sources such as public inquiries, journalism, (auto)biographies, films and documentaries. In the American documentary *Bad Cops* (1993), for example, we witness several officers who have experienced the cycle of corruption, investigation, arrest, prosecution and incarceration and who are prepared to talk about their experiences. The documentary also contains interviews with several prosecutors and FBI agents. These *pentiti*, who mostly became collaborators, form a highly skewed sample. They first betrayed their own organisation and honest colleagues by becoming corrupt and became 'de-corrupted' by breaking the rule of silence; and then they betrayed their former partners in corruption by collaborating with the authorities. But any selection of cops prepared to talk about corruption would be unrepresentative of all the officers ever investigated as so few are willing to reflect openly about their part in corruption. Furthermore, these cops in the documentary not only display regret but were also mostly prepared to cooperate with investigators against their colleagues.[15] The statements of this highly selective group have, then, to be approached with caution; but there appears to be a strong resonance with other material. The aim in examining these accounts is to specify the social dynamics of 'becoming bent' (Sherman 1974b).

Alongside the material from Putnam (above) and Leuci, who also speaks in the documentary, there are two officers from the documentary I wish to cite: Charles Hund and Leo Ryan, both from the Philadelphia PD.[16] I also refer occasionally to the accounts of other corrupt cops. This material is geared to the theme 'joining and leaving the Club' with the 'Club' meaning a group of 'bent' cops. To explore this I will describe the following phases: Joining the police – straight and clean; grass-eating and early rule-bending; first real steps; disillusionment and cynicism; inside the Club; rationalisations; no way back, nowhere to go; police as victims; and exclusion.

Joining the police – straight and clean

In numerous accounts it is noticeable, given the speaker's later deviant career, that the new officer is straight, clean and even idealistic about policing. Putnam always wanted to be a police officer, joined the Met as early as possible and had 'noble ambitions' to help the people of London (BBC 2000). I have not encountered anyone in the western literature who was aware of corruption prior to joining and anticipated its benefits. Some of the later highly corrupt cops were not only straight early on but were also highly motivated and competent officers, looking like ideal recruits on entry. Aguiluz in the NYPD, for instance, had been one of the 'stars' of the spectacular French Connection case, been a 'great detective' and 'as idealistic as most other young cops'. But he had 'kept drugs back from that case and sold them, he had sold suspects their freedom for large sums, he had committed perjury umpteen times and stolen money from dealers' (Daley 1979: 179–281). There seems to be a moment when their idealism and commitment deserts these top detectives and their skills are turned to the wrong use.

Grass-eating and early rule-bending

Most police officers regale you with anecdotes about their earliest days 'on the job'. Policing is seemingly a profession with a high 'reality shock' for those entering practice (Moskos 2008). There are few unblemished paragons in policing and almost everyone recounts some exposure to grass-eating, cooping, mumping, boozing and other easing practices as well as rule-bending on arrests and giving testimony in court on mundane cases. Ryan was initiated on his very first tour of duty in Philadelphia and adapted instantaneously. He went out with a sergeant who picked up some beer from a bar-owner and they met other officers at a scrapyard; the cops were drinking and playing cards and there were some female 'groupies' in one of the patrol cars. Ryan was really 'shocked'; but soon he too was drinking beer and playing cards with his uniform all askew: 'It was the acceptance piece; I was the new guy and I wanted to be accepted.' Then at roll-call the sergeant began to 'drop him five dollars to go easy on a bar' and it developed from there.

When Haken joined the police in Australia he was posted to traffic duties. It was a 'brotherhood'; you had to fit in and 'fitting' in meant drinking, or you were ostracised. From late afternoon the work was conducted from a bar where 'even in uniform, you spent the remainder of the shift drinking and working, and that was the entire shift working out of there' (ABC 2005). On his first day in the SERCS Putnam went to the pub with his new squad; he was asked about debts and mentioned some on his credit cards. The ringleader 'very blatantly turned around' and said, 'Well, don't worry about that. A few months here and we'll have all your debts cleared.' This was his first day and reading between the lines he sensed that 'there was a means of making money corruptly' (BBC 2000).

One officer says in *Bad Cops*, 'once you take that first dollar you lose a part of your soul'. Is this accommodating to early rule-bending the start of the slide or the first step on the ladder? And what takes some officers beyond that?

First real steps, qualms and joining the Club

When confronted for the first time with bribery and 'arrangements' officers are presented with a choice: how strongly do I want to join the club? It may be posed as: 'Are you in or out?' Deviance as a rite of passage for the novitiate can be consciously constructed by experienced officers. Accepting deviance then becomes the price of membership in the club. Frequently, the accounts reveal that the first unambiguous confrontation with corruption is an instantaneous choice but which can also cause considerable emotional turmoil. Hund admits that the first time – he skimmed $200 from a suspected drug-dealer for 'lunch money' – he was 'panic stricken'. He hid the money and did not dare touch it for over a month.

In effect, the first time an officer is offered banknotes or some illegal arrangement it is both an inducement and an instantaneous test. Leuci says that it wasn't really about the money but you could not refuse because you would 'destroy yourself with your peers' (Leuci 2004: 310). Putnam also shows how difficult it was for him, his reaction was: 'What have you done? You stupid fool.' Cops who have spoken on this moment were instantly aware it was wrong but felt they had little choice if they wanted to be 'one of the boys'. In the case of Dowd and his crew the initial test was not money but violence; all his partners went along with this and were then induced into deeper forms of deviance.

Lubricating the slide: disillusionment and cynicism

In some accounts there is, then, a background of bent cops having been motivated and even excellent officers. One crucial element in starting to slide is disillusionment with law enforcement which generates deep cynicism (Niederhoffer 1967). A major shift in orientation occurs as officers become disenchanted with the work, their own organisation and senior officers and with the wider criminal justice system. This was mentioned by both the Knapp and Mollen Commissions as a significant factor in explaining why cops go 'bent'; and the Fitzgerald Commission in Australia (1987: 200) stated that process corruption had its origins in 'contempt for the criminal justice system, disdain for the law and rejection of its application to the police, disregard of the truth, and abuse of authority'.

Inside the Club

The social arrangements underpinning corruption are varied. In New York the 'pad' was almost as if a trade union had bargained for a collective bonus, but with the 'crew' mode there are other elements inducing officers towards corruption. In such groups there is usually a leader of the pack who selects and manipulates the members; in the SERCS Clark was the informal leader who understood human weakness, luring in his catch. Special detective units often develop close relationships with criminals and some members can become addicted to the power, excitement, greed and action associated with the underworld; some cops become fascinated by the 'wise guys'/ villains, become personal friends and even go on vacation with them.

For some there is a moment of doubt or a low point. For Hund that was when Five Squad started stealing and recycling drugs; he felt shame at this 'low point'. But a typical position, echoing the language of addicts, is the inability to break the habit. Typically giving up and stepping out is tougher than stepping in – or sliding, plunging or drifting in. Ryan of Five Squad says, 'I should have had the backbone to duck out but I didn't; there was no way out and I was into drug abuse myself.' Leuci admits he was 'shaking hands with the devil' but 'the indefensible horror was that I was not brainless. I knew better, but weak as it may sound, I didn't seem able to help myself' (Leuci 2004: 232). Some cops become literally addicted. Drury in the SERCS had a serious drug habit; Hund in Philadelphia used the money from corruption for alcohol, took to 'snorting coke' and became addicted to gambling. Some become effectively 'addicted' to the lifestyle and identity associated with corruption and became trapped in the 'sneaky thrills', the web of constant deceit and 'living the lie' (Katz 1988; Cohen 2001: 155). Police corruption can become a form of personal and group addiction.

Rationalisations, justifications and motives

Of all people, a police officer must know what is illegal; in all the accounts, the officers state that they knew the corrupt acts were wrong. In their moral perspective how, then, do they justify and rationalise their behaviour? Corrupt cops use a range of rationalisations, sometimes couched in euphemisms. For instance, the money taken was a form of 'compensation' for taking risks as a cop; it was for 'expenses' or 'lunch money', stealing from drug-dealers was justified because they would be out on bail and dealing again in no time (Daley 1979: 280). Giuliani (then DA in New York) related their justifications to their views on the police organisation and justice system:

> There was weak leadership; you need to be able to respect your bosses; when they lose that respect it becomes another excuse. 'The bosses didn't know what they were doing,' or 'they don't care' or maybe 'they're getting something themselves.' When there is judicial corruption that undermines their determination; they think 'why shouldn't I?' You see a form of alienation – 'one, we put our lives at risk, two, we are not appreciated, three, we get little support from the administration and politics.' (*Bad Cops*, 1993)

Another rationalisation was the claim that they were achieving what the justice system was incapable of doing, 'fining' the dealers by confiscating their money and drugs and 'deporting' the South Americans (Daley 1979: 70). This justified the daring, imaginative but illegal means that the SIU used for 'putting bad people in jail' or expelling them. Putnam in the SERCS even maintained that *everyone* benefited, including the victim; 'everyone gained all round' because the squad achieved arrests and kudos, the informant received reward money, while even the dealer, who had lost his freedom and some of his drugs, was 'not too unhappy because he got less time in prison and wasn't going to scream' (he means the sentence is related to the amount of drugs involved; BBC 2000). These views fit in the 'vocabulary of motive' framework which maintains that deviants use a repertoire of explanations as rhetorical devices to weaken social control before the act – 'neutralisation' – and to deflect blame after the act by justifications and rationalisations (Sykes and Matza 1957; Cohen 2001).

There is *denial of responsibility*. Generally the justifying explanations are focused on group, work and organisational pressures. Officers talk of not being able to say no because that was the way work was done, everyone was doing it, you had to go along if you wanted to fit in and the bosses wanted results. There is *denial of injury*. With some corruption the attitude is 'it hurts no one, everyone benefits, it's easy money, you'd be stupid not to take it'. The 'shakedown' may be redefined as morally neutral. When Leuci and another detective 'touched' two dealers by telling them they were 'short', they argued it wasn't a shakedown or a bribe; the sums were 'offered' and not extorted; they were not being asked to do anything in exchange; so it was 'like a loan they don't have to pay back' (Daley 1979: 195). There is *denial of the victim*. By negative stereotyping the police create categories of those who 'deserve' to be ripped off or who have 'earned' being set up. This was the case with the 'IRA suspects' in the miscarriage cases in Britain when there was public outrage and the police felt justified in 'fitting up' these ostensibly violent terrorists. In New York the narcotics detectives hated the street dealers and the SIU members despised the South America drug barons. This stereotyping makes it much easier to justify abusing the rights of the victim and/or ripping them off. There is *condemnation of the condemners*. When exposed as corrupt, bent officers tend to counter-attack with criticisms of failures in the organisation, among senior officers, in the integrity of the investigation against them (use of illegal methods by the controllers), in the hypocrisy in the criminal justice system and of double standards in the wider society. They take the scapegoat role by arguing that special investigations are always focused on them but that funding and/or political will seems to evaporate when higher level actors – such as lawyers, judges and politicians – are in danger of exposure. There is the *appeal to higher loyalties*. The 'noble cause' defence effectively says good ends justify dodgy means. Noble cause may have emotional and occupational validity in certain situations for the officers concerned but this may all too easily lead to dilution and to using it when it is inappropriate with vulnerable and innocent suspects. Another appeal to loyalty relates to the solidarity of comradeship in asserting that it was done not for individual gain but to support colleagues; the bonds of friendship and the obligation were so strong the officer could not refuse to go along with a close colleague (Kleinig 1996: 67).

No way back; nowhere to go

I was tiptoeing through my days on a thin wire, a circus stunt, and constantly just this side of catastrophe ... *I didn't see any way out.*
(Leuci 2004: 233, 243, my emphasis)

Some of the police groups examined had become effectively full-time deviants (Alex 1976: 93). Part of the psychology of the slope, moreover, is that the person slides past the psychological point of no return and feels there is no way back. And as Putnam says, there was nowhere to turn and no one he trusted inside the organisation. Family relations tended to suffer with the abuse of spouses and the break-up of marriages. Some officers talk of the deviancy as 'frenzy', 'mushrooming' and getting 'out of hand'; Perez of the LAPD Rampart scandal speaks of an 'orgy' of corruption.

Getting out can be related to distrust and disillusion. Some crew members take more than their share of the takings; Clark was taking money and drugs and keeping them for himself. The Australian cop Haken lost his attachment to bent colleagues when one had an affair with his wife: 'that broke my belief in the brotherhood' (ABC 2005). In Chicago one of several cops in custody steadfastly remained silent but decided to talk when other cops ripped off a raffle to support the arrested cops' families: 'the goddam scum. I can't believe it' (Beigel and Beigel 1977: 171). There must, too, be stress and pressure, of constantly playing a deviant role and continually covering up. Yet officers also report a sense of invincibility, of being too smart to get caught and of feeling safe behind the wall of silence. They become overconfident and start to make mistakes or to leave a trail. In Philadelphia it never occurred to Ryan that he might get caught: 'we were too slick'. Putnam was the same: 'We felt we were untouchable and no one was going to touch us, no one was going to find out we were stealing' (BBC 2000).

Police as victims

Although they may attract little sympathy, corrupt cops can also be seen as victims and they often picture themselves as such. At one stage an SIU colleague of Leuci laments, 'Why does everyone hate cops? Why do they turn on us? Why do they persecute us?' (Daley 1979: 278). Clearly it is a considerable humiliation to be arrested by fellow officers; in the US the suspect is often filmed or photographed coming out of his home and the publicity will mean that his family and children are asked embarrassing questions at work and school. There follows being processed as a criminal suspect, having the badge and weapon confiscated, one's locker and home searched with the family present, the interrogation (but now on the other side of the table), trial and possibly a prison sentence where they are typically given a rough time by fellow prisoners (perhaps by some that they have locked up themselves). They have gone through the cycle of joining the police, becoming a good officer, entering corruption and being labelled as a criminal. Apart from the obdurate hardliners they all say they regret it; they regret the suffering caused to their families; and they regret that they were once proud to be a police officer and ended up in prison. But they regret one thing above all.

Exclusion

Corrupt cops who have been caught are then banished as pariahs from the profession they always wanted to belong to, and also from the 'brotherhood'. Putnam says that getting into corruption meant a 'few years of madness that wrecked everything' because he loved 'the job' and misses it 'every day'. Like many people who once had power and are stripped of it, Putnam looks rather forlorn if not pathetic in the documentary. Ryan described the humiliation of arrest, of exposure in the media (a photograph of him in handcuffs appeared in the newspapers), of the impact on his children, and on having to go to jail with 'criminals' and the pain of being visited there by his family at Christmas. When his children at school were shown an article about him it was 'terrible' and 'shameful'.

> At the moment of your arrest it hits you, your world falls in; it's devastating, your reputation is gone, your parents took pride in you. These were high profile cases and there were photos of the arrest in the newspapers and you were taken out in front of your neighbors. It was terrible when I had to tell my family, the sorrow I felt in having to say goodbye to my wife and kids when I went to prison, and then the shame of being inside with criminals. (*Bad Cops*, 1993)

He was proud to become a police officer when he first put on his uniform and badge; but instead of celebrating 20 years as a cop he was doing time in prison; 'there were no winners, and the family loses; there was guilt, shame, remorse and pain that I put the family through this' (*Bad Cops*, 1993). Some have failed marriages, no longer see their children, are alienated from their parents, have no home and are nearly destitute with dead-end jobs. Some of the 'collaborators' have broken lives but also live in constant fear of reprisals; as Haken says, deciding to rat has condemned him to a 'life sentence' of fear and hiding. He is like one of the *pentiti* who have broken the Mafia's code of silence, *omerta*; despite a new identity they live anxiously in the knowledge that one day the assassins may find them. Haken will never have a proper life again.

Finally, Hund says that above all he misses police work. Tearfully he states that he would go anywhere in the country to work as a cop. If offered the chance he would pack his bags immediately, work for the minimum wage, take the worst shifts and perform the most menial tasks. He would do anything just to be a police officer again.

183

Yet he knows he would never be accepted by other cops. Corrupt officers who are caught and sanctioned end up with the cruellest punishment of all; they are cast out of the police family and the police community. Through their deviant conduct they have excluded themselves from the one thing they always wanted to be and which came to dominate their lives and shape their identity – being a cop.

Conclusion

The material presented above reveals features of policing[17] that have been widely described in the literature. There is the importance of the primary group with a sense of fraternity, kinship and inclusion; this can extend to other cops with the feeling of membership in a club, caste or the powerful 'biggest gang in town'. The informal leader is important as are bonding rituals and group behaviour. And in policing there is often an almost idealistic start followed by erosion through sliding down the 'slope', starting small but accelerating. Engaging in deviance and corruption may be a prerequisite of membership, and the 'first time' is an initiation test. Many officers report difficulties when first clearly confronted with corruption or other forms of deviance but generally they felt they could not refuse. And once on the slope the deviant acts became progressively easier to accept.

The portraits above and elsewhere largely show men at work trying to make sense of a weird world of mixing with criminals and others, coming to arrangements with them, trying to gain results and coming up against dilemmas in terms of legal restrictions, ambivalences in the organisation and its leadership and deficiencies in the administration of justice – including bent lawyers, prosecutors and judges. This can lead to a feeling that they are involved in a dark and devious game but, if one is serious about getting results, it has to be played in earnest with the mega-rule that rules, confidence and trust will always be broken in a web of deceit and double-dealing. When cops take the 'game' too seriously, as a deadly competition where you have to come out on top, then they step onto the slide if not a roller coaster.

This can be exacerbated by the frustrating presence of the safely circulating 'birds', colleagues who are ritualistic drones[18] and bosses who are distant and timorous. This backcloth of sloth and indifference can help drive the motivated 'rate-buster' into seeking results by straight or devious means; the 'slackers' incite the 'adrenaline junkies'

(Collins 2008: 379). The eager cops want to see results for their efforts and seek that by diverse means, fair and foul. The reason for getting themselves into trouble, some other cops say, lies ironically in taking policing too seriously. The old timers' advice to newcomers amounted to 'keep your mouth shut, look the other way, and collect your pension'; the rules of survival were to 'bend, don't take risks and do nothing'; and it was important to internalise 'that this police thing is not real' (Sorrentino 1980: 196).

There is a range of adaptations in terms of the sorts of crimes and criminals dealt with and the corrupt practices that emerge, from the pad to the 'score'. There does appear to be a tendency in the drugs area to commence with a combative strategy but then – faced with the temptation of large amounts of money and drugs with cunning criminals who are difficult to catch – to shift to predatory corruption. Both the SIU in New York and the SERCS in London had moved on to predatory style.

Both Leuci and Putnam started as motivated and clean cops who became bent in special units; they were both deeply corrupt and admit it; Putnam said: 'I was in it up to my neck' (BBC 2000). In common with other deviants they had to rationalise and find motives for breaking the law to salve their consciences because they knew it was wrong. Leuci (2004: 226) articulated how he did that: 'There was no denying I had been corrupted, but I also believed that I was basically a good person, and I thought of myself as a good cop. Incredibly, I had managed to convince myself that somehow I could be all three.' They were both able to rationalise it, with Putnam believing that 'everyone benefited', including the victim!

But neither was into violence. They were corrupt and criminal but different social animals from the hard-core, rogue cops who indulge in an orgy of corruption and rob, beat up, rip off and even murder people, sometimes almost at random and gratuitously. These are criminal cops who function like ferocious orca whales or a predatory pack of hyenas in a frenzy of violence; as with the military in the 'fog of war', the group becomes almost out of control and seemingly incited by the very weakness and vulnerability of its opponents (Collins 2008: 402). This was evident with the LAPD Rampart cops and CRASH, the SOS in Boston and also with the Miami River cops. The 'seductions and compulsions' of action, hedonism and violence, and conforming to the 'ways of the badass', strongly reflect the similar pattern among criminals as graphically portrayed by Katz (1988). And the bent cops even come to mirror the crooks they are ostensibly combating.

This is patently not about harmless corruption and this book has shown there are victims and considerable harm. Criminals have been 'set up' quite illegally and been sentenced to crimes they did not commit; they have been subject to intimidation, violence and even death, at the hands either of officers or of criminals who are cooperating with the police. Officers have also engaged in robbery, burglary, car theft, blackmail, rape and other crimes. Innocent people have suffered extortion from police officers, and suspects who were innocent were deprived of their liberty for many years. Police corruption does, then, create victims; and not least in the sense of officers who are drawn in to corrupt practices by cynically manipulative colleagues who prey on their vulnerabilities. And there is, then, a range of harms: deprivation of property, loss of reputation, fear, humiliation, torture, invasion of privacy, loss of liberty and false imprisonment, physical injury and even death. A great deal of police effort may prove wasted when cases collapse because of the role of corrupt officers in them while forces may also face substantial damage claims. Revelations of corruption destroy the reputation of a police force, undermine the trust the public should have in the police (as happened in Sea Girt where the officers were figures of trust in the community), demoralise straight officers, humiliate the families of bent cops, and display that parts of the organisation were outside of formal control and unaccountable.

I focused on three cop 'careers': the 'straight' one, getting into corruption and stepping out of corruption. The latter has received little attention in the literature where the focus is mostly on 'becoming bent' (Sherman 1974c) rather than 'becoming unbent'. In a sense, then, corrupt cops can have a double-deviant career, first of undetected deviance and second, following detection. And that second stage also has a number of variations. There is no data on this phase of a deviant career after detection but what is clear is that detection, arrest, investigation, trial and prison are highly discomforting if not traumatic experiences for a cop. Often they are looked up to within the family; and if they are the breadwinner then the loss of income, much inflated by graft, and of their pension can be a severe financial blow for their family. They typically wrestle with guilt, shame, remorse and humiliation. Some seem to want to confess. And in cooperating, if it is not simply to save their skins, it may be to salve their consciences. Leuci did not have to cough; he was never caught and never prosecuted. But he took on a dangerous undercover assignment, spent years under protection and testifying in court against his former colleagues and put his family under a great deal of stress during witness protection. A colleague he respected greatly and a former partner both committed suicide; and he put many former colleagues into prison doing hard time.

He seems to be unable to accept the 'evilness' element in his conduct and is almost seeking redemption through penance for his sins.[19] Another explanation was that Leuci was hanging on to the police identity to which he was devoted; for some policing is almost an addiction or an 'incurable disease' (Punch 1985: 169). Instead of being cast out like the others he could continue in a role where he worked his informants and contacts as he had done in the SIU; except now he was 'wired'. It probably gave him a sense of continued importance as he was crucial to a substantial investigation; perhaps he was addicted to the true 'authenticity' of undercover work and enjoying its 'sneaky thrills' (Katz 1988).

Corrupt cops are deviants and criminals but, unlike other deviants and criminals, they are special because they are members of a law enforcement agency. They swore an oath to uphold the law and were often motivated and even excellent officers; becoming bent must, then, surely bring with it considerable mental effort to neutralise and justify engaging in crime and delving into evil and malice. They all say they knew it was wrong, but suppressed it or rationalised it. And they were all leading a double life, at work and at home, of constant deception. The crooks in the Mob rarely have such identity problems. As Leuci says to a prosecutor who feels compassion for bent cops under investigation, 'Don't you see? We're not criminals. We're policemen, and we can't cope with being criminals. When was the last time a Mafia guy committed suicide because he got into trouble. It isn't criminals who kill themselves, it's cops' (Daley 1979: 316–17). This is what makes cops such strange social animals; they have become in some sense criminals within policing but do not perceive themselves as such – until they are caught, and sometimes not even then. They are cast out of the police community but are usually not welcome in the criminal fraternity. This is what makes corrupt cops 'creatures in between'.

Notes

1 Someone who collaborated and has done time is the former NYPD cop, Officer Phillips, the star witness at the Knapp hearings. Some maintain he was set up in 1975 by fellow cops for an unsolved murder as a reprisal for 'ratting' and cooperating with Knapp. He has been in prison

for 33 years, is 77 years old, nearly blind and chronically sick. He has always maintained his innocence and has continued to appeal up to the Supreme Court, recently against negative parole decisions (*New York Magazine* 2007).

2 I attended a presentation in the UK by the Complaints Investigation Branch on this case and have discussed it with other anti-corruption officers; this topic is also dealt with in detail by McLagan (2004), who worked on several BBC documentaries into police corruption, and also by Gillard and Flynn (2004).

3 Made by Sidney Lumet who had earlier directed *Serpico*. Leuci has lectured and talked many times of his experiences to diverse audiences while his autobiography was written many years after the events; it sounds authentic and provides useful insights but he does employ some literary flourishes, while it is clearly a form of special pleading; it needs to be treated with the customary caution.

4 Hereafter in this section the quotes are from the transcript of the BBC TV *Panorama* programme *The Bent Cop*, broadcast on 3 December 2000; the transcript is available from the BBC World News: Panorama Archive.

5 One Philadelphia cop in the documentary says that if there was, say $10,000 at a bust, that the cops would take half and get the dealer to sign for the other half; if he protested they would threaten to go after his wife or children.

6 Leuci's first cousin was a captain in the Colombo Mafia family.

7 Cops referred to it as the Tuminaro case (Moore 1971).

8 They joked that they knew their partners better than the women in their lives; but Leuci speaks of a special 'love' for his partner that is stronger than that for his wife.

9 Of which he gave half to the sergeant; the golden rule was, 'always take care of the sergeant'.

10 In Hong Kong the saying is that you can get on the bus (corruption) and step off the bus; but what you must never do is stand in front of the bus (Manion 2004).

11 He later heard cops cheering and applauding as if a New York baseball team had won a trophy; news had reached them that Serpico had been shot.

12 A colleague, Aguiluz, was persuaded to talk and 'shopped' his two mates (they had been like 'brothers' to him) who had helped sell the five kilos held back from the French Connection case; Aguiluz pleaded guilty to tax fraud, received a suspended sentence, and was relocated but his two 'brothers' both got ten years (Daley 1979: 328).

13 The team were federal agents, not street-wise and not always quick to react; once he was stranded with two highly suspicious gangsters who were threatening to kill him if he was a 'snitch'; ironically another gangster appeared on the scene and vouched for him which may have saved his life; Leuci had helped him three years earlier to evade

having his parole revoked and now he returned the favour (Leuci 2004: 281).

14 There was panic in the prosecutor's team when a fourth incident emerged with an informant claiming that Leuci had accepted money from him. But the prosecutor declined to indict him and the judge accepted the offence as 'collateral' to the other offences (Daley 1979: 326).

15 In contrast, some undetected officers might be quite unrepentant; and perhaps still be involved in crime as serving officers or as ex-cops (as has happened in London). They might admit, and even regret, their wrongdoing informally but might state firmly that they simply could never have informed on their mates.

16 Hund and Ryan were detectives in 'Five Squad' in Philadelphia: this was an elite, anti-crime unit that enjoyed high autonomy; at first it produced good work and its members were highly motivated to catch crooks. Hund was 'shopped' to the FBI by his ex-wife following their divorce; at first he discussed murdering her with his fellow bent cops so she couldn't testify but then he too agreed to wear a wire. Six of his colleagues were convicted as a result.

17 And which also apply to varying extents to other predominantly male groups.

18 Like an 'Olympic Torch' because he 'never goes out' or a 'Gurkha' because 'he never takes prisoners'.

19 Putnam had turned to religion and became a born-again Christian.

Chapter 7

Scandal, reform and accountability

> Accountability should run through the bloodstream of the whole body of a police service and it is at least as much a matter of the culture and ethos of the service as it is of ... institutional mechanisms.
>
> (Patten Commission 1999: 22)

The police have been under constant critical scrutiny for some 40 years in the UK, US, the Netherlands and elsewhere, while there have been persistent demands for change. Yet the material presented here indicates that deviance and corruption are endemic in policing; is the conclusion then that this problem is unsolvable? For there is also evidence of police organisations reforming, of police chiefs 'cleaning up' departments and of governmental efforts to enhance accountability. Police reform is perhaps not solely a matter of pessimism.

It is evident, however, that some reforms are short-lived and that corruption returns, sometimes in new forms. Indeed, countries with a record of corruption, or non-corruption, remain so for long periods and change, if any, is gradual (Manion 2004: 11). Regarding Hong Kong, in contrast, it is generally held that the Independent Commission Against Corruption (ICAC), founded in 1974, has been highly successful at tackling ingrained corruption in policing and politics and did so fairly swiftly. This is a major success because there was endemic corruption in Hong Kong, and there still is on mainland China, yet the ICAC has had a significant and lasting impact (Wing Lo 1993).[1] It did face opposition, from the police and the business community, but it has definitely influenced standards of integrity in public life. It did so by a 'three-pronged strategy: enforcement to investigate corruption and prosecute the corrupt, education to mobilize the citizens to report corruption ... and institutional design to reduce opportunities for corruption in the organisation of work' (Manion 2004: 26). In Australia, however, there have been a number of substantial scandals revealing extensive corruption; these were sometimes followed by Royal Commissions and intense efforts at reform; but almost within months some of the corrupt practices had returned (Voyez 1999). The New South Wales (NSW) Police, for instance, experienced ten years of reform and congratulated itself on developing 'professional, accountable, responsible and innovative' officers; but the Wood Royal Commission 'delivered a damning judgement on these attempted reforms; they were uncoordinated, ill-informed, superficial and ineffective' (Dixon 1999d: 144). Also the reform campaign was said to have prematurely withered when political and media pressure on crime control intervened, with a reversion to 'business as usual'.[2] Walker (2005) reports a similar process in the US, of resilient deviance rapidly resurfacing after efforts to reform police departments. Perhaps police reform is like the Procession of Echternach (Luxembourg), which is two steps forward and one step back; except with policing the number of steps forward, and especially the number backwards, is variable.

In this chapter I examine the dynamic of scandal and reform and the changing nature of police accountability. For me and others accountability in policing is essential; without accountability there is no legitimacy and without legitimacy the police cannot function in a democratic society. This remains true even if a depressing number of police organisations have patently endeavoured to avoid responsibility and evade accountability.

A major theme has been that deviance, corruption and crime in policing is ignored, tolerated or encouraged in bad and sometimes 'dirty' organisations. Another important element was to take the interactionist perspective, and concept of moral career, to trace how good people become bad cops through exposure to dirty work. But if the wider environment and/or the organisation itself are dirty, deeply devious and consistently corrupt, or they sponsor dirty means for gaining espoused ends, then the 'dirt' is institutionalised. In turn this implies that an anti-corruption campaign focused on symptoms and 'bad apples' that does not also seek significant institutional reform will achieve little durability.

For instance, in many accounts police organisations come across as 'dysfunctional,' combining the worst features of bureaucratic and military institutions. When in the 1970s Mark (1978: 97) joined the Met, he encountered an organisation where departments functioned as independent islands; there was no coordination, no 'corporate identity', and 'policy meetings' were a farce as everyone battled solely for their own unit. A Met officer remarked, 'rivalry sometimes reached the heights of idiocy' (Punch 1985: 63). Previously we have seen graphic examples of poorly functioning forces in the US, UK and the Netherlands. The Mollen Report's message, moreover, was that the functioning of the NYPD made effective internal control almost impossible; a conspiracy of incompetence generated dramatic failure. A study of corruption in Philadelphia reported that the police department was 'unfocused, unmanaged, under-trained, under-equipped and unaccountable' (Dombrink 1988: 210). Continual exposés of corruption reveal major deficiencies at the leadership, managerial and accountability levels. This can foster among the 'troops' disillusion, demoralisation and cynicism; they encounter capricious leadership, arbitrary punishment, poor personnel policies, lack of resources, favouritism and no reward for good police work (Moskos 2008: 22). Cops may constantly be told informally that they must 'bend, ignore or violate laws and rules' and this institutional double-speak then aids in justifying their own rule-breaking (Goldstein 1977: 200). And Rubinstein (1973: 419) writes that the 'real cost' of graft is the 'degradation of the job, the destruction of morale, the erosion of discipline and supervision, and the breakdown of clear standards of what constitutes "good work" which allows some policemen to become criminals in every sense of the word.'

The point is simply to indicate that institutional variables – including leadership, resources, recruitment, training, standards, supervision, morale, control mechanisms, relations with the environment, and willingness to admit mistakes – influence the organisation regarding deviance, corruption and crime. The nature and extent of corruption will vary but on occasion one can speak of 'deviant' organisations. The bleakness of much of the material, historical and recent, does induce a measure of pessimism; but there have been successful reforms, as Sherman (1978) demonstrated for the US.

Scandal and reform

There have been examples of reforming chiefs who 'cleaned up' police departments hit by scandal. They sound remarkably similar in character, with Murphy in New York and Mark in London as prototypes. Both displayed steely determination in tackling the organisation and its deviants; they displayed courageous leadership, demanded accountability from senior officers, put resources into internal control, took a number of measures such as circulating personnel and altering the opportunity structure and above all showed ruthlessness in ridding the organisation of bent cops.[3] In the US there has been a series of successful reform chiefs, with the legendary O.W. Wilson having a major impact even on the notorious Chicago Police Department. Wilson was a criminologist and influential thinker on policing; Mayor Daley expediently needed a clean outsider following a police scandal and granted him independence; in seven years (1960–67) he turned the department around, removing most of the crass corruption, enhancing the rights of minorities, thoroughly modernising the force and attracting much respect (Rokyo 1971: 115, 155). Clearly, firm leadership with personal integrity can make a significant difference, if only for a time.

Reforming chiefs usually have to accept that they are disliked, if not hated, by their personnel who see them as moral zealots divorced from the daily realities of policing.[4] They frequently face opposition and resistance and have to be paragons to avoid counter-accusations if they or their acolytes stray from virtue.[5] Wilson was a strict disciplinarian, totally unlike the stereotypical Chicago cop, and 'always maintained that a police officer should not be allowed to accept any gratuity, not even a free cup of tea'. And Murphy stated: 'Except for your pay-check, there is no such thing as a clean buck' (Goldstein 1977: 201). It is debatable as to whether these are realistic and enforceable policies, or even socially desirable (refusing a cup of tea?), or maybe they are rhetorical devices. The reforming chief perhaps needs a one-liner or symbolic act to convey his message on integrity, that the rules have changed and he will personally enforce them. The reform chief in Oakland (California) publicly scorned the traditional presents at his inauguration; and he addressed recruits with just two sentences: 'Gentlemen (sic), welcome to the Oakland Police Department. If you do anything wrong, I shall personally escort you to the gates of San Quentin.' His bluntness was enhanced by the fact that several former Oakland cops were then residing in the prison (Sherman 1978: 111). However, many chiefs must realise that their reforms probably will not last long after their departure.

Sherman (1978) has drawn attention to this dynamic in his research on 'scandal and reform'. He examines four cases of scandal, following which three police departments were successfully reformed while in the fourth reform failed. He views scandal both as a socially constructed phenomenon[6] and as an agent of change leading to realignments in the structure of power in organisations. Sherman uses the concept of organisational deviance where police departments adopt deviant means or goals or where they have been 'captured' by external stakeholders. In three of the cities criminals could purchase complete immunity; the deviancy had become effectively a 'shadow' organisational goal inverting the formal one of impartial law enforcement.

Scandal may elicit a crisis and open debate about leadership, the direction to be taken and institutional survival. Factions are likely to crystallise with disgruntled people looking outside and even inviting external control as a weapon in the internal power struggle. Scandal is largely a 'labelling' exercise around the extent of deviance with the 'apples, barrels, orchards' debate. Successful labelling normally depends on convincing evidence of a failure in internal control such as a cover-up, endorsement by high status figures to lend credence to the accusers or whistle-blowers and dramatisation of the scandal (Sherman 1978: 60–6). Examples of the latter are Serpico and Durk, the *New York Times* articles and the televised hearings of the Knapp Commission, *The Times* photos and audiotapes in London or news of a Chicago cop vacationing with a Mob 'godfather' (Rokyo 1971: 105). For the media a 'good' scandal reaches to high levels within and beyond the organisation with resignations, has momentum through fresh revelations with widespread practices, generates juicy leaks, forces embarrassing admissions after denials and can be personified by a whistle-blower or by victims who have suffered grievously and unjustly.

'Reform' typically conveys that heads will roll, with chiefs and senior personnel replaced or moved, new styles of control will be implemented, opportunity structures and enforcement patterns will be altered and that new values will be propagated as reassurance that the organisation has genuinely put its house in order. Sherman (1978: 242) states that corruption may be 'impossible to eliminate entirely' but in Newburgh, New York and Oakland in the 1970s there was significant reform. In 'Central City' reform was unsuccessful. The key was the extent to which the dominant coalition mobilised support either for or against reform. However, there is no guarantee of permanence and Sherman's (1978: 263) message is that organisations will have to learn to *control themselves*. For the lessons from scandals is exposure of a blatant failure of control: 'The dominant coalition's failure to control the deviance is perhaps the most damaging kind of fact, because it raises the critical question of resources for control; if the organisation does not control the conduct of its members, who will?' (Sherman 1978: 25).

Sherman provided the earliest analysis of what transpires inside police organisations gripped by scandal. But his cases are 'local', relating to four unrelated city jurisdictions in a society with no police 'system'. Patterns of reform vary in diverse societies and this relates to politics, power structures, the media and the manner in which policing is organised. Compared to the US, for example, most Western European police systems are highly centralised with the state playing an important role in reform, or lack of it (Mawby 1999). Furthermore, the American-style crusade of 'sound and fury' (Reisman 1979), related to adversarial politics with periodic regime changes, tends to foster ritual 'house-cleaning' with large-scale firing and hiring as the incumbent party engages in swift damage limitation. This is less evident in Europe partly because of different styles of exercising politics, as in coalition administrations, and partly because of the security of tenure of police personnel. Amsterdam in the 1970s, for instance, was a case of scandal but no direct reform because of political, cultural and institutional reasons. Also in America there have been special commissions, with investigatory powers linked to prosecution, whereas in Europe there have more often been policy-advising governmental commissions making recommendations on legislation and procedures at the system level. This has certainly been the case in the UK.

Police accountability in the UK

Defining accountability

The architecture of policing has altered rapidly in the UK and elsewhere in recent years (Bayley and Shearing 2001); if anything the pace of change is only likely to accelerate. This cannot but have profound implications for accountability. The British police traditionally enjoyed considerable autonomy: under the 'tripartite' system formalised in the 1964 Police Act, accountability ran through the police chief, the local Police Authority and the Home Office (except in the Met which came directly under the Home Secretary). Importantly, the chief and his personnel were held to be answerable to the courts rather than directly to the government. But a chief officer told me, 'accountability simply wasn't on the agenda 20 years ago'.

Then the Conservative governments of Margaret Thatcher and her successors launched a sustained assault on public services including the police during their near 20 years in office (1979–97). This 'maelstrom' of reform drew from the ideas and practices of New Public Management or 'NPM' (Leishman *et al.* 1966), but it also represented a substantial shift to central direction of policing. There has been no respite under the Labour governments since 1997 and the Home Office and other agencies, including the Cabinet Office, have harassed the police organisation mercilessly to alter its structure, culture, performance styles and modes of accountability. There is no doubt but that this wave of reform is being driven from the centre, that the government is exerting increasing control and that many traditional assumptions about British policing are no longer valid. Williamson (2006) argues that the tripartite system has faded while a 'paradigm shift' has occurred. 'Legislation has concentrated power in the Home Secretary who sets the National Policing Plan and specifies the outcomes. In this new public management paradigm Chief Constables have an executive function only, which is to deliver against the plan. They are expected to aspire to nothing more grandiose than to producing the prescribed outcomes.'

Viewing how police themselves have reacted to these pressures we can discern three broad phases. First the 1970s and 1980s saw attention to operational 'command-and-control' issues relating to weaknesses in coping with new challenges from Irish terrorism, public order situations, major investigations and a series of disasters. Parallel to this largely internal shift was escalating concern about police misuse of power as several forces had been exposed in corruption scandals or miscarriage of justice cases (as illustrated in Chapter 5). Then, in the 1990s, the police were powerfully influenced by NPM and 'managerial' accountability regarding financial efficiency, targets and performance. The previous elements are still pertinent; but they shade into the current phase of radical transformation to a multilevel structure with plural and third-party policing and the formation of new national agencies such as the Serious Organised Crime Agency or SOCA (Bayley and Shearing 2001; Cramphorn 2006). These substantial shifts have fostered a new generation of police chiefs imbued with the 'new professionalism' of intelligence disciplines, focused leadership, performance and reward culture and of partnerships (O'Connor 2005). These top cops are geared to waves of change, the media, government fads and fashions and take constant accountability to stakeholders as an essential if time-consuming function (Blair 2003).[7]

These latest developments make accountability complex if not intricate, multi-layered, shifting and potentially opaque. Chan has remarked that the modern state is 'deeply ambivalent' about police accountability (1999: 267); and McLaughlin notes: 'What was notable by its absence during the First New Labour administration was any form of principled discussion about the forms of democratically constituted accountability and governance appropriate to the radically altered policing environment of 21st century Britain' (2005: 477). Here I examine accountability primarily in relation to deviance and critical incidents, internal control and organisational policies. Internal operational accountability is paramount; on its foundations rest the other forms of accountability. Policing, even in well-run forces, always carries with it the chance of mistakes and scandal, but serious risk is clearly amplified in large-scale incidents involving public order situations, major sporting or entertainment events, complex sieges, the use of firearms at a crime in progress or a set-piece operation or in coping with a major disaster.

For instance the British police system has developed a structure of 'command and control' which is widely used in major incidents. It is based on three levels of command: 'Gold' (strategic), 'Silver' (operational) and 'Bronze' (implementation); and it is intended to keep the levels separate during incidents. But it is also an accountability structure. Gold has a monitoring function and not only facilitates Silver's decision-making but also monitors it. There is an incident file that is meant to contain all correspondence, briefings (on videotape), appointments, radio traffic and logs of telephone calls and such like (Punch and Markham 2000). In principle there should be complete transparency on decision-making. For instance, the ultimate power of the police is employing fatal force and there simply have to be clear and unambiguous mechanisms of accountability surrounding the use of firearms.[8]

But there is an important principle encapsulated in this model; it draws accountability *upwards*. Gold devolves responsibility while accepting final accountability. In theory a force faced by critical scrutiny after an incident can confidently hand over a complete file saying, 'do you have any questions because we have the answers?' And potentially Gold can face legal action for operational decisions.[9] 'In theory', concerns organisational structure; but the model also assumes a *culture of accountability* where senior officers are imbued with an ethic of accountability as fundamental to their functioning and where there is institutional compliance. Structure is not enough; a police force has to *want* to be accountable.

This is vital because next to genuine mistakes and errors of judgement there are sensitive aspects of policing involving deception, intrusion, civil and human rights and invasion of privacy as well as matters related to excessive use of force, racial and sexual discrimination, corruption and perversion of justice where issues of personal, organisational responsibility and criminal culpability arise (Kleinig 1996; Reiner 2000). And evidently there have been serious organisational failures with police forces evading internal accountability (Grabosky 1989). In essence, I am reiterating the literature's persistent message, that policing is a hazardous, unpredictable and risky enterprise, that this needs to be recognised and that the organisation has to anticipate and institutionalise its response to critical incidents. Indeed, the nature of the police organisation's response to dealing with trouble and its repercussions is often as crucial as the nature of the original incident to determining the legitimacy and credibility of the police in the eyes of the public.

There must be clarity on these issues because contemporary police chiefs have to cope with multiple oversight agencies in a complex network. There is an accountability 'flow-chart' for England and Wales in Neyroud (2004) which is baffling in its complexity and not unlike the London Underground map.[10] There are numerous agencies – of central and local government, new national bodies and local communities – with convoluted lines of accountability. Neyroud focuses on the consequences and ambivalences in this and argues that good policing means more than 'good performance' and that it requires 'a renewal of the contract between the police officer and the citizen which, in turn, requires greater openness and scrutiny, continuously improving professional standards and a new commitment to ethics at the core of policing' (2005: 11).

In brief, there is a shift to strengthening accountability with a stronger measure of external oversight through a battery of agencies and through community engagement. In addition, the police service itself has launched a process, particularly as a result of a number of shootings and critical incidents, of defining responsibilities in operations. What is difficult to establish is how far a new *culture* of accountability permeates policing in the UK. There are senior officers who strongly espouse this: but, if we take the Stockwell shooting as a test case, then the conduct of the Met belied that view. Anecdotal evidence from discussions with a number of senior officers indicates that there is a 'reform' movement in this area but, as yet, no unanimity on implementing it.

The dictionary definition of accountability is 'the quality or state of being accountable: *especially* an obligation or willingness to accept responsibility or to account for one's actions'. In totalitarian regimes accountability is then plainly absent; the authorities act in an arbitrary and illegal fashion with no fear of being called to account. There is no democratic or judicial redress in the face of the absolute and capricious exercise of power by control agencies. In contrast, the police organisation is primarily accountable on two main fronts in western democratic societies. One is *politically* to other democratic institutions, and the other is *legally*, to the law and the courts.

Furthermore, next to these fundamental and overriding commitments the police can be said to be accountable to the following agencies with varying levels of obligation:

- *Central and local government*, for efficient management and for a healthy and transparent financial and budgetary administration. In Britain there is the inspectorate role of the Audit Commission and the HMIC with the Treasury more recently also having a substantial impact. The rise of NPM had indisputably led to an escalating emphasis on managerial accountability (Morgan and Newburn 1997).

- *Permanent parliamentary commissions*, to specific judicial and public commissions of inquiry and to Royal Commissions.

- *External independent commissions* on complaints and possible abuses of power (for example IPCC or OPONI). Police can be held to account to external stakeholders with respect of internal controls, inquiries and investigations, complaints procedures and transparency on specific complaints.

- *Civil liberties and human rights groups* and other monitoring agencies, including delegations of foreign politicians and officials (as is common in Northern Ireland).

- *The media*, providing regular information, holding briefings and mounting press conferences, which are now held to be routine and essential features of giving information and accounts in the public arena.

- *Last but not least, the public and communities*. British policing was traditionally geared to 'policing by consent' and this was reiterated by Mark (1977) and by Scarman (1981). This implies a contract of trust and communication between police and the public with the police representing an *essentially benign and accountable force* in the community. This feature has been amplified recently by the adoption of diverse forms of neighbourhood-oriented policing with some seeing this as a move from consent to 'active cooperation'[11] (McLaughlin 2005: 482).

This theme of public accountability was reiterated in the reform process in Northern Ireland, where the police were held to have lacked consent in parts of the divided community:

> In a democracy, policing, in order to be effective, must be based on consent across the community. The community recognises the legitimacy of the policing task, confers authority on police personnel in carrying out their role in policing and actively supports them. Consent is not unconditional, but depends on proper accountability, and the police should be accountable in two senses – the 'subordinate or obedient' sense and the 'explanatory and cooperative' sense. (Patten Commission: 1999: 22)

Interestingly, Marshall (1978) argues that British policing was initially shaped in the 'subordinate or obedient' style but shifted in the twentieth century more to the 'explanatory and cooperative' mode with the chief constable, and indeed any constable, viewed as an independent law officer answerable directly to the courts, a servant of no one and ostensibly immune to being given direct operational orders. This power was jealously guarded with chiefs becoming almost unassailable. Indeed, Mark retired early because of his opposition to increased lay involvement in complaints which would have diminished the chief's authority on discipline. The balance has shifted back to the 'subordinate or obedient' sense in recent decades.

In brief, accountability is a broad and diffuse concept related to formal obligations within a democracy; notions of good governance; of being transparent to the public and other stakeholders on policies and conduct; and of internally generated norms of professional accountability. For Bovens it's a 'Sunday' concept based on well-intended Sabbath rhetoric while on Monday there's a reversion to 'business as usual' (1998: 22). It is also a 'chameleon' concept with many sorts of accountability. But principally we can distinguish the following:

• democratic and political accountability
• legal accountability
• internal operational and policy accountability
• managerial accountability
• and community accountability (Bowling and Foster 2002; Neyroud 2005).

In the UK there have been several significant institutional changes and alterations in the policing environment in recent decades. It does seem, for example, that the PSNI has made a major effort at a paradigm shift in adopting a human rights approach and showing compliance relating to a bevy of oversight agencies but especially to OPONI (Punch and Wood 2004). These changes may well reflect the new, glossy official paradigm but the more the police espouse this then the more glaring is the discrepancy if the institution or officers within it are exposed for excessive force, discrimination, taking bribes or lying in court.

Generally there has also developed a more open attitude to the sensitive topic of corruption. In the early 1990s, for example, Commissioner Condon of the Met mounted a campaign against corruption. And for the first time he and other senior officers discussed openly its existence, referring to 'noble cause' corruption and the use of force and intimidation as common during their earlier careers in policing (Rose 1996). Furthermore, HMIC issued what is known as a 'Thematic Report' entitled *Police Integrity* (1999) and ACPO launched a *Presidential Task Force on Corruption* (1998). The HMIC Report was driven by falling levels of public confidence in the police and it linked integrity to this. It was less about corruption as such but more about standards of conduct and the need for supervisors and police leaders to set an example and to intervene when they see unacceptable behaviour. It stressed leadership, sound managerial practices and facing up to misconduct, arrogance, harassment of fellow officers, racial and sexual discrimination, 'grass-eating' and corruption. It itemised all the forces and their officers who had been suspended, disciplined or convicted of crimes (HMIC 1999: 88–94).

One way of viewing this shift in orientation is that the British police elite had moved from a law-and-order orientation, functioning in the political arena as an 'overt pressure group', to being 'Scarmanised' (Reiner 1997: 1002). This meant that its members had imbibed the twin lessons of Lord Scarman's Report (1981) on the Brixton riots in which he argued for 'policing by consent' matched with enhanced 'accountability'. Shaping this move was a 'deep sense of crisis' with the traditional public acceptance of the police being eroded and with the police facing 'acute controversy and conflict: corruption and miscarriage of justice scandals; accusations of race and sex discrimination; increasing public disorder and the militarisation of police tactics ... rising crime and an apparently declining police ability to cope with it; decreasing public accountability as forces have grown larger, more centralised and more reliant on technology' (Reiner 1997: 1036).

But developments in policing are rarely unilinear and undisputed; the police elite may have been taking bold strides towards Echternach (the religious procession in Luxembourg with two steps forward and one back) but the government, the populist media and segments of public opinion were demanding that it step several paces 'backwards'. The Conservatives began to demand that the police focus on the core business of 'catching crooks' and bringing down crime; the performance culture and value for money were born (Reiner 2007). I merely wish to indicate that police agencies can be subject to competing demands and pressures. One given in organisational and policy research is that all change has unanticipated consequences; another is that people in organisations will react to a performance culture by a number of strategies, including cutting corners and manipulating the data. One example of mixed messages, contradictory pressures and distortions generated by policy emerges from the HMIC 'Thematic Report' entitled *Police Integrity* (1999). It locates the origins of some forms of police deviance in the performance culture and pressure for results; for instance the guidelines on informants are broken routinely as are other rules in investigations. Yet it had been the HMIC itself that had harried the forces on the government's behalf to meet performance targets.

In short, reform and change in policing are not simple matters of cumulative and progressive improvements. All the glossy and professional rhetoric of official paradigms cannot disguise the fact that a corruption scandal, a poorly handled critical incident or a controversial fatal shooting can suddenly plunge a force into an institutional crisis. Indeed, the more convincing the official paradigm has become – stressing professionalism, integrity and accountability – the greater the discrepancy may be with the reality of the errors, negligence and failures exposed by the critical incident. To put it in a nutshell, accountability is not something an organisation can simply claim to possess; it is something the organisation satisfactorily *delivers* when called to account.

In dealing with accountability in the UK I touch on legislation, complaints, assertive internal control, an independent component in accountability through the IPCC, and the lessons of the clash between the Met Commissioner and the IPCC in relation to the Stockwell shooting.

Legislation

In contrast to Sherman's (1978) four portraits of 'local' reform in US policing, which were unrelated and somewhat staccato individual shake-ups, the dynamic of reform in the UK is different, with more emphasis on commissions and legislation having a system-wide impact. In Smith (2005), for example, the changes in police complaints in England and Wales during 40 years are attributed to several reform cycles characterised by mounting public concern, formal inquiries, the legislative process and implementation; and by the longevity of the reform process. There have been several Royal Commissions on policing and criminal justice. The Commission of 1959–62 brought about the Police Act 1964; the Commission on Criminal Procedure 1979–81 led to the Police and Criminal Evidence Act 1984 (PACE); and the Commission on Criminal Justice 1991–93 fostered the Police and Magistrates Court Act (1994). Much of this activity was related to the aftermath of scandal and fallout from critical incidents with attempts to limit and regulate police powers and to rectify deficiencies in the administration of justice. For instance, following the miscarriages of justice the Criminal Appeals Act 1995 set up the Criminal Cases Review Committee; the management of informants by the police was regulated by the Regulation of Investigatory Powers Act (RIPA) in 2002; and also in 2002 the Police Reform Act led to the founding of the IPCC.[12]

The last two decades have, then, witnessed a stream of commissions, legislation and directives on procedure cascading onto the police. There were four other pieces of legislation to be taken into account. The Human Rights Act 1998 brought a European dimension to accountability and limited the use of coercive and intrusive power; the Public Interest Disclosure Act 1998 gave more rights and protection to whistle-blowers; the Freedom of Information Act 2000 came into force for police forces from 2005; and from 1997 onwards the Labour administration was promising to legislate on 'corporate manslaughter' which would ostensibly have made it easier to convict organisations for manslaughter. In fact it was some time before the Corporate Manslaughter and Corporate Homicide Act was passed, in 2007, but importantly the police were not granted 'crown immunity'. This could mean that a death in custody or a death in a high-speed chase could lead to a prosecution of a police force for the new offence of 'corporate killing' related to management failure (Gobert 2008).

In short, there was a growing wave of laws and directives ostensibly steering the police to becoming more accountable and regulating their powers; but there remained an enduring concern about the police complaints issue, based on a sense of marginalisation among complainers and on the continued lack of independence in police investigations.

Complaints

A crucial debate, indeed more of a long-standing battle, has surrounded the issue of accountability in relation to citizens' complaints against the police (Goldsmith 1991). This has witnessed a shift from *internal accountability* in the hands of the police to *external accountability* in the hands of civilians with the commencement of the IPCC in 2004. That was 175 years after the formation of the New Police in 1829. In all that time the police organisation in Britain investigated itself. There was no external agency to investigate serious police misconduct, critical incidents or citizens' complaints: in certain cases one force investigated another force. Under the concept of 'constabulary independence' police chiefs enjoyed considerable operational autonomy and retained a monopoly over disciplining their personnel. This has long been a bone of contention as it goes against the basic principle that no agency should judge itself; and as we have seen, this principle was blatantly abused within the Met with the CID investigating its own crimes.

The move towards some form of external involvement in complaints can be traced to the 'Thurso' incident in Scotland in 1957. A young boy was mistreated by the police and a complaint was inadequately handled; this apparently minor incident nevertheless led to a parliamentary debate (Whitaker 1979: 63). Then in 1958 there was an altercation between a well-known actor (Brian Rix), a passer-by and a police officer relating to a motoring offence. Again this seemingly minor event raised the issue of police accountability; and following another parliamentary debate, the Home Secretary announced the setting up of a Royal Commission on the police resulting in the Police Act 1964. The Commission reviewed matters related to the structure and organisation of policing and these included accountability. But Reiner (2000: 60) comments that 'the commission's proposals on accountability and complaints ... were widely seen as vague, confused and contradictory'. A minority of the Commission's members were in favour of an independent agency to investigate the police and this became a recurrent theme in subsequent years.

It was echoed in the influential Scarman Report (1981: 113–14) into the Brixton disturbances:

> I have received considerable evidence of a lack of confidence in the impartiality and fairness of the procedure ... The chief criticisms centre on the fact that the police investigate themselves ... The existing system lacks a sufficiently convincing independent element ... It is clear to me that many will continue to criticise it so long as the investigation of complaints remains in police hands ... Unless and until there is a system for judging complaints against the police, which commands the support of the public, there will be no way in which the atmosphere of distrust and suspicion between the police and the community can be dispelled.

And even when an external agency was set up to investigate complaints against the police by the Police Act 1976, the Police Complaints Board (PCB), it was reactive and dependent on a complaint being lodged, on the police to conduct the investigation and to provide it with information, and it functioned on a case-by-case basis (Smith 2001). It was called 'toothless' by Alistair Logan, solicitor for the Guildford Four and the Maguire Seven, and 'not capable of dealing with determined police officers' (Royakkers 1997: 268). There were, too, constant criticisms of its successor, the Police Complaints Authority (PCA), which was a spin-off from PACE; it did have the right to supervise investigations and was involved in overseeing the investigation into the West Midlands Serious Crime Squad (Kaye 1991), but persistent questions were raised about its effectiveness and credibility. Chris Mullin MP said in 1993 that it was 'a complete waste of time as any honest member of the PCA will tell you privately. And it is one of the least effective institutions that exist. And indeed no solicitor these days who knows anything about police complaints would ever advise a client to take a case to the PCA. What you do is sue, that is the trend now' (Royakkers 1997: 268).

Embracing accountability increasingly makes economic sense for institutions in a changing, and increasingly, litigious society; as Mullins says, the trend is to sue. In fact, civil actions against the police have escalated rapidly in a growing 'claim-culture' (Bowling et al. 2004: 21):

In recent years the number and cost of civil actions against the police have mushroomed partly because of the ineffectiveness of the police complaints procedure but also because of fears about criminalisation or harassment if this route was taken ... In 1979, there were just seven cases against the Metropolitan Police with less than £2,000 in damages paid; in 1986, 126 cases, resulted in damages of £373,000 ... By 1996/7 the Metropolitan Police had reached a thousand threatened actions ... with damages amounting to nearly £4 million by 1999/2000 ... Nationally, claims against all police forces reached almost 6,000 in 1999–2000. Of these 1302 were settled and 65 gained damages totalling £4.5 million ... While the civil courts clearly represent a more appealing route for individual complainants it is questionable whether it can improve the fairness, effectiveness and probity of the police service. It is likely too that recent restrictions on the extent of damages and reforms of the complaints system will reduce the growth of civil actions.

Bowling and Foster (2002: 1018) also comment on complaints:

With the exception of those that have only recently been introduced, legal accountability mechanisms have been the subject of sustained criticism ... The police complaints process, seen as the 'touchstone' of police accountability, lacked public confidence in its impartiality and fairness in particular because the police investigate themselves ... Currently, the Police Complaints Authority 'supervises' police investigations of the most serious cases but has a very low substantiation rate. In the 1990s it was around two per cent, and of the substantiated cases, one in five resulted in criminal or disciplinary hearings ... As Lustgarten commented: 'either all those who do bother to complain are liars, or there is something wrong with the system.'

Research among complainants whose case was supervised by the PCA showed high levels of dissatisfaction while several British Social Attitudes Surveys during the 1990s showed that 'only three per cent of the public disagreed that the police should be investigated by an independent body' (Bowling et al. 2004: 20).

Adding to the groundswell of opinion building towards a genuinely independent element in complaints investigations was the impact of the Stephen Lawrence murder (Foster *et al.* 2005). Stephen Lawrence was a black teenager who was murdered by a gang of white youths in a racially motivated attack in London in 1993; for a number of reasons these youths were never convicted. An inquiry set up to look into the killing concluded that the investigation by the Metropolitan Police was 'marred by a combination of professional incompetence, *institutional racism* and a failure of leadership' (Macpherson 1999: 317, my emphasis). It also revealed mistakes in the initial response, in mobilising an investigation and in relations with the family; there were also suspicions of a corrupt relationship between a police officer and the father of one of the youths.[13] Stephen was a model citizen about to go to university and his parents were articulate and determined to seek justice; their plight when the offenders were publicly identified but not convicted attracted intense publicity and strong support from the new Labour government (in office since 1997). Importantly, Recommendation 58 of the Lawrence Inquiry was 'ensure that complaints against the police are independently investigated. Investigations of police officers by their own or another Police Service is widely regarded as unjust, and does not inspire public confidence' (Macpherson 1999: 333). What also emerged was that the incident was treated in isolation whereas a complaint procedure can also be a proactive device for raising critical issues about police policies and procedures. The inquiry and the highly negative label of institutional racism had a major impact on policing in London and beyond with regard to hate crimes and offences against young blacks and had a 'galvanic impact on the criminal justice system' (Bowling and Phillips 2003; Rock 2004: 409).

There were other agencies, some with a European dimension, calling for more independence in the complaints procedure. The European Committee for the Prevention of Torture concluded after visiting the UK that a 'fully fledged independent investigating agency' would have more credibility than the PCA; and in relation to a case before the European Court of Human Rights, the ruling was that the PCA was not sufficient under Article 13 of the European Convention on Human Rights. The Home Affairs Committee called for a feasibility study into an independent complaints procedure and Liberty, the human rights organisation, added its voice to the swelling demands to replace the PCA. KPMG (2000) was then asked to conduct a feasibility study on an independent agency and its report was fed into the deliberations leading to the Police Reform Act 2002.

Assertive internal control

A recurring theme in the literature is the frequent failure of internal control, as with Internal Affairs Departments (IAD, or sometimes Internal Affairs Bureau) in the US or Complaints and Discipline Departments in the UK (Kennison 2001). There are several reasons for this. Officers are generally reluctant to work in such units as they are usually despised and disparaged ('those bastards from IAD' or the 'Gestapo'), while the stigma adheres long after returning to conventional work. Assignment to the control area often went to the 'halt and lame' as the organisation did not want to 'waste' its good personnel; and the malfunctioning of these units could be related to insistent institutional signals not to 'rock the boat'. For example, Murphy revitalised the IAD in the NYPD in the 1970s yet two decades later it was being castigated for multiple failure by the Mollen Commission. A similar picture of waning effort emerges from London.

In the 1970s Mark set up A10 as the spearhead of internal investigations and it recruited top-rate officers determined to tackle corruption. He also formed a separate Anti-Corruption Unit to pursue the 'Porn Squad' and described its successful campaign as 'probably the best ever single piece of detective work' (Cox *et al.* 1977: 142). But in 1993 Ian Blair (1999: 4), the later Commissioner, became responsible for, among other departments, what had become the Complaints Investigation Branch (CIB) and found it a 'rude awakening'. CIB was a 'sleepy and inefficient hollow' that was no longer anything like the elite unit of the Mark era; the élan and the quality of personnel had evaporated.

But again the Met was confronted with some highly corrupt officers (Morton 1994) – in the mid-1990s the then Commissioner spoke of some 250 officers – and there emerged a new determination to rid the force of them. Commissioner Condon saw this as a 'crusade' and launched a 'Corruption and Dishonesty Prevention Strategy' in 1998. There would be no hiding place for bent cops in the Met. Condon stated:

> It would have been easier to have gone through my commissionership without opening this can of worms. I felt I owed it to the public and to the majority of good men and women in the Service to confront the problem. Police chiefs and politicians must continue to face up to the challenge. The battle against corruption needs to be constant and enduring, otherwise it will lose ground again. (HMIC 1999: 57)

The allegations related to officers in elite detective units stealing part of the proceeds of a robbery; seizing drugs from dealers and 'recycling' them; the complete reversal of the informant–handler relationship; accepting bribes for taking confidential data from the Police National Computer, with £5,000 mentioned for destroying evidence; planting weapons; carrying tools for burglary; and selling anything including the identity of an undercover officer (McLaglan 2004).

CIB1 dealt with discipline investigations and CIB2 was an internal proactive unit for serious offences. Then a special investigation unit, CIB3, was formed in 1994 and grew to some 250 officers by 1998; it was allocated top-grade detectives. Its first leader spoke of the 'country's best detectives' and of never having had a 'finer team'. Where an internal control unit is given substantial resources and a challenging mandate it is suddenly likely to be seen in a positive light and its officers can become highly motivated 'enforcement entrepreneurs' (Marx 1988); and CIB certainly attracted several high-flyers who went on to leading roles in policing or outside.[14] CIB3 adopted an aggressive strategy that viewed corrupt cops as organised criminals within the force and, as they were hardened and skilful opponents, tough measures were required to gather convincing evidence against them. Intelligence was crucial with a Complaints Investigations Intelligence Cell (CIBC) priming operations while the proactive methods included surveillance and 'bugging', criminal informants, and officers in deep undercover roles.[15] The highly secretive 'ghost squad' was housed outside of central London with operatives who had been removed from personnel records to make it difficult for bent cops to trace them. Integrity testing and 'sting' operations were also employed. For instance information was circulated about an apartment containing 80 kilograms of drugs; when bent detectives arrived to steal it, they were filmed by concealed cameras. Two of them 'rolled over' and became 'super-grasses', revealing some 80 names of fellow officers and others. It was felt that innovative measures were required because these bent detectives knew all the tricks and with smart lawyers were evading conviction. Having mentioned 250 officers the Commissioner was pursued by the media and criticised by the Federation about the low conviction rate. It emerged that CIB3 had secured only seven convictions in six years of which four were 'super-grasses' who had confessed and cooperated by incriminating others (*Guardian Unimited* 2000a; McLagan 2003).

One problem was that officers under suspicion were retiring early to evade investigation under disciplinary regulations. A critical report of the Home Affairs Committee chaired by Chris Mullin MP exposed how officers under suspicion subverted the system by exploiting loopholes aided by 'extremely skilful lawyers'. It found the willing ear of the Home Secretary Jack Straw who introduced several measures including fast-track disciplinary procedures, holding hearings even if the officer was absent having reported sick, and preventing officers charged with offences retiring on medical grounds with a pension.

One tactic of defence lawyers working for cops facing proceedings was to attack the integrity of the special unit. This raised the interesting issue, *who controls the controllers' controllers?* One CIB3 chief, Commander Hayman, said his unit was at the 'cutting-edge of policing' and he was keen 'to push the parameters' to outwit the targeted officers. But then the 'legally audacious' CIB3, which was clearly going through a steep learning curve, came under scrutiny for entrapment, inducements to super-grasses, non-disclosure and breaches of evidence-gathering procedures; and it attracted criticism when several trials based on testimony from super-grasses collapsed (*Guardian Unlimited* 2000a).[16]

But in the 1990s the Met, with other forces and ACPO, had altered internal investigatory units from being complaint-based, reactive and not well resourced to becoming elite units with top-rate investigators using intelligence to chart networks of corrupt officers before moving into action (Gillard and Flynn 2004). The bent cops would get postings together; they spoke together of manipulating supervisors; they had close links with former officers and certain private security firms; and they forged relationships with certain lawyers and also had contacts with deviant members of the CPS. Sometimes crooks and former cops targeted officers and an arrest was consciously used as an opportunity to corrupt the arresting officer.

This shift to more assertive methods indicated that police chiefs were now prepared to discuss corruption openly and make it central to their policies.[17] There was also the formation of Professional Standard Units (PSUs), replacing Complaints and Discipline Departments, which adopted a far more robust approach; by 2001 there were already seventeen PSUs in England and Wales. Among leading officers the new style was to avoid denial or defensive quibbling about 'bad apples' and to state boldly 'we acknowledge the problem but we are dealing with it'. This approach was encapsulated in this phrase: 'Given the nature of police work, it is no shame to find corruption within the service: the shame is not doing anything about it' (Blair 1993: 3).

IPCC

The Independent Police Complaints Commission (IPCC) for England and Wales dates from the Police Reform Act (2002). It started functioning in 2004 and enjoys a much broader mandate than the PCA. It is run by a Chair appointed by the Crown and seventeen Commissioners appointed by the Home Secretary; none must have served as a police officer. It handles complaints proactively as well as reactively, has an independent investigatory capacity and is tasked to investigate all critical incidents (IPCC 2006). It was not a clone of the OPONI model. OPONI was geared to an extraordinary situation; it took all complaints and reported directly to Parliament. Also Northern Ireland is a relatively small province of 1.7 million inhabitants with one police force of around 13,000 officers (full-time and reserves).[18] The IPCC has to deal with 43 forces policing some 53 million people and employing almost 250,000 personnel (officers and civilian staff). On cost grounds it was impossible for the IPCC to take responsibility for all complaints; indeed, original predictions of costs proved woefully inadequate. There is a protocol announcing the areas it will investigate itself; it is also possible for a chief constable to invite the IPCC to oversee an internal investigation.[19] But effectively the vast majority of complaints are still investigated by the police either independently for minor offences or under IPCC supervision for serious cases. The IPCC remit also covers independent investigations into serious incidents involving death or serious injury (for example by a shooting, in custody or during a car chase) or allegations of misconduct by people serving with the police including allegations of serious or organised corruption, relating to senior officers, involving racism and concerning perverting the course of justice.[20]

The key factor is that the IPCC provides for the first time in British policing history an independent, impartial element regarding complaints. The IPCC can investigate without a complaint and make policy recommendations to a force. It clearly had to establish itself and construct a working relationship with the police.[21] OPONI's early experiences indicate that formal powers do not elicit automatic compliance; the powers were contested, some RUC officers were antagonistic and there was some initial non-cooperation. Compliance is a process of negotiation and the Ombudsman and her staff had to assert their rights forcefully. And to be effective the relationship should not be too cosy but also not too antagonistic so a balance has to be found (Hawkins 2002). The IPCC has had to undergo such a process.

And it has a different composition from OPONI. The IPCC drew on a mixed composition of former staff from the PCA, seconded and former police officers and others with a background in public sector oversight or civil rights. The first Director of Investigations at the IPCC, Roy Clark, was a highly experienced Met detective who had led CIB3. Indeed, some police argue that only cops can investigate cops; but OPONI and others now maintain that it is not essential to have had police experience to conduct investigations on police.

For a comparatively new agency the IPCC soon faced a severe test with the initial non-compliance of the Met Commissioner on the Stockwell shooting in 2005. Jean Charles de Menezes was shot dead by police on 22 July 2005 at the Stockwell Underground Train Station. In reaction to the suicide bomb attacks of 7 July in London, with many casualties, and the failed attacks of 21 July, the Met had mobilised surveillance units to locate the four suspects of 21 July. Armed police units were also on call. Jean Charles de Menezes was viewed as one of the suspect bombers by a surveillance unit; he was followed on to an underground train where he was shot seven times in the head at close range by a firearms unit. It later emerged that he was a Brazilian citizen who had worked in London for several years with no links to terrorist activity; he had been wrongly identified as the suspect bomber (Kennison and Loumansky 2007).

This tragic error raised three main strands of accountability. First, there was operational accountability in relation to command and control; where had the operation gone wrong and how high up the chain of command could the fault be traced? Second, there was accountability in relation to the accuracy of information dispensed by the Met through the media. The Commissioner claimed that the victim was a terrorist suspect for some time after rumours had began to circulate within the Met soon after the shooting that officers had shot the wrong man. Allied to this was the spreading of misinformation – allegations that the suspect wore a thick overcoat (suggesting a hidden device), had jumped the ticket barrier at the station and had run for the train, which were all false; and some incident logs were altered and some CCTV footage was missing. Third, there was the key factor of legal liability. Having used fatal force it can be that officers face criminal prosecution while the organisation itself may face prosecution for 'corporate manslaughter'. This incident was especially controversial because, in contrast to standard firearms' practice in the UK, the victim was hit several times in the head at very close range with hollow-point bullets banned by the Hague Convention in warfare (IPCC 2007a: 79). With regard to liability various officers were interviewed in relation to murder, gross negligence, manslaughter, misconduct in public office and perverting the course of justice. In fact the CPS declined to prosecute any individuals for criminal offences. However, the Met was subsequently prosecuted under Health and Safety legislation, found guilty and fined £175,000. The inquest returned an open verdict.

But the significance of the Stockwell shooting was greatly amplified by the fact that the Commissioner initially endeavoured to evade the obligatory review by the IPCC. Clearly the Commissioner and his force were under great strain. And he doubtless felt that he had legitimate reasons for requesting the Permanent Secretary to the Home Office to suspend the legal requirement on referral to the IPCC while refusing access to the scene at Stockwell station. In fact the wording of Section 17(4) suggests that the chief officer retains the right not to cooperate under certain circumstances but instead of invoking this clause the Commissioner asked for the article's suspension. The Home Secretary rejected suspension but there does seem to be a lack of clarity in the legislation as if the tradition of chief officer autonomy on investigations has not been fully abandoned. The Police (Northern Ireland) Act 2000 is unambiguous about the right to information and of access of the Ombudsman. Perhaps there was some typical British fudging in the legislation for England and Wales with an allowance for the chief officers' lobby. However, the IPCC made its position clear: 'the fact that an independent body established by an Act of Parliament to investigate complaints and serious incidents involving the police ... has been excluded from the scene, is a major concern for an independent investigation and should never occur again' (IPCC 2007a: 85).

Indeed, a police chief simply cannot be 'a little bit' accountable; and cannot say that it is suddenly inconvenient to be held to account. This was a test case on compliance with external oversight not just for the Met but, given the Met's leading role and the case's magnitude, also for British policing generally. This defensive response appeared to be reverting to the old-style, protective stance. It also took several months for the IPCC to gain access to certain information while one officer simply refused point blank to cooperate. Moreover, there have been several cases where chief constables have tried to deflect the IPCC – in one the IPCC was refused access to a disciplinary hearing and in another a chief declined to take disciplinary action against an officer as recommended by the IPCC – and the IPCC won both times following judicial review. This defensiveness contrasts with the contemporary 'developmental' position, espoused by a number of senior officers, of achieving positive compliance with oversight. The Met response in trying to deny access to the site can be seen as a retrograde step. But perhaps the IPCC should have been more assertive and put in an appearance at Stockwell station to advertise that it was being denied access; this was a moment for decisive leadership and perhaps the IPCC should have demonstrably made itself visible. The Commissioner soon received the message from the Home Secretary, had to climb down and allow IPCC investigators access.

Subsequently the IPCC issued two reports on the incident – *Stockwell One* (IPCC 2007a) and *Stockwell Two* (IPCC 2007b); one analysed the operational side and the other looked at the internal flow of information to the Commissioner and his public statements. Like other post-mortems into institutional failures neither are particularly flattering accounts.[22] In one the operation was badly flawed early on, leading to operational commanders making a faulty decision based on inaccurate information, leading to the death of an innocent man. In the other the flow of information to the Commissioner did not go smoothly, as various senior officers became aware of the mistake in identity but did not for a variety of reasons inform him. The Met promotes itself as one of the best, if not *the* best, police force in the world, yet here it failed badly on two accounts. It ran a flawed operation with fatal consequences and it failed on one of the most elementary rules of crisis management: that the leader and spokesperson is fully informed.

The Met was under extreme pressure and faced not only a highly complex investigation into the two sets of bombings but also the possibility of more explosions by suicide bombers. While one makes allowances for this it is also of the essence that the police organisation and its leaders will be held to account for any mistakes made during such events. In addition, the greater the magnitude of the incidents, the greater is the need for a truly independent and impartial oversight agency. And this was not the Thurso boy getting a slap but a watershed case of great significance. One can also hold up the IPCC and its reports to critical scrutiny; no agency is infallible; and its impartiality was damaged by leaks to the press.

But what is unthinkable is that another police force would have investigated the Stockwell shooting with the old-style PCA as overseer. Here it was vital as a matter of principle that the responsibility for the investigation was external to the police and that it was independent and impartial. It is, then, of the essence that there is external oversight through the IPCC. Perhaps it will eventually gain the international reputation of the ICAC in Hong Kong. This would be gratifying for the IPCC itself; but it would be just as important for the credibility and legitimacy of British policing.

In general the IPCC has attracted confidence from the public and can see a rise in the number of complaints referred to it (IPCC 2006, 2007c). At one stage, however, a third of respondents surveyed still thought that the IPCC was part of the police; and the Director admits that there have been difficulties processing the volume of complaints, leading to delays. There also appears to be CPS reluctance to vigorously push cases forwarded to it by the IPCC with a recommendation to prosecute officers. More generally, substantiation of complaints rates over the years, including both civilian and police agencies, remain relatively low; in England and Wales the rate for police complaints during 20 years has been around 11 per cent and even with OPONI the rate is 18 per cent (Jones 2008: 712). Also, a new agency has to establish itself and meet expectations and cope with resistance; it would, for instance, be valuable and interesting to see a survey of police officers' confidence in the IPCC. But Smith (2006: 26) feels that much has been achieved in a short period with the IPCC establishing itself as a 'key stakeholder in policing, something that the PCA did not manage to achieve in 18 years'. Others are not so complimentary, feeling that the Home Secretary's dual responsibilities for both policing and complaints could compromise the IPCC's independence; McLaughlin and Johansen (2002: 635) even refer to it as the 'latest Home Office controlled "puppet on a string"'. However, its mandate and functioning indicate an important paradigm shift in oversight from the PCA's orientation to 'finding fault' in police investigations to the IPCC's search for the truth with an added 'lessons to be learned from mistakes' slant. This in turn fed into those in the police service who had become oriented to the concept of the 'learning organisation'.[23]

Police accountability in the US

> Many cynics believe that the American police are incapable of reforming themselves and that the police subculture is resistant to all efforts to achieve accountability.
>
> (Walker 2005: 17)

The history of reform, in the US, and of institutionalising police accountability, is bleak. The leading authority remains 'deeply skeptical about the possibilities of lasting change'. He states that 'the history of police reform is filled with stories of highly publicised changes that promised much but evaporated over the long run with minimal impact' (Walker 2005: 17).[24] Certainly there has been implacable hostility in much of American policing to any form of 'civilian review' of complaints and discipline investigations. In the 1960s, for example, Mayor Lindsay's efforts to establish a civilian review board in New York were torpedoed by the Patrolmen's Benevolent Association, which spent $500,000 on the successful campaign (Black 1968). And that hostility has continued unabated over several decades. Several police departments, as we saw in Chapter 3, have been afflicted by scandal and have been found to be lax about implementing subsequent reforms. These include Cincinnati, Oakland, Miami, LAPD, Detroit, Pittsburgh, New Jersey State Police, Philadelphia (held to be deeply resistant to change) and Pennsylvania State Troopers, with a 'massive pattern of sexual misconduct including several high-ranking command officers' (Walker 2005: 10).

And yet Walker remains cautiously optimistic about certain changes in the patterns of accountability in the last fifteen years. A number of police departments have taken features of the new accountability seriously including San Diego, Kansas City, Miami-Dade, Memphis (Tennessee), Boise (Idaho) and Phoenix (Arizona). The Office of Independent Review within the Los Angeles Sheriff Department (LASD), moreover, responds to all police-related shootings. Walker bases his views on three main innovations: police auditors, early intervention systems (EIS) and citizen oversight (Walker 2001, 2003). But like all innovation in American policing the changes are patchy and essentially 'local' because there are often no national standards or mechanisms for national implementation; there is an accreditation agency for standards in police departments but only about 500 of the roughly 18,000 departments are accredited.

The thrust of the recent changes is that previous reform efforts proposed by 'blue-ribbon' committees and special investigations were too much focused on a 'quick fix' and on the 'bad apples' rather than on the 'orchard'. In other words, they were insufficiently geared to significant and permanent organisational change. An alteration in this pattern came with the Violent Crime Act 1994 which authorised the US Department of Justice to bring civil suits against errant departments requiring them to introduce a set of organisational reforms. These include a 'comprehensive use of force reporting system ... an open and accessible citizen complaint procedure ... and an early intervention system' (Walker 2005: 5; cf. USDOJ 2001).

These seem to be fairly straightforward if not self-evident requirements in policing. But it was precisely in these areas that police departments had conspicuously failed when violence, corruption and misconduct was revealed by scandal. The new focus was on written policies and procedures, instructing personnel, getting officers to record critical incidents, monitoring performance, enhancing the role of supervisors and investing resources in accountability mechanisms.

Police departments engaged in reform were required to specify guidelines on use of force and to get officers to record incidents involving force. Using this data it often became evident, as with the Christopher Commission (1991) on the Rodney King beating, that a minority of officers was responsible for a disproportionate amount of violence, that the officers concerned could be easily located yet little was done about them. Using data it was possible to identify the officers and offer them training and counselling to change their ways; this often resulted in positive results.

The same effect could be produced by an Early Intervention System (EIS). This is a proactive system that takes a number of data sources and indicators (sometimes between 18 and 24 indicators) and examines patterns of behaviour.[25] For example, a female driver complained of sexual harassment at a traffic stop by a particular officer; a scan of his performance indicated that he was predominantly stopping female drivers which provided opportunities for him as a sexual predator. In another case it emerged that an officer simply was not doing any police work; during questioning it transpired he had a demanding second job and was exhausted when arriving for duty. Importantly the data can also display excellent officers who are performing well and these can receive a commendation. This kind of performance and assessment tool has been enhanced by the spread of 'Compstat'-style information and control systems (Punch 2007). Pittsburgh and Phoenix have large 'comprehensive personnel assessment systems' which require 'both a sophisticated technological infrastructure and an enormous amount of administrative oversight'; Miami-Dade and Tampa (Florida) employ smaller, cheaper and more limited systems which function as 'performance problem systems' (Walker 2005: 105). Another way of looking at this is as *risk-assessment* and such systems have itemised the risks involved in high-speed car pursuits, use of dogs, foot pursuits, dealing with the mentally ill, shooting from vehicles or at moving vehicles. Clear procedures, training and supervision have often reduced substantially the risks to police officers and to citizens. An EIS can also uncover patterns of racial profiling.

Given the history of police opposition to civilian review of complaints, and of widespread evidence of police failure to implement complaints procedures and to take citizen complaints seriously,[26] it comes as no surprise that a central plank in the new police accountability structures is 'an open, accessible and accountable citizen complaint process' (2005: 71). Again it becomes evident from an analysis of patterns that some officers are 'complaints-prone' and that this can be identified and measures can be taken to alter behaviour. For citizens there can be community outreach, publicising the complaints' procedure; information and forms in several languages;[27] convenient locations or mobile offices for making a complaint; accepting anonymous complaints; tape-recording statements from complainants and officers; providing feedback to the complainant and officer; and putting sufficient resources into the handling of complaints (2005: 71–99).

Next to these mechanisms a new model of citizen oversight emerged in the 1990s with the police auditor. The auditor is a full-time government official who is appointed on a permanent basis. There are twelve police auditors in the US with the LASD having two. Walker believes that the Special Counsel to the LASD is 'arguably the most successful citizen oversight agency' in the US (2005: 145). One of the auditors for the LASD explains that 'to change behavior effectively, an oversight agency *must look beyond the particular cases of misconduct to systemic issues implicating policy and training*' (2005: 135, emphasis in original). It is obviously attractive to have permanent oversight but it does not approach the powers, resources and impact of OPONI or the IPCC in the UK.

Nevertheless, Walker is cautiously optimistic. However three aspects are plain. First, there is still a great deal of evidence that some police departments simply do not implement the reforms or actively undermine them. Second, there have been success stories of turning around a troublesome precinct by changing the personnel and improving the quality of the supervision; but within a relatively short period of time the virtuous cycle could revert to the vicious cycle if the effort was relaxed. This happened in the Century Station of the LASD which had a poor reputation and record but had been turned around by putting in more supervisors and better personnel. Yet it reverted to its old ways, leading Walker (2005: 152) to comment that reform is fragile and the 'improvements were undermined not by evil intent but by a combination of neglect, a failure of top commanders to ensure continuity, and to a certain extent the silent operation of traditional personnel procedures'. Third, a department claiming to have improved accountability did not necessarily mean that it had done so. Chief Parks of the LAPD announced that all the recommendations of the Christopher Report had been implemented; yet the Rampart scandal exposed this as puffery; and thirteen years after Christopher (1991), the LAPD still had no fully operational EI system.

Conclusion

In the UK there have been voices calling for accountability as a core institutional value in policing in terms of auditing, reporting and communicating to outside stakeholders and making it the 'very lifeblood' of the service. Mounting pressure from several sources has pushed the police down this path. There was government pressure on efficiency and effectiveness; the judiciary pronouncing that operational accountability should be drawn upwards; new legislation bringing the possibility of prosecution for killing through corporate failure; enhanced oversight with sharper teeth; escalating civil actions with higher payouts; increased emphasis on local accountability; and the attention to, and lessons from, critical and controversial incidents such as the Stephen Lawrence murder and the Stockwell shooting within the police.

But given the rapid changes in British policing, fostered by the 'managerial mania' of the government (McLaughlin 2005), this move is not simple. If anything, accountability has become increasingly complex if not intricate and is now multi-layered, shifting and open to negotiation with the danger of becoming opaque. O'Neill (2002), indeed, has warned against an overemphasis on formal accountability in terms of performance and managerial criteria, which can deflect practitioners from 'genuine' accountability. For accountability is not something an agency can claim to possess simply because it meets certain criteria or has procedures in place; rather it is something an agency convincingly delivers to the satisfaction of external stakeholders – both routinely but especially at critical moments. For there is also much evidence that police organisations and police personnel endeavour to evade accountability in many ways (Goldsmith and Lewis 2000). This makes independent, impartial, competent, well-resourced, fearless, assertive and well-led oversight agencies – that do not leak – of pivotal importance.

Furthermore, it is clear from the material above on the UK and US that genuine reform and lasting change in a police organisation

219

recovering from scandal or wishing to reform needs strong leadership, enhanced supervision, resources devoted to internal control, a structure of accountability and a culture of compliance, with a resilient determination to tackle problems. There has to be significant cultural and organisational change. It is, then, not just a matter of simply cleaning out the stables but of rebuilding them, placing them under new management and inspecting them rigorously; and of not relaxing the effort.

Notes

1 Police corruption with graft from the organised crime syndicates ran through the middle-ranking Chinese officers who then paid off the senior officers, usually expatriates from the UK; anti-corruption efforts were solely a matter for the police; then a senior officer, Godber, was exposed for having amassed a small fortune but while under suspicion he absconded to Britain; he was extradited to Hong Kong and convicted. His corruption and trial attracted wide attention because for the first time a well-placed ex-pat had been prosecuted (Wing Lo 1993: 89–92).

2 In NSW there was a resort to a clean broom from the UK, Commissioner Ryan, but Dixon (1999b) argues that under pressure to 'get back' to fighting crime he had 'lost the desire to push for meaningful and lasting reform'.

3 Frank Williamson, who the HMIC brought in to investigate the Met but who resigned in disgust, was religious, had 'cast-iron integrity' and was a 'sea-green incorruptible'; he thought that Mark had been too circumspect and should have cast his net wider (Whitaker 1979: 263).

4 Murphy, for example, was booed by police officers' wives at a social function he attended.

5 Murphy forgave a senior officer who had dined expensively while allowing someone else to pay for the meal; ordinary cops complained that this was double standards.

6 Within the media it will be related to priorities, resources and support for certain journalists and perhaps to the willingness to employ expensive investigative journalism – with the risk of facing legal action – and particularly to relationships with powerful figures in the local elites. There are a number of contingent variables that determine why one topic becomes converted into a 'real' media scandal and others never make it from the editor's desk (Burnham 1976)

7 Chief Constable Orde (2003) states publicly that he welcomes OPONI and is geared to working with it constructively. But he warns of increased bureaucracy and oversight becoming dysfunctional with twelve agencies overseeing the PSNI. He told me at a meeting in September 2005 that he spends a great deal of time on oversight while the domestic political

parties expect ready access to him, as do some American politicians with an interest in Northern Ireland.

8 For a detailed consideration of this area see Markham and Punch (2007a, 2007b) and Punch and Markham (2009).

9 The Gold Commander at an animal rights demonstration in Essex was taken to court for breaking a local ordinance; he was acquitted (personal communication, former Assistant Chief Constable (ACC) Geoffrey Markham). In a court case in Sussex, where a firearms officer was prosecuted for murder (on a raid to arrest a suspect thought to be armed he shot the man dead who turned out to be unarmed) the judge argued that those responsible for the operation were not present in her court; Justice Rafferty was clearly *drawing accountability upwards* to the Silver and Gold Commanders for the raid and also to the senior officers who approved the operation (Punch and Markham 2009).

10 I showed the chart to Neyroud during a meeting and he said, 'It's really much more complicated than that'!

11 In some forces, notably the Met after the Lawrence inquiry, representatives of communities, of victims and human rights groups and lay advisors were invited on to so-called 'diamond' groups which function by posing critical questions about operations to the professionals (personal communication, Ben Bowling).

12 Whitaker (1979: 91–8) shows a flood of legislation already impinging on the police between 1960 and the late 1970s.

13 Some officers were very bitter about the report, especially the stigma of institutional racism, and felt the police were unfairly pilloried with the public inquiry amounting to a 'witch-hunt' (Foster 2008: 93).

14 Two became Directors of Investigations at OPONI and IPCC respectively (Dave Wood and Roy Clark), and Andy Hayman became Head of Special Operations in the Met with responsibility for counter-terrorism measures.

15 Of interest is that random surveillance showed very little deviance among officers; it was directed surveillance that proved valuable, according to a former head of CIB3.

16 The use of super-grasses was controversial because of their own deep involvement in crime and their reliability as witnesses; their use had largely been discredited in major criminal trials (McLaglan 2004).

17 Symptomatic of this new openness is the edition of *The Job* (the magazine of the Met) for 3 September 1999, which announces on page 3 a series of seminars by CIB on corruption aimed at front-line officers; and the centre-spread, pages 8–9, is devoted to the work of CIB under the headline, 'Corruption crack down'.

18 OPONI also has oversight over several small forces for the ports and airports, for the Ministry of Defence Police in the province and members of SOCA operating in Northern Ireland. But these are tiny compared to the RUC/PSNI.

19 The Highmoor Cross shootings in the Thames Valley Police (TVP) area led to Chief Constable Neyroud calling in the IPCC to oversee the

investigation (IPCC 2004). An armed man entered premises and shot three women; following emergency calls to the control room there was delay in mobilising a Silver Commander and in entering the premises. The IPCC evaluation is damning. The police response was overcautious and geared to eliminating risk rather than managing it; the delay was unjustifiable; there was a lack of clarity to act; and there was too little attention to the plight of the victims and those citizens who had come to their aid. This report led to a complete reorganisation of the TVP response to firearms incidents. An expert on police use of force, 'Tank' Waddington, feels the IPCC report is unduly critical (personal communication) while the police followed standard ACPO guidelines. But Chief Constable Neyroud had brought an independent, impartial element to a highly sensitive investigation.

20 For the criteria see www.ipcc.gov.uk.
21 In a case study of CIRPA (Citizens Independent Review of Police Activities) in Toronto, McMahon and Ericson (1984) show how the police 'defused' the impact of the new agency by co-optation which meant the police could control the reform process and use CIRPA to maintain a form of 'surrogate accountability'.
22 Everyone will recognise the immense pressure everyone involved was under within the Met; my concern here is not with an evaluation of the operations, communications and functioning of individuals – everyone can read the IPCC reports, the accounts of the HSE prosecution and the inquest and make their own judgement – but rather to convey the relationship between a police force under stress and an oversight agency in relation to compliance.
23 With thanks to Peter Kennison and Peter Squires for these insights. They are working on a book about the Stockwell shooting and other cases: Shoot to Kill: Police Force and Firearms (Wiley Blackwell, forthcoming 2009). Peter Kennison, who worked in CIB and wrote his PhD on police complaints investigations (Kennison 2001), also helped me with information on the Met's CIB.
24 There is not a single reference to any oversight agency outside of the USA, not even in Canada, in Walker (2005); not a word about the ICAC in Hong Kong or the Australian experience, while OPONI in Northern Ireland had already been functioning for four years when he finished writing.
25 Reiss (1971) had suggested this possibility 30 years earlier in the first flush of computerisation.
26 Rodney King's brother was threatened with arrest when he tried to lodge a complaint in an LAPD station about his brother's beating.
27 In Washington DC the complaints material is in thirteen languages apart from English.

Chapter 8

Conclusion: sticky fingers and dirty hands

The patrolman is obliged to violate the law, degrade people, lie and even shame himself in his own eyes in order to make arrests he knows are meaningless and he suspects produce money for others. This not only tends to make him cynical about the law and the motives of many people he knows, it also makes him think of himself as a special kind of fool. He sees himself in a world where 'notes' are constantly floating about, and only the stupid, the naive and the faint-hearted are unwilling to allow some of them to stick to their fingers.

(Rubinstein 1973: 401)

Sticky fingers

This book is about 'ordinary' men going about their work within an organisation. The work is unusual and the organisation peculiar; and it is overwhelming men who become deviant in this context. For the police organisation is a law-enforcement agency yet it is frequently found to be breaking the law. And police enjoy predatory powers; they look for prey to pounce on and they fish with live bait – putting out 'a sprat to catch a cod' (Punch 1985: 47). They stalk and hunt people, including at times other cops. Like the organisation they work in, police officers are also continually exposed as not abiding by the rules and the law. There may be many excellent police organisations, with officers strongly motivated by professionalism and integrity, but these are rarely an object of systematic study. Indeed, a review of the literature almost suggests that policing is predominantly a deviant institution populated by habitual delinquents.

The delinquency may be mild. Whyte (1955) describes a cop in Boston who sat daily in a diner drinking coffee and reading the papers; he never did a stroke of police work. It can be grave with Officer Dowd 'running shotgun' on drug transactions in New York; a London detective getting an innocent person a life sentence on the basis of a fake confession; or officers in Northern Ireland shooting dead unarmed suspects of terrorism in highly suspicious circumstances. These relate to gross abuse of power and evading accountability.

For instance, in 1986 an LAPD 'CRASH' unit went to search a house for a firearm. Despite not having the appropriate warrant for forced entry they smashed through the windows early in the morning. The 'suspect', Larez, a disabled veteran, was asleep, as were his wife, children and grandchildren. He was thrown to the floor, kicked, handcuffed and verbally abused with a gun to his head; he required hospital treatment for his injuries. His daughter was grabbed by her hair, thrown to the floor and handcuffed; when she looked to see her baby, 'Officer Keller grabbed Diane's hair and banged her head to the floor, demanding that she "put [her] f——— face to the floor."' Officers kicked in a son's bedroom door with one shouting, 'I'll blow your f——— head off'; the son was also pushed to the floor and kicked. The cops threw utensils and crockery on the floor, turned over beds, ripped posters from the wall, destroyed precious family mementoes, emptied potted plants and ripped open a punchbag. They also broke 'a pitcher, a crockpot, a figurine, a dish, a vase, a music box, a lamp, a rice cooker, a coffee pot, wall panelling, a clock, a sliding glass door, picture frames and a camera lens' (Skolnick and Fyfe 2005: 571–2). The group behaved almost as a marauding pack of predators, like some ferocious pack of wolves, locked into a 'tunnel' of violence (Collins 2008: 371).

The CRASH team found nothing; but they arrested Larez for battery of an officer. This was dismissed at trial and Larez made a complaint; this was handled by a fellow CRASH officer with Chief Gates of the LAPD writing that the complaint could not be substantiated. This is not about the free cup of coffee or a buckshee burger but about gross abuse of the rights of citizens by cops in a near manic 'frenzy' of corruption in an unaccountable organisation. They intimidated the weak and vulnerable, invaded their privacy and destroyed their personal property.

And it was plainly not for 'individual gain'; this simply has to be abandoned as a defining characteristic of corruption.

It is this intriguing but disturbing issue of police deviance and corruption that I have pursued in this work, commencing with the observation that 'policing and corruption go hand in hand'. Corruption is seen not as one thing but as a complex and shifting phenomenon taking many forms, proving remarkably resilient, altering over time and adapting to control regimes. Corruption also has to be placed in the wider spectrum of police deviance. Misconduct represents disciplinary offences; corruption – in which bribery is but one feature – refers to a range of criminal offences, including violence, in which abuse of power and trust are central; 'police crime' is reserved for some very serious offences which are an expression of 'purely' criminal behaviour.

Explanations for the various forms of police deviance and corruption were sought in the nature of the police organisation, police culture and police work; these in turn are shaped by the wider socio-political environment, the varied nature of crime and diverse relationships with criminals. Like others, including Sherman (1978) and Shearing (1981), I have stressed the *organisational* component in police deviance. This perspective rejects the 'bad apple' analogy ('cancer' is also sometimes used), and stresses the need to examine the orchard, if not the fruit industry and its owners. The 'bad apple' metaphor employed as an institutional defence – conveying that the problem refers to a small minority while the vast majority are in rude health – has been convincingly demolished time and again. Police deviance and corruption have repeatedly been shown to be widespread, organised, durable and even systemic. Sometimes everyone is on the take and everyone is bent; the entire orchard is rotten.

An examination of its forms and consequences, moreover, takes us away from some image of cosy, consensual and essentially harmless relationships lubricated by endless free lunches (or nowadays the free line of cocaine), in which picaresque crooks happily hand over bags marked 'graft' to jovial and avuncular cops. It brings us into the realm of vicious, venal, exploitive, rapacious and intimidating behaviour causing serious harm to multiple victims. Some of the victims may be 'bad villains' in the eyes of cops – and hence 'deserving' targets (Laurie 1972: 272) – but others are completely undeserving and guilty of nothing. Indeed, there is at times a reversal of justice; the guilty go free and the innocent are convicted (Brown 1998: 230). A central explanation was sought in the tension between the edicts of the formal paradigm and the norms and practices of the operational code.

There is a strong strain in the descriptions of police practitioners at work that they are continually exploring the boundaries of rule-bending and rule-breaking in order to achieve results for a variety of motives. I have heard cops say, 'when I see a new law my first reaction is "how can I get around it?"'[1] There is also the view that 'if you stick to the rules you lose', as illustrated by an Australian cop:

> We thought we had done a good job. To us these people were criminals; they were wrongdoers ... All right, we might have done the wrong things, but we saw it for the greater good. We didn't see ourselves as criminals by assaulting someone or trying to put criminals behind bars. That was ... the morality that we saw. If it was like a perfect world, sir, the people who were guilty would plead guilty. It's not a perfect world ... It's like squaring up to someone and saying, you know, Marquess of Queensberry Rules and they kick you in the balls ... My view of it is – and it is somewhat cynical – it's a big game and the criminals tell lies, the police tell lies, or did tell lies, and if you, shall we say, played by the rules the whole time, you'd lose, and it's a combination of things ... it's a system; it was a result oriented squad. It had a certain ethos about it that was A grade. It was there to take on the A graders, it was not to lose. (Voyez 1999: 12)

There is reference here to a pressing contingent reality that is widely at variance with what the law and the formal paradigm officially demands in 'playing by the rules'.[2] Probably most if not nearly all front-line and street-level professionals – as well as many senior executives of leading corporations and once prestigious banks – employ some variation of this argument: 'the rules don't apply in this particular world'. It clearly has some validity in much of policing but it can also be a rationalisation for shoddy work, cutting corners and ripping off people.

But it does represent a persistent occupational reality that, like other workers, cops will continually, creatively and for a multiplicity of purposes bend and break rules according to covert codes. This continual friction between the 'rules' and the 'street' is related to the many internal regulations, the strictures of the law and legal procedures, the tenets of the occupational culture and the operational autonomy that cops often enjoy. But this pervasive rule-bending is not just about 'occupational' deviance, fiddling overtime or pilfering a parking permit, but about the administration of the criminal law within the criminal justice system with possibly grave consequences for the victims of this 'creative' manipulation of the law and procedure. Corruption is about abusing the civil, legal and human rights of its victims, with often severe consequences.

This internal, practitioner-viewed tension between rules and occupational reality can be reinforced by pressure and signals from the wider environment. There is often direct political pressure on the police due to moral panics in the media and among the public; 'zero-tolerance' campaigns on crime; the 'war' against drugs[3] or terrorism; or repressive reaction to perceived threats to national security. This can lead to tension between 'due process' and 'crime control' (Rose 1996). McBarnet (1979), however, sees this as something of a false dichotomy because the practical application of criminal law and procedure routinely provides rich structural opportunities for legal, quasi-legal and extra-legal ways for the police to achieve their ends. The 'system' largely cooperates and colludes with this through secret codes and covert conventions about not challenging the police (Rose 1996: 41). Brown (1998: 230), moreover, argues that almost no one criticises the legal profession, prosecutors and the judiciary on effectively condoning police deviance; and on its exposure they offer the weak 'we were duped' defence. In the miscarriages cases in the UK, for example, it was the cream of the legal profession and judiciary that were involved – in prosecution, adjudicating in court and in the appeals. Yet they all continued their successful careers, some to the highest positions in the land, unhindered by the ravage caused to innocent people's lives in the cases they had handled. And if the police are caught out in 'bent for job' deviance then they are rarely prosecuted and convicted; their conduct is typically viewed as 'disaccountable' (Brodeur 1981). No officer was convicted for the miscarriages cases in Britain; and when three officers were tried following the Guildford Four's release there was a patent bias favouring them throughout the proceedings (Bennett 1993).[4]

In this light police scarcely need new or expanded powers for most routine cases because the law is replete with ambiguity, unclear phrases, 'weasel' words and loopholes; and what one law restricts another allows. Indeed, Reiner (2007) maintains that police in Britain have lobbied stridently for enhanced powers but have in recent years been granted more powers than they ever dreamed of, making some even feel uncomfortable about this. This is largely because the new security agenda geared to international and domestic terrorism and transnational organised crime has been driving legislation and practice, especially since '9/11' in the US in 2001 (Bowling and Newburn 2006).

227

This leads to four observations. First, there is a wealth of evidence that the state in diverse ways stimulates police deviance (Green and Ward 2004). This can happen directly, by demanding or encouraging illicit actions (as with the 'Third Force' in apartheid South Africa; Ellis 1988), or indirectly through the unanticipated consequences of, and adaptations to, legislation and enforcement policies. This is clear in areas of prohibition – traditionally related to alcohol, gambling, prostitution, pornography but especially drugs (Moskos 2008). Also the state's reaction to new threats is often to pass temporary special measures which long remain in force and are also applied in practice for quite different purposes through 'mission creep'. Second, that law and the courts to a degree promote, condone and collude with police deviance. Police hardly have to bend the law; the law is elastic enough for most licit and illicit purposes. Brodeur (1981), for instance, shows that during a national security scare in Canada in the 1970s, police units for political offences broke the law massively, but the courts tolerated this. An illegal break-in to remove property, which is burglary and theft, was accepted in the interests of 'national security'.[5] But third, where the police do face tough challenges – from serious criminals with sophisticated lawyers, clandestine 'subversive' movements, assertive and smart action groups and from international terrorists – then this can lead to major deviance in 'deep policing' investigations regarding manipulation of evidence, active informants or *agents provocateur*, undercover roles, interrogations, confessions, torture and planting evidence in order to obtain a conviction. Sometimes police infiltrate 'subversive' groups to the extent that they help run them or almost keep them in existence. And fourth, it may appear that legislation related to deviant policing is progressively trimming police powers and restricting their movements; but limitations in one area are often matched by slipping the leash in another (Brodeur 1981; Reiner 2007). The progress of criminal law and practice in restricting and taming police powers is also, on its path to 'Echternach,' sometimes two steps forward and at least one backwards.

The pressure for results, organisational weaknesses, latitude in the law and habitual rule-bending often leads to police 'excesses' which when exposed galvanise a 'scandal and reform' cycle. This in turn is related to certain crime areas and enforcement strategies. The drugs area, with large amounts of money and drugs circulating and sometimes major dealers who are difficult to pin down, lends itself to either combative or predatory corruption with deep undercover work, use of active informants, buy-and-bust operations and controlled deliveries (Manning 1980). This combative style can lead to some peculiar consequences. The IRT affair with deep penetration by a participating informant led ultimately to the Dutch government becoming a major importer of illegal drugs with umpteen containers containing tons of drugs reaching the illegal market beyond the supervision of the police and to the benefit of the informant. And in the 'François' case in Belgium, the eager head of a police drug squad set up his own drug operation ostensibly to combat the other drugs gangs but also to retrieve covert funding of informants (Fijnaut 1983).

The so-called 'vice' offences in contrast are associated more with routine, consensual corruption. Brodeur (1981: 149) relates that successive reports throughout the years detailing police corruption in the red light district of Montreal are almost identical. Prostitution was forbidden but given its continued existence it was thought best to adopt a policy of containment with the police moving from enforcement to crime 'management'. This created a permanent corruption-prone environment where illicit establishments were prepared to pay for their continued existence as the police could always invoke the law if necessary. The same pattern was repeated time and again in the US with gambling. Police couldn't resist the temptation to enter arrangements and profit from the illegal markets, which in turn fed the political machine. But there were periodic scandals in America exposing this and the series of reports stretching over a century are, as in Montreal, almost identical except for the date.

This 'scandal and reform' cycle tended to elicit ritual house-cleaning, with an almost predictable reappearance of the corruption within a time lapse. This can foster cynicism about reforming the police organisation. There have been reforming chiefs, like Murphy in New York and Mark in London, who have taken strong measures and achieved some success; but the effects can be short-lived. Such chiefs are often seen as zealots whose strictures are viewed by ordinary cops as unrealistic and unenforceable. Goldstein (1977: 201) warns against 'fanaticism' and a 'war' promising total elimination; and there is the danger of a deviancy amplification process (Sherman 1974b: 37). In Amsterdam, moreover, the reimposition of control and the selection of scapegoats following scandal led to such turmoil that it almost tore the organisation apart. The lower ranks responded with hostility towards senior officers, counter-surveillance, adverse propaganda and leaks to the press, while two accused detectives became cultural heroes. There was wide popular support for them and others who were pictured as victims of a failing and hypocritical organisation.

The lower orders fought back vigorously and the turbulence lasted nearly four years (Punch 1983b). This revealed a highly segmented organisation with widely varying patterns of solidarity and intense inter-rank hostility.

This does raise the issue about how much internal enforcement a police organisation can take. The leader of the Countryman investigation into the Met said he could have gone on for ever.[6] But can an organisation carry on tackling corruption, with cops hunting fellow cops, indefinitely? Internal and external investigations generate much turbulence and 'fallout' that may be experienced as undermining morale and handicapping routine operations. Reform campaigns can be toned down in a shift back to 'business as usual' before they have run their full course (Dixon 1999d). Anechiarico and Jacobs (1996), moreover, argue that too much formal, bureaucratic control leads to its own counterproductive pathology of passivity, administrative checks, paralysis of decision-making and misuse of the rules.[7] Tighter control strategies can also stimulate those, with a motivation like computer hackers, to take on the challenge of cracking the system. But Anechiarico and Jacobs (1996) raise the issue, *can you have 'too much' control and 'too much' accountability?*

The move towards more assertive internal investigations – started by Murphy in New York in the 1970s and pioneered in the UK by the Met's CIB3 in the 1990s – has certainly brought in tougher measures than in earlier periods. These units employ 'sting' operations, integrity testing, surveillance, undercover agents and use of deep informants. In the US the move towards a new accountability culture (Walker 2005) has led to 'early intervention systems', improved complaints procedures and use of force reporting. Implementation has been patchy, as one expects in the US, with no police 'system' and much hostility to 'civilian review'. But the auditor concept – rather like a permanent ombudsman but *within* the police organisation to assess compliance and to enforce oversight – is certainly worth considering elsewhere as it is valuable to have the progress of reforms monitored. It is noticeable, however, that the organisational drive and quality of personnel in internal control waxes and wanes with changes of institutional mood and regime.

But the most significant innovation in the development of control and oversight has been the arrival of genuinely independent and impartial agencies like OPONI and the IPCC. It is a glaring lesson from this book and the wider literature that police cannot be trusted to police themselves and should not be asked to police themselves (cf. Bayley 1994). Proactive oversight agencies with sharp teeth, resources and a mandate to advise forces on policy have become a vital element in the landscape of police reform.

The material in this book might lead to the pessimistic view that police corruption is endemic, universal and unsolvable (Goldstein 1977: 218). Yet in the UK new oversight agencies, assertive PSUs, fresh legislation and reformist chiefs are signs of hope. But it is doubtful if police culture has really changed; for that in turn is rooted in how police officers experience and view their daily work situation. For example, no one has come up with an answer to the near universal rule of silence which tolerates deviance and hinders inquiries. The Wood Commission in Australia (1997a: 155) commented on the strength of the code:

> Almost without exception officers approached by the Commission initially denied ever witnessing or engaging in any form of corrupt activity. Even with an undertaking that police would not be disciplined for failing to report certain forms of corruption, the offer of amnesty and the availability of protection against self-incrimination, officer after officer maintained this stand until presented with irrefutable evidence to the contrary. Each knew the truth, and the blind hope that no-one would break it, prevailed.

Almost certainly the characteristics of the police culture will continue to revolve around secrecy, solidarity and danger and will hold strong negative moral stereotypes of certain groups and criminals; this then justifies classifying them as 'police property' or as 'deserving' to be convicted by fair mains or foul (Reiner 1997: 1010).

Another feature of policing that allows the recurrence of deviance is the collective amnesia, amounting to institutionalised denial, that afflicts some senior officers. For example, a senior Met officer was interviewed in the TV documentary on the SERCS affair dealt with in Chapter 6. This relates to the largest RCS in the UK, where one expects high risk-awareness with alertness to the lessons of the past. Indeed, the SERCS unit housed in Surbiton had been the subject of a BBC Panorama documentary exposing serious corruption just a few years earlier (McLaglan 2004). This investigative journalism had even been instrumental in fostering the anti-corruption efforts in the Met of the mid-1990s. Yet the officer says, 'I was stunned, and I use the word carefully, I was stunned at the scale of the corruption ... we didn't think it was happening ... but there wasn't the resources, skills, organisational drive at that time to really get into these types of offences ... I had never imagined that officers could behave like that, behave with such impunity, be so openly corrupt and get way with it. But we didn't think it was actually happening' (BBC 2000). This is baffling. He worked in an organisation that for over two decades had experienced successive investigations into major and hard-core corruption; has he forgotten that, and is there no institutional memory? Effectively he is saying that the organisation failed, hence making it complicit in the deviance. The latter standpoint was graphically conveyed by an investigator on the SERCS case: 'there was wilful blindness. Supervisors denied the reality. People lifted the stone, looked under it, put it back quickly and then denied the stone.'

Policing is inextricably related to opportunities for deviance. And some cops can resist everything but temptation leading to grubby hands, muddy boots and sticky fingers, while 'if you swim in an ocean of shit, you don't come up smelling of roses' (Leuci 2004: 255). But human weakness is enhanced by an organisation that encourages the deviance, or colludes in it by turning a blind eye, and then when faced by exposure casts out a few scapegoats, engages in ritual reform and represses the experience by forgetting about it – until it 'stuns' people by happening again.

Dirty hands

Well I have dirty hands. Right up to the elbows. I've plunged them in filth and blood. But what do you hope? Do you think you can govern innocently? Jean-Paul Sartre (in Kleinig 1996: 287)

In his lapidary book on policing Manning (1977), writes of police work containing both sacred and profane features. This institutional ambivalence is reflected in behaviour with excellent officers doing good work as well as corrupt cops being venal and nasty; and they are sometimes cheek by jowl in the same organisation. Indeed, from the inside the police organisation does not look like a coherent, co-ordinated entity but is more a loosely coupled matrix with clean and dirty segments. It exhibits a 'multi-personality' syndrome, as cops move in a hall of mirrors through the matrix and change their identities accordingly like crafty chameleons. The origin of the internal choices leading to those segments is also set by the externally determined mandate and functions of policing.

Policing is about many things (Manning 1977; Waddington 1999a; Reiner 2000; Newburn 2003, 2005). But as an institution it is granted considerable powers by the state to be employed in sensitive areas related to rights, freedom, privacy and the use of force. And historically it has been associated with cunning and deception, unsavoury repression, gross invasions of privacy, covert surveillance, undue violence, diverse forms of corruption and serious if not systematic abuse of the law and of the rights of citizens. This is clearly not just a matter of practitioners getting dirty hands from exposure to dirty work but far more of the irreducible dilemma of exercising power as expressed by Sartre's 'can you govern innocently?'

Two factors are of crucial importance. First, the official paradigm – which some practitioners endeavour to articulate with dedication and enthusiasm – can be influenced by what might be called a macro 'operational code'. This is that states and other authorities, along with policy- and law-makers, tend to build in 'space' through ambiguity to allow for flexibility if the going gets rough; and officials imbibe the techniques of deviousness, circumlocution and deniability. Even the most enlightened democracy faces 'dirty hands' dilemmas when faced by serious challenges to its security (say in how to deal with suicide bombers). It may react by swiftly passing emergency legislation that overnight infringes a number of long-held traditional rights and freedoms. Politicians also discover that being seen to be tough on crime, certain out-groups and terrorism is electorally advantageous. When the old Mayor Daley grossly infringed the rights of the Black Panthers in Chicago his popularity soared (Rokyo 1971). This tension between ostensibly clean values and dirty means can be illustrated by the situation in the UK where the official paradigm was that the police were the most accountable in the world. Yet in Northern Ireland during the Troubles the police and security services were systematically abusing rights and breaking the law in a climate of low or no accountability. And these 'tough measures' were said to have been encouraged, if not directed, from Downing Street (Dillon 1991). In short there is a built-in reserve in governments and other authorities that in time of need it may be necessary to limit rights and employ tough measures.[8] That doubtless builds a measure of ambiguity, if not double-think, into policing.

Second, policing elites in recent years have become relatively liberal in the UK – and also in the Netherlands. The 'consent' paradigm espoused by these leaders – geared to service to the public, consultation, rights, due process and integrity – is, however, difficult to maintain when the heat is on from politicians and the populist media (Punch 2007). Politicians and influential stakeholders may opportunistically support a 'progressive' paradigm in policing but abandon it swiftly when it is not politically expedient. Faced by crime 'waves' politicians make sudden demands to alter orientation and get back to 'business as usual'. The exclusive emphasis on crime-control fighting can in turn reignite the 'shadow' paradigm within the organisation of traditionalist crime-fighters biding their time for a swing back to 'real' policing. In brief, 'enlightened' policing is never undisputed, is vulnerable and subject to oscillation between paradigms. There is external ambivalence between the formal paradigm of accountable democracy, with the covert need to make dirty hands in tough times, and internal ambivalence between the liberal 'consenters' and traditional 'thief-catchers'. And the choices emanating from these vacillations between paradigms and codes influence the divisions and choices between the sacred and profane elements in practical policing on the ground.

For ambivalence with police is fatal; they will exploit it. If there is sudden pressure from outside for results, with a signal that the means are subordinate to the ends, internal ambivalence with mixed messages and this is then coupled with poor management, weak supervision, operational autonomy and the delegation of extensive and unaccounted powers to cops – and those cops are males – then this is a rock-solid recipe for abuses.

Indeed, corruption is held to be 'perennial and ubiquitous, to be found in any and all systems of government' (Heidenheimer 1970; Palmier 1983: 297). This conveys that corruption is not so much about bad people as about the dilemmas of exercising power on behalf of government and authorities and translating those environmental pressures and signals into practical policing. In a sense, then, policing and abuse of power are intertwined in a symbiotic embrace. It is an illusion that this can be eradicated so we should anticipate that it will continually resurface. The moral and practical choices to be made are rooted in how practitioners cope with the ambivalences and contradictions in what must at times seem like trying to make sense of, and to function in, a 'crazy system' (Singer 1980). Some officers rise to the challenge by becoming professional, dedicated and straight. Others may start like that but, for diverse reasons, they seek deviant solutions; for them if the rules do not work then you have to bend the rules (Goldschmidt 2008). While that may result in using dirty means for noble ends, we have also seen that this can lead officers to venality, violence, contempt for the law, abuse of rights and even effectively becoming criminals. There is, then, something about the nature of policing that distorts perceptions and deflects good cops onto deviant paths while encouraging bad cops to become rogue cops.

This means that police corruption will always be with us. Its potential is built into the system; and some cops will always slot into their allocated roles in the sacred–profane dramaturgy and into playing by the rules of a dark and sometimes deadly 'game'. This bleak picture may reinforce the image of criminology as nothing but a gloomy science. In turning to the negative reference group of police organisations throughout this book, for example, it is clear that corrupt cops do not provide a service to the public, they exploit citizens, come to arrangements with criminals – by regulating, stimulating and even organising crime – and rarely do any police work. The organisations are typically badly led, poorly managed and do not have a serious structure or culture of accountability. Yet this is not a gospel of despair.

All that is required is clarity and consistency on the mandate and the paradigm of policing while changing the structure and culture of the police organisation! Of course, this is rather like saying that 'the police should be required to obey the law'.[9] There always will be external pressure, ambivalence and shifting and competing priorities and these will always impact on the way policing is conducted. Nevertheless, in the two societies I know best, the UK and the Netherlands, there have in recent years been excellent investigations, first-class handling of public order incidents and skilful and humane reactions to disasters and emergencies. There are smart cops doing smart things with competence, conviction and integrity (Neyroud and Beckley 2001). Good policing comes from forces with an ethic of service, sound leadership at all levels, clear standards of performance and conduct, rigorous evaluation, feedback to practitioners and the public and a genuinely professional structure and culture of accountability. The contours of good, professional and accountable policing are, then, clear and unambiguous (Punch and Nowicki 2003; and see Appendix below).

I am convinced that a great deal can be achieved, despite the limitations mentioned, with good leadership, clear standards and sound accountability; and that many officers will respond positively and the public will appreciate it greatly.

But I have also emphasised that in many of the cases reviewed there was a failing organisation where the components for good policing were starkly absent.[10] In examining deviance, corruption and crime in policing, then, this book has taken as its central message that we are not dealing with bad apples seeking individual gain but with collective conduct geared to varied ends and diverse satisfactions. The police environment can form a 'rotten barrel' that powerfully shapes people's identities and induces them to take deviant paths in concert with others. The history of policing reveals that it can have a distorting and seductive influence on practitioners by steering them to evade the formal paradigm and to slip into operational codes of rule-bending and rule-breaking. But it is clear that what generates police deviance, crime and corruption is the institutional context of policing and failings or inducements in the system. Police corruption is crime caused by managerial failure and organisational fault.

Notes

1 I have often heard business managers saying the same during executive programmes I have taught.
2 For instance, when Foster (2008) studied detectives on the Murder Squad in London in the wake of the Stephen Lawrence Inquiry, their plea was effectively that mistakes may have been made but there should be some appreciation that rules are not always followed and that certain matters are simply not played by the book; indeed it was part of the cop's craft to bend the rules to fit the situation. They also said the incident may have just been incompetence rather than racism.
3 Leuci says cops tackling drugs in the NYPD saw themselves as 'mercenaries' in a 'give-no-quarter war' that 'seemed to permeate all of narcotics enforcement. There was a loss of all standards, all sense of right and wrong' (Leuci 2004: 247).
4 In New York the PBA, Patrolmen's Benevolent Association, has negotiated that officers under investigation have 48 hours to consult with union representatives and its lawyers before facing Internal Affairs (Skolnick 2002).
5 Brodeur (1981: 142) explains this double-think by adding the concept of *finis reus* (requisite purpose or goal) to *actus reus* and *mens rea*: 'if *finis* and *mens* conflict (wilfully breaking the law in order to apply it more efficiently) *mens* is neutralised by *finis* ... there are cases where the police knowingly (*mens*) breach the law (*actus*) for what they consider law enforcement purposes (*finis*)'. This removes the malice from 'intent' which is mitigated by a 'just' cause.
6 In turn Met cops pilloried Countryman as that 'long-running farce'.
7 As when a poorly performing employee claims whistle-blower status to avoid sanctioning and perhaps dismissal; he or she then enters a process that may take years to resolve and during which others are virtually powerless to raise any criticism for fear of new accusations of bias and

threats of legal action. Police forces may try to rid themselves of deviant personnel only to find they have to take them back because of an appeal to an external tribunal.

8   In the US the counter-terrorist security agenda has fostered abuse of human rights, abductions, false imprisonment, aggressive interrogation techniques and torture, such as 'water-boarding' (Sands 2008).

9   The Wikipedia entry on a Canadian commission into systematic law-breaking by the RCMP against 'subversive' groups in the 1970s states, perhaps unwittingly, that the report recommends that *the police should be required to obey the law.*

10   This is not to say that deviance does not also occur in excellent police forces.

Appendix

What can be done?

If corruption in policing is endemic, resilient and near universal, can anything be done about it? The answer is 'no' and 'yes', while police forces usually have to 'do something about it'. By 'no' I mean that it is an illusion to think that corruption will not happen at some time in a police organisation or that after scandal and reform it will go away for good; it remains a permanent occupational hazard and a recurring phenomenon. And 'yes' refers to the fact that there is a battery of measures that can be taken to try to prevent corruption or tackle it when it occurs. It is also the case that a police agency faced by corruption normally has 'to do something about it' because of internal and external pressure to reform; doing nothing is usually not an option. The cautionary approach, however, is that there is no magic bullet, no quick fix, and no single measure that works. The evidence indicates that forces have to use a multi-pronged approach, sustain the effort and anticipate recidivism.

There is a body of knowledge about best practice in the anti-corruption literature. But rather like the umpteen reports on corruption in diverse societies, which are remarkably similar, the anti-corruption material not only reads like more of the same but also continually proposes measures that have repeatedly failed.[1] With these provisos in mind I shall briefly outline the key measures that emerge from the literature. A number of sources are of value. There is the *Anti-Corruption Manual* of Ward and McCormack (1979); an annual review of anti-corruption strategies by Transparency International in Prague; guidelines on this area from Interpol and from the Council of Europe; the HMIC (1999) report on police integrity and a number of documents from ACPO emanating from the Presidential Task Force on Corruption (set up in 1998); and there are umpteen individual force proposals (as for the NYPD; Giuliani and Bratton 1995). Diverse agencies also offer seminars about combating corruption. These usually end up with the classroom walls enthusiastically covered with sheets of analysis and recommendations; but after this revivalist 'Sunday' surge there is the return to reality on Monday and often little happens (Bovens 1998).

For success depends on effective implementation and constant commitment. Anti-corruption efforts tend to produce long check-lists, administrative changes, good intentions and vacuous statements of intent. But if 'the resources, skills and organisational drive' are absent (as in the SERCS case), what can be expected? I can but touch selectively on the key features of an anti-corruption strategy given the limitations of space; each item could be expanded considerably and the reader can pursue the themes at more length in the literature.

(a) It is vital to start by abandoning the *individual failure model* and accepting that corruption is an *institutional* failure. Hence, preventing and tackling corruption is about organisational and cultural change.

(b) One of the most crucial factors is *leadership*. Much of the literature conveys the near impotence, if not irrelevance, of police leadership when viewed from below. Yet when there is trouble the cry is often to bring in a 'strong leader'. One has to be cautious with external disciplinarians who can set up tensions and generate resistance so perhaps the term should be 'determined and perceptive leaders who understand policing'. Clearly the reforming chief can restore order and discipline, take tough measures and make substantial gains in improving practices and establishing norms of integrity. *Leadership and commitment can make a considerable difference* (Ward and McCormack 1979).

The difficulty with the 'new broom' model is that it personifies reforms and these tend to fade when the chief departs. Probably the most important characteristics of any police leader is knowing the business he or she is in (a 'professional' rather than a 'manager'), consistency and not sending out ambivalent signals, decisiveness, long-term views, a well-thought-out set of values and setting a tone for integrity. Generally an explicit moralist style does not appeal to practitioners but in a censorious culture – where cops look upwards for signals as to what is acceptable, what they can get away with and what they can criticise – the chief is inevitably a role model and has to set standards of personal and professional integrity. There is considerable evidence from the organisational literature that the top person, with his or her team, is vital to the success of institutional change. The reverse is also true – if the top people do not genuinely support an innovation it will wither. But much of this material is from the management literature with an obsession on individual success stories of successful entrepreneurs galvanising the organisation.

But policing is radically different; it is a 24/7 emergency organisation requiring leaders who can lead in the face of sudden critical incidents (Flin 1996). And such leaders can be trained and groomed for operational responsibility (Punch and Markham 2000, 2004). And, crucially, policing requires competent leaders who can lead confidently *at all levels* of the institution, which means we should not be mesmerised only by leadership at the top. Also, the main complaint of the lower ranks is that the bosses do not support them when tough decisions have to be taken and blame is allocated. With new accountability structures senior officers devolve responsibility but draw accountability upwards – that is, if there is a genuine culture of accountability where superiors cannot hide.

(c) *Supervision.* Probably the most consistent theme in the literature is the pivotal importance of front-line supervision: 'The first-line of supervision is the first-line of anti-corruption.'[2] Time and again we have seen that supervisors either witnessed deviance but ignored it, were drawn into it or encouraged it. Good supervision is clearly dependent on a number of variables such as recruitment, training and ratios of supervisors to ordinary ranks; but the pivotal one is the level of support the supervisor can expect from superiors. The more the supervisor feels isolated and abandoned by those above – either through sloth, indifference or fixation on managerial tasks – the more likely the supervisor will develop an indulgency pattern with the group. There is always group dynamics and in a squad an informal leader or a clique can influence and manipulate supervisors. Clark of the SERCS is on tape discussing supervisors as if he could remove them if they did not suit his purposes. There has also been at times the recruitment of a large cohort of young and inexperienced officers who were rapidly promoted to supervisory roles. But if front-line supervision is so vital – and that derives from the structural characteristics of policing with small units having high autonomy and facing important decisions in uncertain situations – then there has to be investment in the role. Supervision has to be seen as the front-line, cutting edge of operational leadership and there has to be training for, and organisational support for, assertive and intrusive supervision. Armies rely on NCOs and police forces depend on their sergeants (Van Maanen 1983). Integrity, accountability and control of the primary processes begin at the 'coalface' with sound, self-confident and institutionally supported supervisors.

(d) *Risk assessment*. Deviance and corruption in policing, I and others have maintained, is a permanent occupational hazard. Yet it tends to occur in highly predictable areas. There are certain structural characteristics of enforcement areas that create the potential for corruption; where there is frequent contact with criminals, undercover work, running informants, deep infiltration in gangs or 'subversive' groups, drugs enforcement and vice enforcement. The relationships that cops get involved in and the pressures they are exposed to can lead to cosy arrangements but also to distortions and obsessions where they go over to the other side or will do anything to gain results. At times this can lead to mental health problems and post-traumatic stress. In essence, if the danger areas are predictable and the risks to personnel are plain then there simply has to be a serious and persistent risk analysis of the corruption-conducive areas, as well as, from a duty of care, risk assessment for personnel in relation to their assignments.

(e) *Red flags*. All these points are in a way self-explanatory; yet despite the awareness of the need for such measures we can see that organisations still get into trouble. The measures are all interrelated and they are linked to the need for a constant and unrelenting alertness while not relaxing the effort (as in constant and serious risk management). Nearly all disasters and institutional crises display an audit trail of signals and warnings that were overlooked, ignored or deflected; as was the case in the four scandals reviewed by Sherman (1978). Somehow the 'red flags' were not seen or were not perceived to be important – even when they were more like huge red banners waving under someone's unresponsive gaze. The answer is to get organisations into alert mode for warning signs; but if they ignored them in the first place what guarantee is there that they will remain alert in the future? For there are defence mechanisms related to collective and irrational processes in organisations – like the 'Abilene Paradox', group-think, cognitive dissonance and denial – that distort decision-making, deflect warning signals and ignore the bringer of bad news (Punch 1996). This pleads for a strong 'early-warning' orientation towards red flags. Walker (2005) has described how the data collected by police organisations can help detect deviant or positive patterns in police conduct. With not much effort an Early Intervention System can be constructed to utilise this data. Importantly, this can also be used to reward good policing, while with retraining a deviant or poorly performing officer can often be rehabilitated and saved for the organisation instead of being sanctioned or dismissed. An EIS is largely about low-level operational policing work whereas I am pointing also to an institution-wide alertness to warning signals at all levels. For instance, control tends to focus downwards; yet the senior ranks have their own opportunity structures for deviance so the standard rule has to be – *look up as well as down*. Another measure could be random health, drug and locker checks. This exudes the message that *everyone* has to accept that they are subject to control. Another warning signal that is often overlooked is the 'high performer'. Superiors tend to welcome productive, results-oriented workers and not question how the results were reached; but deviants often camouflage their activities with impression-management and ostensibly high activity (as with Nick Leeson at Barings Bank; Punch 1996). This means the high performer has to be suspect; yet he or she may be genuine and may be upset by the critical attention. What is needed, and this has to be an organisation-wide cultural investment, is a constant alertness for red flags, audit trails, footprints in the sand and roaches under the rug. But officers have to keep lifting the rug; and stop ignoring the roaches.

(f) *Somewhere to go*. In Chapter 6 we have seen that cops in trouble feel that there is 'nowhere to go' in the organisation. Also they can have drink, drugs and domestic problems. One solution is a confidential hotline for officers to counselling professionals external to the organisation; generally cops do not trust confiding in people inside the organisation. Another external hotline could be for the families of officers who are suffering abuse and who see drink or drug addiction in their partners. Police forces have a duty of care to personnel and families and these two lines are for professional help. But the effort is also designed to get cops starting to do something about their corruption 'habit' and related problems. Thinking of the 'slope' analogy, efforts should be directed to getting officers to seek help as early as possible, before they start to 'slide' and pass the psychological point of no return. This can be encouraged by an 'error-tolerant' approach as opposed to an 'error-friendly' style; in the former if an officer comes forward early, admits an error of judgement and there are clearly extenuating circumstances (say with regard to institutional negligence), then there could be some leniency. Some excellent officers get carried away by zeal and eagerness for results; putting them back into uniform, which sometimes happens as a sanction, is as much a punishment for the uniformed branch as it is for them. But perhaps they can be retained as a detective but in another area. Rather than a disillusioned officer, demotivated and treading water until his or her pension, there could be a contrite and motivated officer grateful for being given a second chance.

(g) *Special squads.* I'm almost inclined to advise abolishing all special squads! They nearly always seem to get out of hand and cause trouble (Skolnick 2002).[3] But we miss positive reporting on units that perform well without the pathologies reported when squads go off the rails. And obviously malfunctioning is related to the lack of sound management. Often special units are set up with high autonomy and trust and attract the best personnel. The SIU of Leuci and the SERCS of Putnam were viewed as the elite of the elite. These squads may be loosely linked to the organisation – as with inter-regional squads – and function on a secretive 'need-to-know' basis. Such units if not well managed can manipulate that trust and secretiveness to enlarge their autonomy. This mechanism can be used to bend rules to achieve fake results, as in the Dutch case in South Limburg, or to engage in a rich range of deviancy as in the NYPD's SIU. Examples in this book show cops in units determining their own hours, vacationing without permission, selecting their own cases and avoiding the office for weeks on end. They were unsupervised, unmanaged, or rather self-managed, out of institutional control and unaccountable. In policing that is a recipe for disaster. Clearly special units have to be well managed; and it has to be the golden rule, *no autonomy without accountability.* For example, if the squad's commander is a 'Silver' commander then there will be a 'Gold' commander external to the unit who is distant to the operational processes and monitors and verifies Silver's decisions.[4] This assumes there is a solid and practised accountability structure.

(h) *Positive counter-ideology.* The literature on police is replete with material about cynicism, disillusion, frustration and demoralisation among cops. We hear less about well-motivated cops who are proud of their job and find it fulfilling. But perhaps there can be a strong effort to emphasise pride and professionalism and to extend more recognition for those doing the tough jobs at the base of the organisation where many of the most important decisions are taken. Part of this could be to allow a certain amount of low-level grass-eating and gift-taking. Overzealous, moralistic and rule-bound regimes are not popular with practitioners and it should be possible to set acceptable limits given that food and gifts play an important role in society, and in certain cultures are an essential part of lubricating social interaction. To say 'not even a cup of coffee' is unrealistic and may even be seen as asocial in some groups, while alienating them from the police. It should be possible to set clear guidelines and implement them with common sense – such as where *never* to take a cup of coffee. But perhaps police forces could invest more in a positive counter-ideology to combat the cynicism and alienation. One way is to reward officers publicly who have shown courage in some act of integrity alongside those receiving bravery awards.[5] Another is to use 'bad cops', as in the American TV documentary, to spell out the dangers of sliding into corruption and the deleterious consequences for the individual and their families. At the Academy in Baltimore the main message to the recruits was to make sure that when they took to the streets they came home safely in the evening, 'everything else is secondary' (Moskos 2008: 22). The instructors are referring to avoiding unnecessary physical danger and getting home safely; but they could have added moral danger and not making it home because you have been arrested by your own colleagues and will be spending some time in prison. They convey what it is like, as the wife of Putman does, to have the police arrive to search the house; and when she asked what her husband was suspected of they answered 'drug trafficking' (BBC 2000).

(i) *Opportunities and enforcement.* A factor that emerges in the literature is to eliminate or reduce opportunities for deviance and corruption by changing enforcement strategies, such as downgrading certain drugs. Murphy in New York effectively decriminalised gambling and the Sunday closing laws which generated graft in ethnic neighbourhoods where shopkeepers opened on Sunday and paid the cops to look away. In the UK the 'golden-hook' – referring to tow-trucks that paid a kickback to cops who recommended their garage – has been eliminated by moving the selection of tow-truck operators to the control room with allocation by rotation. In Amsterdam cops on overtime could declare a meal by showing a receipt and this led to considerable and creative fiddling with bills with the hearty compliance of waiters; this fiddle was eradicated with an automatic meal allowance to all on overtime. There are a number of enforcement and administrative decisions and arrangements that can alter the opportunity structure and even eliminate certain forms of deviance. But then came mobile phones and credit cards!

(j) *Proactive control.* I have dealt with this and the following item in Chapter 7. But in the constellation of mechanisms that can be put into an anti-corruption strategy, they form the two central and essential fundaments. A major and far-reaching innovation, transmitting a significant message to bent cops and others, is that police forces are prepared to invest in substantial, robust and proactive PSUs with quality personnel. The attitude is that they are combating serious organised crime rooted within the organisation and that the standard methods used against serious criminals – intelligence, surveillance, undercover work and informants – will be utilised against the bent cops. The aim is to gain criminal convictions and remove them from the service.

(k) *External oversight.* All these measures are important and should be combined in a coherent and coordinated strategy. But the change that has most radically altered the architecture of policing and culture of accountability is the rise of truly independent and impartial oversight agencies. For instance, in the LAPD CRASH incident detailed above the family endured a double injustice; they faced a vicious assault with a wrongful arrest followed by a biased internal investigation. This portrays the LAPD as a deviant and unaccountable organization and with the chief colluding in the deviance. When the law breaks the law there is no law;[6] and when there is no redress against the law's lawbreakers there are no rights and there is no democracy. The golden rule has got to be, *the police cannot and should not be responsible for investigating their own deviance and crimes.* It is of the essence – for the victims, for the police and for democracy – that there are effective, independent oversight agencies for policing like OPONI, the IPCC, the ICAC (Hong Kong), the Independent Commission Against Corruption (Australia) and the auditor in the US.

But to institutionalise integrity, to embrace human rights and to make accountability the very 'lifeblood' of the police organisation requires structural and cultural change and enduring commitment. That is difficult for three reasons.

First, the evidence on organisational change is that it is never unproblematic and linear, is always 'political', often contested and frequently fails (Knights and McCabe 2003). And all change has unanticipated consequences; the greater the change, the larger those unanticipated consequences are likely to be.[7]

Second, those who support the traditional values and culture are sometimes able to mobilise resistance to change. Innovations seen as 'soft', as merely geared to political correctness and as not contributing to the 'core business' of crime-fighting, are roundly disparaged; innovative staff officers are dubbed 'the empty holster guys' and change consultants are dismissed as not understanding 'real' policing. American cops have displayed their displeasure at proposed changes by growing their hair long, by massively reporting sick ('blue flu'), by wild-cat strikes and by suddenly conducting enforcement blitzes that elicit loud citizen protests (Alex 1976). In the South African Police Service (SAPS) there was an influx of specialists from abroad to help with police change after apartheid; one reform wave, including experts from Scandinavian countries, came to introduce human rights. The glaring discrepancy between the harsh reality of policing in South Africa and applying the human rights paradigm imported from abroad – and taught by experts almost from another planet (affluent 'WASP' societies with low crime) – led to strong resistance and hostility at all levels. One SAPS officer retorted, 'don't push this constitution down my throat!' (Hornberger 2007). Reform has to convince the practitioners that it does not weaken their operational effectiveness otherwise, perhaps with an alliance with hard-line senior officers, they are often capable of undermining change.

And, third, even if there are dedicated and committed officers espousing professional standards and integrity, their enlightened regime has to cope with political pressure responding to moral panics, populist media campaigns and public opinion. In Chicago the police department had made a long investment in community policing but following a crime scare in the media the mayor instantly abandoned this, removed the reform chief and on the spot appointed a new hard-liner who focused on 'guns, gangs and homicide' (Skogan 2008). Furthermore, a chief espousing human rights and ethical policing is demanding a constant commitment and a permanent cultural change from her staff and personnel; and the institutional ethos and commitment has to be genuine because you cannot be a 'little bit ethical'.[8] In practice reform regimes and change projects tend to display fluctuations and vacillation in relation to changes of senior personnel, alterations in funding and resources, cultural resistance and especially shifts in support, accompanied by sudden demands to alter orientation and return to 'real' policing and 'thief-catching'. The Met's CIB3, which had broken new ground and changed the paradigm of internal control in the 1990s with assertive and penetrating investigations into police deviance, had absorbed considerable resources yet found convictions difficult to achieve. Some commentators felt it was slackening its pace in recent years while not always receiving top personnel; one 'very senior officer' lamented, 'I don't think the organization has the stomach for a fight anymore' (McLaglan 2004: 438). This makes the search for good and clean policing a never-ending quest.

Notes

1 I have attended a number of large, international 'anti-corruption' conferences where the majority of delegates were from countries with a reputation and a record of major corruption and human rights abuses (including the host country); and these meetings usually produce a vacuous report full of recommendations that will never be implemented and, if they were, they would fail for predictable reasons. Mounting such expensive conferences can even be seen as a form of corruption; and attendance at them as rather lush grass-eating – except for serious scholars, of course.
2 Kevin Ford, who previously worked for New York City's Department of Investigation (personal communication).
3 Australian cops in the Armed Offenders Squad (AOS) of Victoria modelled themselves on the violent characters in Tarantino's film *Reservoir Dogs*; they dressed in black suits and wore sunglasses; they also employed excessive force until the AOS was disbanded (OPI 2008).
4 The investigator (on behalf of the Home Secretary) into the conduct of two Met detectives in relation to the possible miscarriage of justice in the case of Silcott, maintained that they went almost completely unsupervised by anyone senior to them in the hierarchy; yet the investigation into the

murder of PC Blakelock was one of the most expensive and intensive ever undertaken by the Met (presentation to Senior Command Course, Cambridge University, 2000). In the light of current accountability practice this amounts to institutional neglect – and asking for trouble.

5 This happened in the West Midlands Police when two officers were publicly commended by the Chief Constable for 'bravery' by exposing drug-related corruption. I'm unaware of how they have fared since.

6 Former US Attorney General Ramsay Clark (Whitaker 1979: 248). Also Justice Brandeis (Grabosky 1989: 4): 'In a government of laws, the existence of the government will be imperilled if it fails to observe the law scrupulously ... Crime is contagious. If the government becomes the lawbreaker; it breeds contempt for the law; it invites every man (sic) to be a law unto himself; it invites anarchy.'

7 In New York in the 1970s and 1980s, for example, affirmative action led to recruiting whereby some people had difficulty in passing the sergeant's exams; the ones who failed then took legal action against the City and the NYPD was forced to make them 'temporary sergeants' as a compromise; generally they made poor supervisors while many cops did not accept them as credible supervisors (Kevin Ford, who previously worked for NYC's Department of Investigation; personal communication). This is a difficult area to assess because many white cops were strongly resistant to the influx of cops from minorities through affirmative action, some with criminal records, and opposed it volubly from early on (Alex 1976).

8 'The government either has integrity or it does not. There is no such thing as a "little integrity". And the administration of society relies upon the integrity of government. When the integrity of government is affected, the government loses the trust of the people. Without the trust of the people there is no democracy. It ceases to exist' (Dutch Minister for Home Affairs, Mrs Dales, responsible for all civil servants including police officers, speaking on integrity; quoted in Punch 2002: 845).

References

ABC (2005) 'Dead Man Talking – Transcript', Australian Broadcasting Corporation: *Australian Story*, 10 October.

Alex, N. (1976) *New York Cops Talk Back*. New York: Wiley.

Allason, R. (1983) *The Branch*. London: Secker and Warburg.

Amir, M. and Einstein, S. (eds) (2004) *Police Corruption: Challenges for Developed Countries*. Huntsville, TX: OICJ.

Anechiarico, F. and Jacobs, J. (1996) *The Pursuit of Absolute Integrity*. Chicago: Chicago University Press.

Ascoli, D. (1979) *The Queen's Peace*. London: Hamish Hamilton.

Bad Cops (1993) Documentary film on police corruption in the US. London: Eaton Films.

Bailey, V. (ed.) (1981) *Policing and Punishment in Nineteenth Century Britain*. London: Croom Helm.

Ball, J., Chester, L. and Perrot, R. (1979) *Cops and Robbers*. Harmondsworth: Penguin.

Banfield, E. C. and Wilson, J. Q. (1963) *City Politics*. Cambridge, MA: Harvard University Press.

Banton, M. (1964) *The Policeman in the Community*. London: Tavistock.

Barker, A. (2004) *Shadows: Inside Northern Ireland's Special Branch*. Edinburgh and London: Mainstream.

Barker, T. and Carter, D. (1990) 'Fluffing up the evidence and covering your ass: some conceptual notes on police lying', *Deviant Behavior*, 1(1): 61–73.

Barker, T. and Roebuck, J. B. (1973) *An Empirical Typology of Police Corruption*. Springfield, IL: Thomas.

Bayley, D. H. (1974) 'Police corruption in India', in L.W. Sherman (ed.) *Police Corruption: A Sociological Perspective*. New York: Doubleday.

249

Bayley, D. H. (1994) *Police for the Future.* New York/Oxford: Oxford University Press.

Bayley, D. H. and Shearing, C. (2001) *The New Structure of Policing.* Washington, DC: National Institute of Justice.

BBC (2000) 'The Bent Cop', *Panorama*, broadcast 3 December. BBC World News: Panorama Archive.

Beigel, H. and Beigel, A. (1977) *Beneath the Badge.* New York: Harper and Row.

Belfast Telegraph (2007) 'Nuala O'Loan: The job I didn't want to leave', 5 November.

Belur, J. (2007) *Police Use of Deadly Force: Analysing Police 'Encounters' in Mumbai*, PhD thesis, Department of Sociology, London School of Economics.

Bennett, R. (1993) *Double Jeopardy.* Harmondsworth: Penguin.

Besse, A. and Kuys, J. (1997) *Cowboys aan het Spaarne.* Breda: De Geus.

Bittner, E. (1965) 'The concept of organization', *Social Research*, 32 (Winter): 239–55.

Bittner, E. (1967) 'The police on Skid Row: a study of peace-keeping', *American Sociological Review*, XXXII(5): 699–715.

Black, A. (1968) *The Police and the People.* New York: McGraw-Hill.

Blair, I. (1999) 'Police corruption: the UK experience and response', NIJ/NYU Seminar on Police Integrity and Democracies Florence, May.

Blair, I. (2003) 'Leading towards the future', speech at the Future of Policing Conference, London School of Economics, September.

Blair, I. (2005) *Richard Dimbleby Lecture.* London: BBC.

Blanken, M. (1976) *Force of Order and Methods.* The Hague: Martinus Nijhoff.

Bovens, M. (1998) *The Quest for Responsibility: Accountability and Citizenship in Complex Organizations.* Cambridge: Cambridge University Press.

Bowden, T. (1978) *Beyond the Limits of the Law.* Harmondsworth: Penguin.

Bowes, S. (1968) *Police and Civil Liberties.* London: Lawrence and Wishart.

Bowling, B. (1999) 'The rise and fall of New York murder', *British Journal of Criminology*, 39(4): 531–54.

Bowling, B. (2008) 'Fair and effective police methods: towards "good-enough" policing', *Scandinavian Studies in Criminology and Crime Prevention*, 8/S1, 17–23.

Bowling, B. and Foster, J. (2002) 'Policing and the police', in M. Maguire, R. Morgan and R. Reiner (eds) *The Oxford Handbook of Policing*, 3rd edn. Oxford: Clarendon Press.

Bowling, B. and Newburn, T. (2006) 'Policing and national security', paper presented at Columbia University–IALS London Workshop: Police, Community and the Rule of Law, March.

Bowling, B. and Phillips, C. (2003) 'Policing ethnic minority communities', in T. Newburn (ed.) *Handbook of Policing.* Cullompton: Willan Publishing.

Bowling, B., Phillips, C., Campbell, A. and Docking, M. (2004) *Policing and Human Rights.* Geneva: UNRISD.

Brants, C. (1999) 'The fine art of regulated tolerance: prostitution in Amsterdam', *Journal of Law and Society*, 25(4): 621–53.

Brodeur, J.-P. (1981) 'Legitimizing police deviance,' in C. D. Shearing (ed.) *Organizational Police Deviance*. Toronto: Butterworths.

Brodeur, J.-P. (1983) 'High and low policing: remarks about the policing of political activities', *Social Problems*, 30(5): 507–20.

Brown, D. B. (1998) 'The Royal Commission into the NSW Police Service process corruption and the limits of judicial reflexivity', *Current Issues in Criminal Justice*, 9(3): 228–40.

Browning, C. (1992) *Ordinary Men*. Harmondsworth: Penguin.

Bunyan, T. (1977) *The Political Police in Britain*. London: Quartet Books.

Burnham, D. (1976) *The Role of the Media in Controlling Corruption*. New York: John Jay Press.

Cain, M. (1973) *Society and the Policeman's Role*. London: Routledge & Kegan Paul.

Carte, G. E. and Carte, E. H. (1975) *Police Reform in the USA: The Era of August Vollmer*. Berkeley, CA: University of California Press.

Chambliss, W. J. (1971) 'Vice, corruption, bureaucracy and power', *University of Wisconsin Law Review*, 4: 1150–73.

Chan, J. B. L. (1997) *Changing Police Culture: Policing in a Multicultural Society*. Cambridge: Cambridge University Press.

Chan, J. B. L. (1999) 'Governing police practice: limits of the new accountability', *British Journal of Sociology*, 50(2): 249–68.

Chan, J. B. L. (2003) *Fair Cop: Learning the Art of Policing*. Toronto: University of Toronto Press.

Chatterton, M. (1976) 'Police arrest powers as resources in peace-keeping', *Social Work Today*, 7: 234–49.

Chemerinsky, E. (2000) *An Independent Analysis of the LAPD's Board of Inquiry Report into the Rampart Scandal*. Los Angeles: University of Southern California.

Chicago Tribune (2006) 'Chicago brass ignores culprits, key expert says', 29 November.

Chicago Tribune (2007) 'Cops disband elite unit', 10 October.

Christianson, S. (1973) 'Albany's finest wriggle free', *The Nation*, 3 December.

Christie, S. (2004) *Granny Made Me an Anarchist*. London: Scribner.

Christopher Commission (1991) *Independent Commission on the Los Angeles Police Department*. Los Angeles: City of Los Angeles.

Cohen, S. (2001) *States of Denial*. Cambridge: Polity.

Collins, R. (2008) *Violence: A Micro-sociological Theory*. Princeton/Oxford: Princeton University Press.

Command Corruption Profile (1973) *Report of Intelligence Section of Internal Affairs Division*. New York: NYPD.

Commission on Police Integrity (1997) *Report of the Commission on Police Integrity*. Chicago: Chicago Police Department.

Cox, B., Shirley, J. and Short, M. (1977) *The Fall of Scotland Yard*. Harmondsworth: Penguin.

Cramphorn, C. (2006) 'Set for an unfair cop', *Yorkshire Post*, 24 March.

Crank, J. P. (1998). *Understanding Police Culture*. Cincinnati, OH: Anderson.

Crawshaw, R. and Holmström, L. (2006) *Essential Cases on Human Rights for the Police*. Leiden/Boston: Martinus Nijhoff.

Cressey, D. R. (1969) *Theft of the Nation*. New York: Harper.

Critchley, T. A. (1978) *A History of Police in England and Wales*. London: Constable.

Daley, R. (1979) *Prince of the City*. London: Panther.

Dalton, M. (1959) *Men Who Manage*. New York: Wiley.

Davies, N. (1999) *Ten-Thirty Three*. Edinburgh and London: Mainstream.

Dillon, M. (1991) *The Dirty War*. Arrow: London.

Ditton, J. (1977) *Part-Time Crime*. London: Macmillan.

Dixon, D. (ed.) (1999a) *A Culture of Corruption*. Leichhardt, NSW: Hawkins Press.

Dixon, D. (1999b) 'Issues in the legal regulation of policing', in D. Dixon (ed.) *A Culture of Corruption*. Leichhardt, NSW: Hawkins Press.

Dixon, D. (1999c) 'The normative structure of policing', in D. Dixon (ed.) *A Culture of Corruption*. Leichhardt, NSW: Hawkins Press.

Dixon, D. (1999d) 'Reform, regression and the Royal Commission into the NSW Police Service', in D. Dixon (ed.) *A Culture of Corruption*. Leichhardt, NSW: Hawkins Press.

Dombrink, J. (1988) 'The touchables: vice and police corruption in the 1980s', *Law and Contemporary Problems*, 51(1): 201–32.

Dominion Post (2007) 'Former cops under spotlight', 12 December.

Downes, D. (1988) *Contrasts in Tolerance*. Oxford: Clarendon Press.

Downes, D. and Rock, P. (2007) *Understanding Deviance*, 5th edn. Oxford: Oxford University Press.

Duchaine, N. (1979) *The Literature on Police Corruption, Vol. 2: A Selected, Annotated Bibliography*. New York: John Jay Press.

Dutch Report (1994) *Contribution of the Netherlands Delegation to World Ministerial Conference on Organised Transnational Crime*. Naples, November.

Economist (1980) 'Policing the police', 4 July.

Economist (1982) 'Police corruption: copy Hong Kong', 7 August.

Economist (1999) 'The LAPD: over-creative policing', 25 September.

Einstein S. and Amir, A. (2003) (eds) *Police Corruption: Paradigms, Models and Concepts*. Huntsville: TX: OICJ.

Ellis, S. (1998) 'The historical significance of South Africa's Third Force', *Journal of South African Studies*, 24(2): 261–99.

Emsley, C. (1996) *The English Police: A Political and Social History*. London: Longman.

English, R. (2004) *Armed Struggle: The History of the IRA*. London: Pan.

Ericson, R. V. (1981) 'Rules for police deviance', in C. D. Shearing (ed.) *Organizational Police Deviance*. Toronto: Butterworths.

Ermann, M. D. and Lundman, R. J. (eds) (1996) *Corporate and Governmental Deviance*, 3rd edn. New York/Oxford: Oxford University Press.

Extra (1978) 'Exclusief Onderzoek in Corruptie-Schandaal bij Amsterdamse Politie', 29 December.

FBI (2005) 'Four Chicago police officers, five others, arrested on drug and conspiracy charges', Federal Bureau of Investigation press release, 27 January. Chicago: US Department of Justice.

Fijnaut, C. (1983) *De Zaak Francois*. Antwerpen: Kluwer.

Fijnaut, C. and Marx, G. T. (eds) (1995) *Undercover: Police Surveillance in Comparative Perspective*. The Hague/London/Boston: Kluwer.

Fisher, Sir H. (1977) *The Confait Case: Report*. London: HMSO.

Fitzgerald Commission (1987) *Commission of Inquiry into Possible Illegal Activities and Associated Police Misconduct*. Brisbane: Government Printer.

Flin, R. (1996) *Sitting in the Hot Seat*. New York: Wiley

Fogelson, R. M. (1977) *Big-City Police*. Cambridge, MA: Harvard University Press.

Fosdick, R. B. (1915) *European Police Systems*. New York: Century.

Foster, J. (2003) 'Police cultures', in T. Newburn (ed.) *The Handbook of Policing*. Cullompton: Willan Publishing.

Foster, J. (2008) '"It might have been incompetent but it wasn't racist": murder detectives' perceptions of the Lawrence Inquiry and its impact on homicide investigation in London', *Policing and Society*, 18(2): 89–112.

Foster, J., Newburn, T. and Souhami, A. (2005) *Assessing the Impact of the Stephen Lawrence Inquiry*. London: Home Office.

Gaffigan, S. and McDonald, P. (1997) *Police Integrity: Public Service with Honor – Report of National Symposium on Police Integrity*. Washington, DC: National Institute of Justice/Office of Community Oriented Policing Services.

GAO Report (1998) *Law Enforcement: Information on Drug-related Police Corruption*. Washington, DC: US Government Audit Office.

Gardiner, J. A. (1970) *The Politics of Corruption*. New York: Russell Sage Foundation.

Gardiner, J. A. and Olson, D. J. (1974) (eds) *Theft of the City*. Bloomington, IN: Indiana University Press.

Geis, G. (1996) 'White collar crime: the heavy electrical equipment anti-trust cases', in M. D. Ermann and R. J. Lundman (eds) *Corporate and Governmental Deviance*, 3rd edn. New York/Oxford: Oxford University Press.

Gillard, M. and Flynn, L. (2004) *The Untouchables*. Edinburgh and London: Mainstream.

Giuliani, R. W. and Bratton, W. J. (1995) *Police Strategy No.7: Rooting Out Corruption: Building Organizational Integrity in the New York Police Department*. New York: NYPD.

Glazer, S. (1995) 'Police corruption: can brutality and other misconduct be rooted out?', *Congressional Quarterly Researcher*, 5(44): 1041–64.

Gobert, J. (2008) 'The evolving legal test of corporate criminal liability', in J. Minkes and L. Minkes (eds) *Corporate and White-Collar Crime*. London: Sage.

Gobert, J. and Punch, M. (2000) 'Whistleblowers, public interest and the Public Interest Disclosure Act 1998', *Modern Law Review*, 63(1): 25–54.

Goffman, E. (1959) *The Presentation of Self in Everyday Life*. Harmondsworth: Penguin.

Goffman, E. (1961) *Asylums*. Harmondsworth: Penguin.

Goldschmidt, J. (2008) 'The necessity for dishonesty: police deviance, "making the case" and the public good', *Policing and Society*, 18(2): 113–35.

Goldsmith A. (1991) (ed.) *Complaints Against the Police: The Trend to External Review*. Oxford: Oxford University Press.

Goldsmith, A. and Lewis, C. (eds) (2000) *Civilian Oversight of Policing: Governance, Democracy and Human Rights*. Portland, OR: Hart.

Goldstein, H. (1977) *Policing a Free Society*. Cambridge, MA: Ballinger.

Gouldner, A. (1954) *Patterns of Industrial Democracy*. New York: Free Press.

Gourevitch, P. and Morris, E. (2008) *Standard Operating Procedure: A War Story*. New York: Penguin.

Grabosky, P. (1989) *Wayward Governance*. Canberra: Australian Institute of Criminology.

Green, G. (1997) *Occupational Crime*, 2nd edn. Chicago: Nelson-Hall.

Green, P. and Ward, T. (2004) *State Crime: Governments, Violence and Corruption*. London: Pluto.

Gross (1980) 'Organization structure and organizational crime', in G. Geis and E. Stotland (eds) *White Collar Crime*. Beverly Hills, CA: Sage.

Guardian (1974) 'Police chief made £400,000 from Hong Kong vice', 8 October.

Guardian Unlimited (2000a) 'Corruption squad under fire', 4 March.

Guardian Unlimited (2000b) '"Untouchables" of the Met drop corrupt supergrass', 20 March.

Guardian Unlimited (2006) 'New York on edge as police kill unarmed man in hail of 50 bullets on his wedding day', 27 November.

Haagse Post (1977) 'Dossier Corruptie', 30 April.

Haenen, M. and Meeus, T.-J. (1996) *Het IRT Moeras*. Amsterdam: Balans.

Hain, P., Humphry, D. and Rose-Smith, B. (1979) *Policing the Police, Vol. 1*. London: Calder.

Harrison, J. and Cunneen, M. (2000) *An Independent Police Complaints Commission*. London: Liberty.

Hawkins, K. (2002) *Law as Last Resort*. Oxford: Oxford University Press.

Hayes, M. (1997) *A Police Ombudsman for Northern Ireland*. London: HMSO.

Hayward, H. (2000) 'Canteen Culture', *Times Literary Supplement*, 31 March.

Heidenheimer, A. J. (ed.) (1970) *Political Corruption*. New York: Holt, Rinehart & Winston.

Hinton, M. S. (2005) *The State on the Streets*. Boulder, CO/London: Rienner.

Hinton, M. S. and Newburn, T. (eds) (2009) *Policing Developing Democracies*. London and New York: Routledge.

HMIC (1999) *Police Integrity: Securing and Maintaining Public Confidence*. London: Home Office.

Hobbs, R. (1988) *Doing the Business*. Oxford: Oxford University Press.

Holdaway, S. (ed.) (1979) *The British Police*. London: Arnold.

Holdaway, S. (1980) *The Occupational Culture of Urban Policing*, PhD Thesis, University of Sheffield.

Holdaway, S. (1983) *Inside the British Police*. Oxford: Basil Blackwell.

Honeycombe, G. (1974) *Adam's Tale*. London: Hutchinson.

Hopkins-Burke, R. (2004) *Hard Cop, Soft Cop: Dilemmas and Debates in Contemporary Policing*. Cullompton: Willan Publishing.

Hornberger, J. (2007) *Don't Push This Constitution Down My Throat*, PhD Thesis, University of Utrecht, School of Law.

Huberts, L., Lamboo, T. and Punch, M. (2003) 'Police integrity in the Netherlands and the United States', *Police Practice and Research*, 4(3): 217–32.

Hughes, E. (1963) 'Good people and dirty work', in H. S. Becker (ed.) *The Other Side*. Glencoe: Free Press.

Ingram, M. and Harkin, G. (2004) *Stakeknife: Britains Secret Agent in Ireland*. Dublin: O'Brien Press.

IPCC (2004) *Highmoor Cross Report*. London: IPCC.

IPCC (2006) *IPCC Annual Report 2005/06*. London: IPCC.

IPCC (2007c) *IPCC Annual Report 2006/07*. London: IPCC.

IPCC (2007a) *Stockwell One: Investigation into the shooting of Jean Charles de Menezes at Stockwell underground station on 22 July 2005*. London: IPCC.

IPCC (2007b) *Stockwell Two: An investigation into complaints about the Metropolitan Police Service handling of public statements following the shooting of Jean Charles de Menezes on 22 July 2005*. London: IPCC.

IPCC (2008) *IPCC Annual Report 2007/08*. London: IPCC.

Jackall, R. (1988) *Moral Mazes*. New York/Oxford: Oxford University Press.

The Job (1999) 'Ideas wanted on how to foil corruption' and 'Corruption crack-down', 3 September: 3, 8–9.

Jones, T. (2003) 'The governance and accountability of policing', in T. Newburn (ed.) *Handbook of Policing*. Cullompton: Willan Publishing.

Jones, T. (2008) 'The governance and accountability of policing' in T. Newburn (ed.) *Handbook of Policing*, 2nd edn. Cullompton: Willan Publishing.

Justice Report (1989) *Miscarriages of Justice*. London: Justice.

Kappeler, V. E., Sluder, R. D. and Alpert, P. (1994) *Forces of Deviance: Understanding the Dark Side of Policing*. Prospect Heights, IL: Waveland Press.

Katz, J. (1988) *The Seductions of Crime*. New York: Basic Books.

Kaye, T. (1991) *Unsafe and Unsatisfactory: Report of Independent Inquiry into the Working Practices of the West Midlands Police Serious Crimes Squad*. London: Civil Liberties Trust.

Kennedy School (1977a) 'Note on police corruption in New York in 1970', mimeo, Kennedy School of Government. Cambridge, MA: Harvard University.

Kennedy School (1977b) 'The Knapp Commission and Patrick Murphy', mimeo, Kennedy School of Government. Cambridge, MA: Harvard University.

Kennison, P. (2001) *Policing Black People: A Study of Ethnic Relations as Seen Through the Police Complaints System*, PhD Thesis, University of Middlesex.

Kennison, P. and Loumansky, A. (2007) 'Shoot to kill: understanding police use of force in combating suicide terrorism', *Crime, Law and Social Change*, 47: 151–68.

Kerner Report (1968) *Report of the National Advisory Commission on Civil Disorders*. Washington, DC: USGPO.

Kleinig, J. (1996) *The Ethics of Policing*. Cambridge: Cambridge University Press.

Klerks, P. (1995) 'Covert policing in the Netherlands', in C. Fijnaut and G. T. Marx (eds) *Undercover: Police Surveillance in Comparative Perspective*. The Hague/London/Boston: Kluwer.

Klockars, C. B. (1985) *The Idea of Police*. Beverly Hills, CA: Sage.

Klockars, C. B. (2005) 'The Dirty Harry problem', in T. Newburn (ed.) *Policing: Key Readings*. Cullompton: Willan Publishing.

Klockars, C. B., Kutnjak Ivkovic, S. and Haberfeld, M. B. (2004) *The Contours of Police Integrity*. Thousand Oaks, CA: Sage.

Knapp Commission (1972) *The Report of the Commission to Investigate Alleged Police Corruption and the City's Anti-Corruption Procedures*. New York: Braziller.

Knight, S. (1983) *The Brotherhood*. London: Granada.

Knights, D. and McCabe, D. (2003) *Organization and Innovation: Guru Schemes and American Dreams*. Maidenhead: Open University Press.

KPMG (2000) *Feasibility of an Independent System for Investigating Complaints Against the Police*. London: Home Office.

Kutnjak Ivkovic, S. (2005) *Fallen Blue Knights*. New York/Oxford: Oxford University Press.

Lamboo, T. (2000) *Will History Repeat Itself?*, Master's Thesis, University of Amsterdam.

Lamboo, T. (2005) *Integriteitsbeleid van de Nederlands Politie*. Delft: Eburon.

Landesco, J. (1929) *Organized Crime in Chicago*. Chicago: Chicago University Press.

Langendoen, K. and Vierboom, A. (1998) *Het Konings Koppel*. Amsterdam: Balans.

LAPD (2000) *Board of Inquiry into the Rampart Area Corruption Incident*. Los Angeles: LAPD.

Laurie, P. (1972) *Scotland Yard*. Harmondsworth: Penguin.

Lee, M. and Punch, M. (2006) *Policing by Degrees*. Groningen: Hondsrug Pers.

Leishman, F., Savage, S. and Loveday, B. (eds) (1966) *Core Issues in Policing*. London: Longman.

Leo, R. A. and Ofshe, R. J. (1998) 'The consequences of false confessions', *Journal of Criminal Law and Criminology*, 88(2): 429–96.

Leuci, R. (2004) *All the Centurions*. New York: Harper Collins.

Lipsky, M. (1980) *Street Level Bureaucrats*. New York: Russell-Sage Foundation.

Loader, I. and Walker, N. (2007) *Civilizing Security*. Cambridge: Cambridge University Press.

Lyman, M. and Scott, S. (1970) *Sociology of the Absurd*. New York: Appleton Century Crofts.

Maas, P. (1974) *Serpico*. London: Collins.

McBarnet, D. (1979) 'Arrest: the legal context of policing', in S. Holdaway (ed.) *The British Police*. London: Arnold.

McConville, M. and Bridges, L. (eds) 1994) *Criminal Justice in Crisis*. Cheltenham: Edward Elgar Publishing.

McLagan, G. (2004) *Bent Coppers*. London: Orion.

McLaughlin, E. (2005) 'Forcing the issue: New Labour, new localism and the democratic renewal of police accountability', *Howard Journal*, 44(5): 473–89.

McLaughlin, E. and Johansen, A. (2002) 'A force for change? The prospects for applying restorative justice to citizen complaints against the police in England and Wales', *British Journal of Criminology*, 42(3): 635–53.

McMahon, M. and Ericson, R. (1984) *Policing Reform*. Toronto: Centre for Criminology.

McNee, D. (1983) *McNee's Law*. London: Collins.

Macpherson, W. (1999) *The Stephen Lawrence Inquiry: Report of an Inquiry by Sir William Macpherson of Cluny*. London: HMSO.

Manion, M. (2004) *Corruption by Design*. Cambridge, MA: Harvard University Press.

Manning, P. K. (1977) *Police Work*. Cambridge, MA: MIT Press.

Manning, P. K. (1980) *The Narc's Game*. Cambridge, MA: MIT Press.

Manning, P. K. and Redlinger, L. J. (1978) 'Invitational edges of corruption', in P. Manning and J. Van Maanen (eds) *Policing: A View from the Street*. Santa Monica, CA: Goodyear.

Manning, P. K. and Van Maanen, J. (1978) (eds) *Policing: A View from the Street*. Santa Monica, CA: Goodyear.

Mark, R. (1977) *Policing a Perplexed Society*. London: Allen and Unwin.

Mark, R. (1978) *In the Office of Constable*. London: Collins.

Markham, G. and Punch, M. G. (2007a) 'Embracing accountability: the way forward – part one', *Policing: Journal of Research and Practice*, 1(3): 1–9.

Markham, G. and Punch, M. (2007b) 'Embracing accountability: the way forward – part two', *Policing: Journal of Research and Practice,* 1(4): 485–94.

Mars, (1982) *Cheats at Work*. London: Allen and Unwin.

Marshall, G. (1978) 'Police accountability revisited', in D. Butler and A. Halsey (eds) *Policy and Politics*. London: Macmillan.

Marx, G. T. (1988) *Undercover: Police Surveillance in America*. Berkeley: University of California Press.

Masuch, M. (1985) 'Vicious circles in organizations', *Administrative Science Quarterly*, 30: 14–33.

Matza, D. (1969) *Becoming Deviant*. Englewood Cliffs, NJ: Prentice-Hall.

Mawby, R. I. (1999) *Policing Across the World*. London: University College London Press.

Meeus, J. and Schoorl, J. (2002) *Zand Erover*. Amsterdam: Meulenhoff.

Miami Herald (2001) 'Officers accused of drug crimes', 7 February.

Middelburg, B. (1993) *De Dominee*. Amsterdam: Veen.

Middelburg, B. and Vugts, P. (2006) *De oorlog in de Amsterdamse Onderwereld*. Amsterdam: Nieuwe Amsterdam.

Miller, J. (2003) *Police Corruption in England and Wales*. London: Home Office.

Miller, W. (1977) *Cops and Bobbies*. Chicago: University of Chicago Press.

Mollen Commission (1994) *Report of the Commission to Investigate Allegations of Police Corruption and the Anti-Corruption Procedures of the Police Department*. City of New York: Mollen Commission.

Moore, B. (1997) *Victims and Survivors*. London: Arnold.

Moore, R. (1971) *The French Connection*. New York: Bantam.

Morgan, R. and Newburn, T. (1997) *The Future of Policing*. Oxford: Oxford UniversityPress.

Morris Tribunal (2004) *The Tribunal of Inquiry into complaints concerning some Gardai of the Donegal Division*. Dublin: Ministry of Justice.

Morton, J. (1994) *Bent Coppers: A Survey of Police Corruption*. London: Warner.

Moskos, P. (2008) *Cop in the Hood*. Princeton: Princeton University Press.

Muir, W. K. (1977) *Police: Streetcorner Politicians*. Chicago: University of Chicago Press.

Mulcahy, A. (2006) *Policing Northern Ireland*. Cullompton: Willan Publishing.

Mullin, C. (1990) *Error of Judgment*. Dublin: Poolbeg.

Murphy, P. and Plate, T. (1977) *Commissioner*. New York: Simon and Schuster.

Nadelmann, E. (1993) *Cops Across borders: The Internationalisation of US Law Enforcement*. University Park: Pennsylvania State University Press.

Nadelmann, E. (1995) 'The DEA in Europe', in C. Fijnaut and G. T. Marx (eds) *Undercover: Police Surveillance in Comparative Perspective*. The Hague/London/Boston: Kluwer.

Naeyé, J. (1995) *Het politieël vooronderzoek in strafzaken*. Arnhem: Gouda Quint.

New Statesman (1980) 'The story of Operation Countryman', 18 January.

New York Daily News (2004) 'Dowd: I don't expect any sympathy', 30 April.

New York Magazine (2007) 'William Phillips, Knapp Commission informant, paroled', 21 September.

New York Times (1970) 'Graft paid to police here: said to run in millions', 25 April.

New York Times (1982) 'A decade after Knapp: sense of "revolution" pervades police department', 29 November.

New Yorker (1997) 'The crime buster', 24 February and 3 March.

The New Zealand Herald (2007) 'Operation Austin assessing four other police complaints', 12 December.

Newburn, T. (1999) *Understanding and Preventing Police Corruption: Lessons from the Literature*. London: Home Office.

Newburn, T. (ed.) (2003) *Handbook of Policing*. Cullompton: Willan Publishing.

Newburn, T. (ed.) (2005) *Policing: Key Readings*. Cullompton: Willan Publishing.

Newburn, T. (ed.) (2008) *Handbook of Policing*, 2nd edn. Cullompton: Willan Publishing.

Newburn, T. and Sparks, R. (eds) (2004) *Criminal Justice and Political Cultures*. Cullompton: Willan Publishing.

Newman, G. F. (1977) *A Detective's Tale*. London: Sphere.

Neyroud, P. (2004) 'Closer to the citizen? Developing accountability and governance in policing', presentation at British Society of Criminology Conference, Birmingham, July.

Neyroud, P. (2005) 'ACPO and the NPIA: a new professional future', presentation to ACPO, June.

Neyroud, R. and Beckley, P. (2001) *Policing, Ethics and Human Rights*. Cullompton: Willan Publishing.

Niederhoffer, A. (1967) *Behind the Shield*. New York: Doubleday Anchor.

Nieuwe Revue (1977) 'Politie bezwijkt voor geld', 28 January.

Nolan, Lord (1998) *First Report of the Committee on Standards in Public Life*. London: HMSO.

Observer (1982) 'Obstruction in Countryman Inquiry', 4 April.

O'Connor, D. (2005) *Closing the Gap*. London: HMIC.

Ofshe, R. J. and Leo, R. A. (1997) 'The social psychology of police interrogation', *Studies in Law, Politics and Society*, 16(1): 189–251.

O'Neill, O. (2002) *A Question of Trust: BBC Reith Lectures*. London: BBC.

OPI (2008) *The Victorian Armed Offenders Squad*. Victoria: Office of Police Integrity.

OPONI (2001) *Omagh Bomb Report: Statement by the Police Ombudsman for Northern Ireland on matters relating to the Omagh bombing of 15 August 1998*. Belfast: OPONI.

OPONI (2007a) *Statement by the Police Ombudsman for Northern Ireland on her investigation into the circumstances surrounding the death of Raymond McCord Junior and related matters*. Belfast: OPONI.

OPONI (2007b) *Developments in Police Complaints – 7 Years On*. Belfast: OPONI.

Orde, H. (2003) 'Working with an independent investigation agency', presentation at OPONI conference, Policing the Police, Belfast, November.

Palmier, L. (1983) 'Bureaucratic corruption and its remedies', in M. Clarke (ed.) *Corruption*. London: Frances Pinter.

Parker, R. (1981) *Rough Justice*. London: Fontana.

Patten Commission (1999) *A New Beginning: Policing in Northern Ireland. Report of the Independent Commission on Policing for Northern Ireland*. London: Home Office.

Pennsylvania Crime Commission (1974) *Report on Police Corruption and Quality of Law Enforcement in Philadelphia*. St Davids, PA: Pennsylvania Crime Commission.

President's Commission (1967) *Law Enforcement and the Administration of Justice: Task Force Report – The Police*. Washington, DC: USGPO.

Pretoria News (2008) 'Kill the bastards, minister tells police', 10 April.

Punch, M. (1979) *Policing the Inner City*. London: Macmillan.

Punch, M. (ed.) (1983a) *Control in the Police Organisation*. Cambridge, MA: MIT Press.

Punch, M. (1983b) 'Officers and men: occupational culture, inter-rank antagonism and the investigation of corruption,' in M. Punch (ed.) *Control in the Police Organisation*. Cambridge, MA: MIT Press.

Punch, M. (1985) *Conduct Unbecoming: The Social Construction of Police Deviance and Control*. London: Tavistock.

Punch, M. (1986) *Politics and Ethics of Field-Work*. Beverly Hills, CA: Sage.

Punch, M. (1989) 'Researching police deviance', *British Journal of Sociology*, 40(2): 177–204.

Punch, M. (1996) *Dirty Business*. London: Sage.

Punch, M. (1997) 'The Dutch criminal justice system: a crisis of identity', *Security Journal*, 9: 177–84.

Punch, M. (2000) 'Police corruption and its prevention', *European Journal on Criminal Policy and Research*, 8(3): 301–24.

Punch, M. (2002) 'De appel en de mand', *De Gids*, 10: 843–78.

Punch, M. (2003) 'Rotten orchards: "pestilence", police misconduct and system failure', *Policing and Society*, 13 (2): 171–96.

Punch, M. (2005) 'The Belgian disease: Dutroux, scandal and "system failure" in Belgium', in R. Sarre, H. J. Albrecht and D. Das (eds) *Policing Corruption: International Perspectives*. Lanham, MD: Lexington.

Punch, M. (2007) *Zero Tolerance Policing*. Bristol: Policy Press.

Punch, M. (2008) 'The organization did it: individuals, corporations and crime', in J. Minkes and L. Minkes (eds) *Corporate and White-Collar Crime*. London: Sage.

Punch, M. (2009) 'Why corporations kill and get away with it: the failure of law to cope with crime in organizations', in P. A. Nollkaemper and H. van der Wilt (eds) *System Criminality in International Law*. Cambridge: Cambridge University Press.

Punch, M. and Gobert, J. (2007) 'Because they can: motivations and intent of white-collar criminals', in H. N. Pontell and G. Geis (eds) *International Handbook of White-Collar and Corporate Crime*. New York: Springer.

Punch, M. and Markham, G. (2000) 'Policing disasters', *International Journal of Police Science & Management*, 3(1): 40–54.

Punch, M. and Markham, G. (2003) 'The Gemini solution: embracing accountability', in M. Amir and S. Einstein (eds) *Police Corruption: Challenges for Developed Countries*. Huntsville, TX: OICJ.

Punch, M. and Markham, G. (2004) 'Animal rights, public order and police accountability', *International Journal of Police Science and Management*, 6(2): 84–96.

Punch, M. and Markham, G. (2009) 'Police accountability: never ending quest', in B. Bowling and G. Fagan (eds) *Policing the Community and the Rule of Law*. Oxford: Hart.

Punch, M. and Nowicki, D. (2003) 'Fostering integrity and professional standards', in W. A. Geller and D. W. Stephens (eds) *Local Government Police Management*. Washington, DC: ICMA.

Punch, M. and Wood, D. (2004) 'A model of accountability', *Policing Today*, 10(4): 26–8.

RCMP (1998) 'Shared Leadership Vision', *Royal Canadian Mounted Police*. Ottawa: RCMP.

Reiner, R. (1978) *The Blue Coated Worker*. Cambridge: Cambridge University Press.

Reiner, R. (1991) *Chief Constables*. Oxford: Oxford University Press.

Reiner, R. (1992) *The Politics of the Police*. Hemel Hempstead: Harvester.

Reiner, R. (1997) 'Policing and the police', in M. Maguire, R. Morgan and R. Reiner (eds) *The Oxford Handbook of Policing*, 2nd edn. Oxford: Clarendon Press.

Reiner, R. (2000) *The Politics of the Police*, 3rd edn. Oxford: Oxford University Press.

Reiner, R. (2007) *Law and Order*. Cambridge: Polity.

Reisman, D. (1979) *Folded Lies*. New York: Free Press.

Reiss, A. J. Jr (1971) *The Police and the Public*. New Haven, CT: Yale University Press.

Reiss, A. J. Jr (1977) 'Foreword', in **A.** Simpson (1977) *The Literature of Police Corruption, Vol. 1: A Guide to Bibliography and Theory*. New York: John Jay Press.

Reuss-Ianni, E. R. (1983) *Two Cultures of Policing*. New Brunswick, NJ: Transaction Books.

Richardson, J. F. (1974) *Urban Police in the United States*. Port Washington, NY: Kennikat.

Rock, P. (2004) *Constructing Victims' Rights*. Oxford: Oxford University Press.

Rokyo, M. (1971) *Boss: Richard J. Daley of Chicago*. New York: Ditton.

Rose, D. (1992) *Climate of Fear*. London: Bloomsbury.

Rose, D. (1996) *In the Name of the Law*. London: Jonathan Cape.

Royakkers, C. M. H. (1997) *De controle over de politie in Engeland en Wales*, PhD Thesis, University of Maastricht. Arnhem: Gouda Quint.

Rubinstein, J. (1973) *City Police*. New York: Ballantine.

Ryder, C. (2000) *The RUC*. London: Arrow.

Salaman, G. (1979) *Work Organisations*. London: Longman.

Sands, P. (2008) *Torture Team: Deception, Cruelty and the Compromise of Law*. Hamondsworth: Penguin.

Sarre, R., Das, D. and Albrecht, H. J. (2005) (eds) *Policing Corruption: International Perspectives*. Lanham, ML: Lexington.

Scarman, L. (1981) *The Scarman Report: The Brixton Disorders*. London: HMSO. Reprinted 1982, Harmondsworth: Penguin.

Schein, E. (1985) *Organizational Culture and Leadership*. San Francisco: Jossey Bass.

Scraton, P. (1999) *Hillsborough: The Truth*. Edinburgh and London: Mainstream.

Shearing, C. D. (ed.) (1981) *Organizational Police Deviance*. Toronto: Butterworths.

Shecter, L. and Phillips, W. (1974) *On the Pad*. New York: Putnam.

Sheptycki, J. (1999) 'Political culture and structures of control: police-related scandals in the Low Countries in comparative perspective', *Police and Society*, 9(1): 1–32.

Sheptycki, J. (ed.) (2000a) *Issues in Transnational Policing*. London and New York: Routledge.

Sheptycki, J. (2000b) 'The "Drug War": learning from the paradigm example of transnational policing', in J. Sheptycki (ed.) *Issues in Transnational Policing*. London and New York: Routledge.

Sherman, L. W. (ed.) (1974a) *Police Corruption: A Sociological Perspective*. New York: Doubleday.

Sherman, L. W. (1974b) 'Introduction: toward a sociological theory of police corruption', in L. W. Sherman (ed.) *Police Corruption: A Sociological Perspective*. New York: Doubleday.

Sherman, L. W. (1974c) 'Becoming bent: moral careers of corrupt policemen', in L. W. Sherman (ed.) *Police Corruption: A Sociological Perspective*. New York: Doubleday.

Sherman, L. W. (1977) *City Politics, Police Administrators, and Corruption Control*. New York: John Jay Press.

Sherman, L. W. (1978) *Scandal and Reform: Controlling Police Corruption*. Berkeley, CA: University of California Press.

Shover, N. (1980) 'The criminalization of corporate behaviour', in G. Geis and E. Stotland (eds) *White Collar Crime*. Beverly Hills, CA: Sage.

Simpson, A. (1977) *The Literature of Police Corruption, Vol. 1: A Guide to Bibliography and Theory*. New York: John Jay Press.

Singer, B. P. (1980) 'Crazy systems', *Social Policy*, September/October: 149–67.

Skogan, W. (2008) 'Why reforms fail', *Policing & Society*, 18(1): 23–34.

Skolnick, J. H. (1966) *Justice Without Trial*. New York: Wiley.

Skolnick, J. H. (2002) 'Code Blue: prosecuting police brutality requires penetrating the wall of silence', *American Prospect*, 27 March–10 April: 49–53.

Skolnick, J. and Fyfe, J. (2005) 'The beating of Rodney King', in T. Newburn (ed.) *Policing: Key Readings*. Cullompton: Willan Publishing.

Small, S. (1983) *Police and People in London, Vol. 2: A Group of Young Black People*. London: Policy Studies Institute.

Smith, D. J. (1983) *Police and People in London, Vol. 3: A Survey of Police Officers*. London: Policy Studies Institute.

Smith, D. J. and Gray, J. (1983a) *Police and People in London, Vol. 1: A Survey of Londoners*. London: Policy Studies Institute.

Smith, D. J. and Gray, J. (1983b) *Police and People in London, Vol. 4: The Police in Action*. London: Policy Studies Institute.

Smith, D. J. and Gray, J. (1985) *Police and People in London: The PSI Report*. London: Gower.

Smith, G. (2001) 'Police complaints and criminal prosecutions', *Modern Law Review*, 64(3): 372–92.

Smith, G. (2004) 'Rethinking police complaints', *British Journal of Criminology*, 44: 15–33.

Smith, G. (2005) 'A most enduring problem: police complaints reform in England and Wales', *Journal of Social Policy*, 35(1): 121–41.

Smith, G. (2006) 'Police complaints in the reform era', *Criminal Justice Matters*, 63: 26–7.

Sorrentino, J. (1980) *The Gold Shield*. New York: Dell.

Stalker, J. (1988) *Stalker: Ireland, 'Shoot to Kill' and the 'Affair'*. Harmondsworth: Penguin.

Stanton, M. (2003) *The Prince of Providence*. New York: Random House.

Steffens, J. L. (1957) *The Shame of the Cities*. New York: Hill and Wang (first published 1903).

Steinberg, J. (1989) 'Capos and cardinals', review in *London Review of Books*, 17 August.

Stevens, J. (2003) *Stevens Enquiry 3: Overview and Recommendations.* London: Home Office.

Sunday Times (1976) 'My anguish – by a Porn Squad detective', 26 November.

Sunday Times (1977) 'Mason Moody Partners, corruption a speciality', 15 May.

Sunday Times (1979) 'Nobblers fail to stop big probe into police', 2 December.

Sunday Times Magazine (1977) 'Top of the cops', 3 November.

Sykes, G. and Matza, D. (1957) 'Techniques of neutralization', *American Sociological Review*, 22: 664–70.

Tak, P. (2003) *The Dutch Criminal Justice System.* Meppel: Boom.

TI (Transparency International) (2007) *Corruption Perceptions Index 2007.* www. transparency.org

Uchida, C. D. (1993) 'The development of the American police: an historical overview', in G. Durham and G. P. Alpert (eds) *Critical Issues in Policing: Contemporary Readings*, 2nd edn. Prospect Heights, IL: Waveland Press.

Urban, M. (1993) *Big Boys' Rules.* London: Faber and Faber.

USDOJ (2001) *Principles for Promoting Police Integrity.* Washington, DC: US Department of Justice.

van de Bunt, H., Fijnaut, C. and Nelen, H. (2001) *Post-Fort: Evaluatie van het strafrechtelijk onderzoek (1996–1999).*

van Laere, E. and Geerts, R. (1984) *Wetshandhaver of Wetsontduiker.* Den Haag: Ministerie van Binnenlandse Zaken.

Van Maanen, J. (1973) 'Observations on the making of policemen', *Human Organisation*, 32(4): 407–18.

Van Maanen, J. (1978a) 'Kinsmen in repose: occupational perspectives of patrolmen', in P. K. Manning and J. Van Maanen (eds) *Policing: A View from the Street.* Santa Monica, CA: Goodyear: 115–28.

Van Maanen, J. (1978b) 'The asshole', in P. K. Manning and J. Van Maanen (eds) *Policing: A View from the Street.* Santa Monica, CA: Goodyear.

Van Maanen, J. (1978c) 'Watching the watchers', in P. K. Manning and J. Van Maanen (eds) *Policing: A View from the Street.* Santa Monica, CA: Goodyear.

Van Maanen, J. (1983) 'The boss: first-line supervision in an American police agency', in M. Punch (ed.) *Control in the Police Organisation.* Cambridge, MA: MIT Press.

van Traa Commission (1996) *Inzake opsporing: Enquête-commissie opsporingsmethoden.* Den Haag: Sdu Uitgevers.

de Volkskrant (1995) 'Politie hield tip justitie buiten doorvoer drugs', 7 September.

de Volkskrant (1997) 'Justitie in Limburg vervolgt verdachte rechercheurs niet', 15 November.

de Volkskrant (1998a) 'Ex-minister in Spanje kan 23 jaar cel krijgen', 26 May.

de Volkskrant (1998b) 'Spanje tegen Spanje', 20 June.

de Volkskrant (1998c) 'Ex-minister Spanje veroordeeld tot tien jaar cel', 30 July.

de Volkskrant (1998d) 'Kamer moet crisis bij politie zelf onderzoeken', 8October.

de Volkskrant (1999) 'Talentvolle CID-rechercheur veloor zichzelf in corruptie', 22 June.

Voyez, M. (1999) 'Lessons from Royal Commission into the New South Wales Police Service', presentation to Western Australian Police Service, October.

Vrij Nederland (1984) 'De politie van New York', 21 January.

Waddington, P. A. J. (1999a) *Policing Citizens*. London: UCL.

Waddington, P. A. J. (1999b) 'Police (canteen) sub-culture: an appreciation', *British Journal of Criminology*, 39(2): 286–308.

Walker, C. and Starmer, K. (1993) *Justice in Error*. London: Blackstone.

Walker, C. and Starmer, K. (1999) *Miscarriages of Justice: A Review of Justice in Error*. London: Blackstone.

Walker, S. (2001) *Police Accountability: The Role of Civilian Oversight*. Belmont, CA: Wadsworth.

Walker, S. (2003) *Early Intervention Schemes for Law-Enforcement Agencies*. Washington, DC: US Department of Justice.

Walker, S. (2005) *The New World of Police Accountability*. Thousand Oaks, CA: Sage.

Ward, R. H. (1975) 'Police corruption: an overview', *Police Journal*, 48 (January): 52–4.

Ward, R. H. and McCormack, R. (1979) *An Anti-Corruption Manual for Administrators in Law Enforcement*. New York: John Jay Press.

Weitzer, R. (1995) *Policing Under Fire*. Albany, NY: SUNY Press.

Weitzer, R. (2002) 'Incidents of police misconduct and public opinion', *Journal of Criminal Justice*, 30: 397–408.

Westley, W. A. (1970) *Violence and the Police*. Cambridge, MA: MIT Press.

Whitaker, B. (1979) *The Police in Society*. London: Eyre Methuen.

Whyte, W. F. (1955) *Street Corner Society*, 2nd edn. Chicago: University of Chicago Press.

Wierenga Commission (1994) *Rapport van de bijzondere onderzoekscommisse IRT*. The Hague: Ministry of Home Affairs.

Williamson, T. (2006) 'Who needs police authorities?', *Police Review*, 20 January: 15.

Wilson, J. Q. (1968) *Varieties of Police Behaviour*. Cambridge, MA: Harvard University Press.

Wing Lo, T. (1993) *Corruption and Politics in Hong Kong and China*. Buckingham/Philadelphia: Open University Press.

Wise, D. (1976) *The American Police State*. New York: Random House.

Wood, D. (2003) 'Police governance', presentation at OPONI conference: Policing the Police. Belfast, November.

Wood, J. R. T. (1997a) *Final Report of the Royal Commission into the New South Wales Police Service, Vol. 1: Corruption*. Sydney, NSW: RCNSWP.

Wood, J. R. T. (1997b) *Final Report of the Royal Commission into the New South Wales Police Service, Vol. 2: Reform*. Sydney, NSW: RCNSWP.

Young, J. (1971) *The Drugtakers*. Harmondsworth: Penguin.

Young, M. (1991) *An Inside Job: Policing and Police Culture in Britain*. Oxford: Clarendon Press.

Index

A10 Department
  Robert Mark, Metropolitan Police
    208
Abu Ghraib prison, Iraq 16
abuses
  of authority, office, power and
    trust 31–3, 224
accountability 235
  demise of 70
  policing as 2, 4, 9, 190–222
  UK 219
Association of Chief Police Officers
  (ACPO) Presidential Task Force
  on Corruption 1998 150
African National Congress (ANC)
  25
Afro-Americans 82
alcoholism 43, 44
American documentary, *Bad Cops*
  175
Amsterdam 93–125, 94
  scandal, 109–12
Amsterdam City Police
  antagonsim between ranks 110,
    111
  mild deviance 95, 96
anger in Belgium over Dutroux case
  30

Anglo-American 'adversary' system
  115
Anti-Corruption Manual (Ward and
  McCormack) 1979 238
anti-corruption strategies 239
Anti-Corruption Unit
  Robert Mark, Metropolitan Police
    208
appeal requests in Britain 138
appeal to higher loyalties
  'noble cause' defence 181
armed bank robbery, by police
  officer LAPD 77
Armed Offenders Squad (AOS),
  Victoria, Australia 246
army of occupation, police seen as
  87
Audit Commission, UK 199
auditors, LASD 218
Australia, scandals revealing
  extensive corruption 191
Australian, corrupt cop 4, 5
autonomy 35

'bad apple' analogy, Knapp rejection
  of 66
'bad apples' and 'rotten orchards'
  2, 9, 10

Murphy, Pat, NYPD Commissioner
  on police corruption in USA 54–5
Murphy, Patrick, clean-up of NYPD
  67–9

narcotics
  corruption 64–5
  police operational code 170
  stolen from NYPD property office
    170
  see also drugs, 64–6
Narcotics Division 65
National Detective Agency,
  Amsterdam 98
national outrage at IRA activities
  137
'national security' 228
National Symposium on Police
  Integrity 1996 82
  excessive force as corruption 31
nature of work as corrupting 42
negative stereotype 40–41
negative stereotypes of leaders,
  Amsterdam 103–4
Netherlands
  Amsterdam police 94
  centre for Europe drug trade 122
  corruption-free, 1975 94
  sociological-criminological
    perspective 8
New Orleans shooting by
  policewoman 50
New Police of the Metropolis
  low-key, unarmed and
    dependable 127
'new public management' in
  policing
  further claims 4
New Public Management (NPM)
  196
  managerial accountability 199
New South Wales, (NSW) Police 191
New York Police Department
  (NYPD) 12–14, 56–74
  corruption in 1960s 88

corruption scandals 11
deviance and excessive violence
  81
Nixon, President Richard
  pardon for crimes in office 88
  resignation 53
'noble cause', excuse 107
  in Dutch policing, 121
  in Great Britain 157
  in IRA violence cases 157
  rule benders, serving public good
    24–5, 33
Nolan Principles 4
non-enforcement by police,
  Amsterdam 95
Northern Ireland 142–57
  lack of accountability 143
  police deviance and corruption
    126–62
  'Troubles' (1968-98) 25
number crunchers
  search for success and kudos 25

Obscene Publications Squad (OPS)
  graft, friendship with vice
    entrepreneurs 132–3
  'Porn Squad' in the Met. 131
occupational culture as deviance
  42
  police vocabulary on 34
offences, serious 32
Office of Police Ombudsman for
  Northern Ireland (OPONI) 2, 7,
  149–51, 211
Office of Professional Standards
  (OPS) Chicago 76–7
officers leaving force under Robert
  Mark 134
official power, abuse of 11
officials ignoring corruption 76
O'Loan, Nuala 150, 162
Omagh bombing, 1998 152
Ombudsman
  criticism of RUC
  report on Special Branch 156

Exam

Bagley, police utility,
accountability & brutality

* Stuart, prosecutorial
Accountability

section 1-15
section 24. 1,2, 8-10 x charter Dialogue
section   by Hogg,
↓
exclusionary rule

x charter standards
for Investigative
powers - Stuart.

* Wrongful
Convictions.

Cases

delay in   Askov
strip search   Golden
911 enterbm's   Godoy
search   Testing
(grow ops.)
disclosure - Stinchcombe

YCJA - 2003.

SCPS
& Gladue Journal
- Volunteer